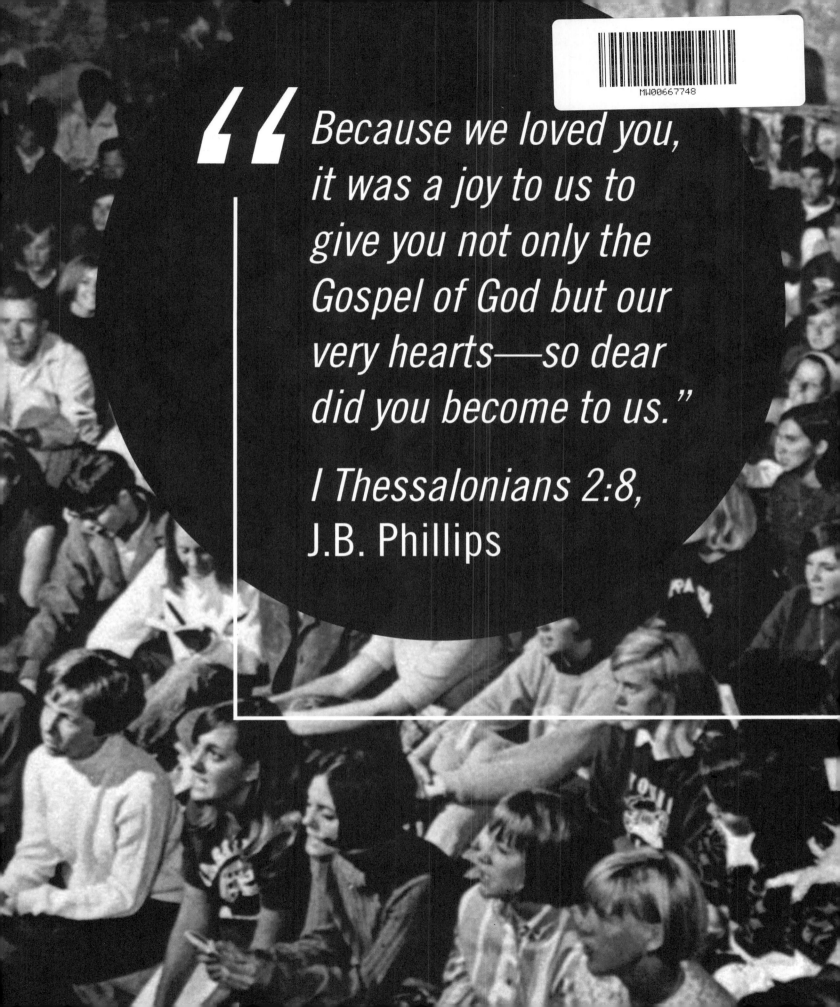

" *Because we loved you, it was a joy to us to give you not only the Gospel of God but our very hearts—so dear did you become to us."*

I Thessalonians 2:8, J.B. Phillips

MW00667748

MADE FOR THIS

THE YOUNG LIFE STORY

by
JEFF CHESEMORE

Published by Young Life.

ISBN: 978-0-9770338-3-6

Young Life Communications
P.O. Box 520
Colorado Springs, CO 80901
877-438-9572

Library of Congress Control Number: 2015945506

Printed in the United States of America
Walsworth Printing
Marceline, Missouri

2015—First Edition
10 9 8 7 6 5 4 3 2 1

DEDICATION

In gratitude for the men and women who have gone before,
As encouragement for those presently involved,
And in prayer for those who will one day join
this great endeavor known as "Young Life."

ACKNOWLEDGMENTS

True Young Life work is always done in the context of relationships. While I've had the privilege of putting the mission's story into words, from day one this has been a team effort with a group of men and women I have continually thanked God for throughout this project. I am so grateful for the immense contributions from the following:

ADVISORY

Denny Rydberg
Greg Kinberg

EDITOR

Terry Swenson

PROJECT MANAGEMENT

Connilee Walter

PRODUCTION COORDINATION

Donna McKenzie
Michael Ward

DESIGN

Diné Wiedey
Joann Oh
Isaac Watkins
Jason O'Hara

COPY EDITOR

Jessica Williams

PROOFREADING

Jessica Williams
Debbie Anderson

ADDITIONAL CONTENT

Stacy Windahl
Josh Griffin

RESEARCH

Tonia Shaw
Amy Petersen-Weddle
Kristen Griffin
Jill Comer

LEGAL

Jan Morton

HISTORICAL REVIEW TEAM

Marty Caldwell
Dave Carlson
Millie Carter
Lee Corder
Jim Dyson
Larry Entwistle
Arnie Jacobs
Ted Johnson
Bob Mitchell
Bo Nixon
Mary Nixon
Jim Rayburn III
Angel Ruiz
Kathy Schierholz
George Sheffer III
Mary Stam
Bill Starr
Kit Sublett
John Vicary

Thank you to the countless photographers whose pictures grace these pages. For more than seventy years you have captured shots of our favorite subject—kids—and your gifts in photography have painted pictures words never could.

Thank you to my wife, Jodi, and sons, Timothy and Aidan, who sacrificed countless hours to allow me the time needed to tell this story. Your love and encouragement leave me forever in your debt. Thanks to my friends and family who prayed and continually asked, "How's the Young Life book coming along?" I'm glad you now have the answer in your hands! Finally, thank you to Jack Dyson and Todd Main, the leaders who, in 1983, befriended a sophomore at Frederick High School and introduced him to Jesus through this beautiful ministry.

Table of CONTENTS

FOREWORD by Joni Eareckson Tada   **3**

the
1940s: A Perfect Convergence   **5**

Rayburn-isms   **20**

the
1950s: An Absolute Dream   **23**

"I Want You to Read This Letter!"   **42**

the
1960s: Warning: Contents Under Pressure   **45**

Fit to a Tee   **68**

the
1970s: A Continuing Education   **71**

Young Life Camps Through the Years   **94**

the
1980s: Branching Out 97

Make 'Em Laugh 116

the
1990s: Whatever . . . It Takes 119

A Young Life Glossary 142

the
2000s: Ready! 145

Cover-ing Young Life 166

the
2010s: The Now and the Not Yet 169

AFTERWORD 189

BIBLIOGRAPHY 190

NOTES 193

INDEX 207

FOLD-OUT TIMELINE

FOREWORD

Every great movement has a story. And if the story is personal, then you know it's a movement that goes beyond great. That's what Young Life is all about: heartfelt stories that grip the imaginations of kids everywhere.

I know. I've been there. And my story is so like every other young person's. Whether you're a wide-eyed freshman who is new to the school, or a senior who appears to own the hallways, you're hit with the same truth when you open your locker and see your face in the little mirror. Those crowded, noisy hallways do not belong to you.

Then maybe a week or two later, a classmate slides her cafeteria tray next to yours. You recognize her from Biology. Your chat about dissecting frogs and Friday night's game flows easily. You like this person. But you have to wonder, Why is she taking time with me? Who am I? The question dissipates when the class bell rings—as you head separate ways, you know you've made a friend.

Next thing you know, you are shoulder-to-shoulder with scores of kids, sitting in someone's big living room, singing songs that actually mean something, and listening to a Young Life leader with an open Bible in his hand. You don't know much about religion, but you feel your heart begin to warm—his words have, after all, the ring of truth.

A few more Young Life clubs and a weekend retreat later and you're hooked. Your story—the really great story of your life—has just begun. And you realize from the start, it'll be an adventure. That's because it's wrapped up in the Biggest Story Ever Told: Jesus' story.

Suddenly, the hallways back in high school belong to you . . . because they belong to God. That makes them—and the cafeteria—a mission field. So you smile and slide your lunch tray next to that shy girl whose locker is across from yours; you ask her name, get to know her a bit, and then at the end of lunch, pose the question: "Ever heard of Young Life?" You're off and running. You've made a friend.

That was the way it was back in the sixties when I first connected with club. And I just bet it's not far off from your experience, too—even if you're brand new to Young Life. The movement is that powerful.

It is the hand of God that has stirred and swelled the Young Life movement for more than seventy-five years. True, fashions change, music evolves, and school looks different than it did decades ago, but the Spirit-blessed method and message pretty much remains the same. Young Life is still a life-transforming narrative about the stories of kids and how they bond to the best Story of all. And the movement continues to grow. Big time.

It's why we're celebrating. Young Life staff and volunteers, donors, parents, newcomers to the mission, school and community people, and you and I simply must celebrate. We can't help but rejoice over this extraordinary milestone that marks the faithfulness of the God of the Bible and a ministry that loves young people, loves Jesus, and treasures His Gospel.

My husband, Ken—who also came to Christ through Young Life—and I consider it a privilege to support this remarkable ministry, because we know and we're thrilled that the Young Life story is far from concluding. So savor what you're holding in your hands and keep the movement strong!

by Joni Eareckson Tada
Joni and Friends
Young Life
Capernaum Advisor

the
1940s

A Perfect Convergence

In the small Texas community of Gainesville, Clara Frasher had a front-row view of the town's teenagers. Every morning and afternoon, the elderly woman sat on her front porch directly across from the local high school and watched the crowds of students pass by. From her rocking chair she observed a newly emerging youth culture, complete with its own slang, music, fashions, and attitudes.

She was also aware of another trend among 1930s teenagers—a growing disenchantment with organized religion. As a churchgoer herself, she saw firsthand that their interest and participation in church was waning. How, she wondered, would these kids ever hear the Good News?

Seeing these lost students was more than Mrs. Frasher could bear, so she prayed, "I don't know what I can do, but I pray someone will rescue these kids. They don't know where they're going. They're wandering back and forth, and going where, nobody knows."

Mrs. Frasher soon invited a small group of women to meet on Monday mornings and pray for the kids at Gainesville High School. The answer didn't come in a few days. Or weeks. Or even months. For six years these friends faithfully called on the Lord's help. And when the time was right, the Lord moved in a way that would prove to be more than they could ask or imagine.

A WATERSHED MOMENT

It was during this critical juncture, pregnant with possibility, that one man found his calling. In 1934, Jim Rayburn Jr. brought his young bride, Maxine, to Chama, New Mexico, where he served with the Presbyterian Board of National Missions. Months shy of his twenty-fifth birthday, Rayburn was following in the footsteps of his father, James Sr., himself a traveling evangelist.

Through his mission work over the next two years in New Mexico and Arizona, Rayburn learned he had a natural connection with young people. During these wilderness years, the pastor made another important discovery. He came across a copy of Lewis Sperry Chafer's classic work, *He That is Spiritual*, and couldn't put it down. He devoured the book, and entered into a new understanding of the Christian faith. Rayburn realized Gospel preaching often lacked the outpouring of grace, joy, and freedom meant for every believer, which can only come through the Holy Spirit.

I DON'T KNOW WHAT I CAN DO, BUT I PRAY SOMEONE WILL RESCUE THESE KIDS. THEY DON'T KNOW WHERE THEY'RE GOING. THEY'RE JUST WANDERING BACK AND FORTH, AND GOING WHERE, NOBODY KNOWS."

—CLARA FRASHER

Opposite: Happy kids about to enter the Star Ranch dining hall in the late 1940s.

"Dilly"

"Armored heifer"
(canned milk)

"Ducky shincracker"
(a good dancer)

"Cook with gas"
(to do something right)

"Hi, sugar, are you rationed?"
(Are you going steady?)

"Pennies from heaven"
(easy money)

"Lettuce"
(money)

"What's buzzin', cousin?"
(How are you?)

"Khaki wacky"
(boy crazy)

"Kisser"
(mouth)

"Hepcat"
(cool guy)

"Dilly"
(pretty girl)

The experience left the young man longing to go to seminary. Jim and Maxine Rayburn soon found themselves, and all their possessions, in their Chevy sitting at a literal fork in the road outside Clifton, Arizona. Two opportunities awaited them. To the west lay San Francisco Theological Seminary, and to the east, Dallas Theological Seminary (DTS). The couple prayed for God's leading. Rayburn then asked Maxine, "Which way shall we go, hon?"

Knowing her husband's deep desire to study under Chafer who taught at DTS, she replied, "I think we should go east."

They discussed the options a little longer and Rayburn again asked the Lord for guidance. A few minutes later, he turned the car toward Dallas.

A SEMINARIAN GOES TO HIGH SCHOOL

Jim and Maxine Rayburn arrived in Dallas in the fall of 1936, and found their decision validated. The twenty-seven-year-old student soaked up the wisdom of his professors, including Chafer. Rayburn knew he needed to learn more about grace, as his early Christian life had been heavily legalistic—activities like dancing, card playing, and even going to the movies, were frowned upon.

Like his book, Chafer's lectures resonated with Rayburn. Wally Howard, who would become one of the original five Young Life staff, said, "I remember [Dr. Chafer] saying, 'God has never done anything for human beings from the beginning of time until now but by grace.' He had a tremendous impact on Jim."

Rayburn longed to share the grace of Christ with others, especially teenagers. He had heard some of his seminary friends were working with an organization called the "Miracle Book Club" (MBC) in their efforts to reach out to kids.

The MBC had been founded by an education director for the Portland YWCA, Evelyn MacFarlane McClusky, who longed for teens to know better the teachings of "the miracle book"—the Bible. The ministry, which had chapters nationwide, was not based around church youth groups, but around high schools, where the MBC leaders welcomed unbelievers with open arms.

During the spring of 1939, Rayburn started his own chapter of the MBC in a small town seventy-five miles to the north of the seminary. The name of the town was Gainesville, Texas.

In addition to developing the Miracle Book Club program in Gainesville, Rayburn worked with the town's Presbyterian pastor, Clyde Kennedy. Like Clara Frasher and her prayer circle, Kennedy was concerned about the town's teenagers, who showed no interest in engaging with the traditional church programs. Realizing something must be done, Kennedy hired the young seminarian to fill a part-time position within the church in order to accomplish something vital beyond its walls.

Jim Rayburn, 1940.

In his book, *Dance, Children, Dance*, Jim Rayburn III shares his father's recollection of Kennedy's vision. "He was pushing on me all the time," Rayburn recalled. "He didn't care if I did any work around the church. He just wanted to see those kids reached for Christ. He said, 'Don't monkey around with the people who come to church. I'll take care of them. You go on down to that high school.'"

Though already involved at the school through MBC, Rayburn was not pleased with the results of his weekly afterschool meetings held in an English teacher's classroom. The kids sat at desks as Rayburn taught from the Scriptures; it felt like one more class tacked on at the end of a long school day. After months of averaging ten kids each week, Rayburn began holding the meetings in the evenings and in the homes of club members.

Once Rayburn moved both the time and location of club, more kids came out and the relaxed surroundings put them at ease, which in turn created more energy and, consequently, more talk about the event in school the next day.

All this was undergirded by prayer, Wally Howard explained. "When he had that Gainesville club he asked the rest of us to meet that night and to pray." The seminary students' prayers were being answered, noted Rayburn. "They'd get down on their knees and spend hours praying for that club meeting. It's no wonder we had a revival in that school! . . . That club went from 75 to 96, and then to 100, and then to 119, and 135, and the week before finals there were 170 kids there."

When Rayburn returned to the seminary from Gainesville on Monday nights, he drew his fellow students together to debrief on the evening and pray once more. The students included Howard, Add Sewell, George Cowan, and Ted Benson, all of whom played important roles in the early years of the mission. "There's no way to overemphasize the importance of that Gainesville club," Sewell said. "If it hadn't happened, Young Life might not have happened. It gave us an idea of what could be."

IN-TENTS-ITY!

With his graduation from DTS now complete and the summer of 1940 quickly approaching, Rayburn sought a new opportunity to bring the Gospel to kids: a tent revival for teens. Popular among traveling evangelists at the time, revivals often drew large crowds to a presentation of the Gospel message and an invitation to profess faith in Christ. Adapting this approach with a message tailor-made for kids, Rayburn organized three summer tent meetings in Gainesville, Houston, and Dallas, respectively.

However, he faced the problem of coming up with a name for the event. "Miracle Book Club" didn't exactly instill the excitement needed to bring out a city's teenagers. Wally Howard remembered the dilemma well. "We didn't have

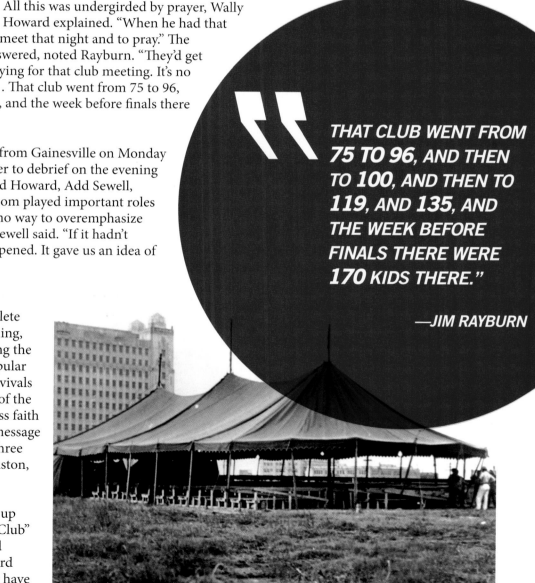

THAT CLUB WENT FROM **75 TO 96**, AND THEN TO **100**, AND THEN TO **119**, AND **135**, AND THE WEEK BEFORE FINALS THERE WERE **170** KIDS THERE."

—JIM RAYBURN

The tent used for the early campaigns, pictured here in Houston.

any great vision at the moment. The name 'Miracle Book Club' didn't seem very enhancing to Jim. We weren't focused around a book; we were focused around a person named Jesus Christ, who gives life. I remember the day we sat up in a classroom on the second floor of the seminary, and Jim had heard about this organization in England called Young Life. He liked the name and requested permission to use it. And we all agreed, this is going to be the 'Young Life Campaign.' It was just a much more attractive name that would intrigue kids."

With a name chosen, Rayburn and his men went to work assembling a music component to the tent meetings. They brought together two pianists, a men's quartet from the seminary, and a youth choir, in the hopes of reaching kids through music. After vibrant singing of hymns and spirituals, Rayburn would stand up in the sweltering Texas heat and bring another kind of warmth to the evening. In his own simple style, Rayburn sought to build bridges with the audience. He spoke in his own special way—passionate yet inviting. His message and delivery were tuned specifically to the frequency of a teenager.

A boy by the name of Bob Mitchell and his entire family attended the Dallas campaign after hearing so much about the upcoming event from his father, who had helped to fund and promote (and even build benches for) the meeting. This young man would one day go on to become president of Young Life, after having held almost every other position in the mission. Mitchell remembered vividly his introduction to Rayburn:

"I first met him at that tent, and I'd never heard anybody talk like this. His sense of humor is what captivated me. I wanted to go each night just to hear him tell these stories, because I'd never heard a Bible story told with humor. Everything [back then] was pretty formal. Jim would talk about the changing of water to wine, I remember that's the first one I heard him tell—how Jesus took this old West Texas, brackish well water and He turned it into this fine wine and, man, we were captivated. In all the humorous touches and beautiful ways, he gave us a picture of Jesus."

The three campaigns were a huge success and Mitchell's life, as well as thousands of other Texas teenagers', would never be the same.

COMMUTING TO CLUB

The tent campaigns became a springboard for more ministry in more places. As the new school year began, Rayburn recruited more than forty volunteers from the seminary to help lead clubs throughout Texas.

The summer tent meetings had also introduced a new name—"The Young Life Campaign"—which had been well received. While Rayburn and his volunteers were still officially doing ministry as the Texas chapter of the Miracle Book Club, they also used the new name.

The men continued to drive to Gainesville on Mondays and then spent Tuesday nights in Dallas. Two nights later they added Houston clubs to their repertoire. In *The Diaries of Jim Rayburn*, Kit Sublett describes the exhausting process:

"On Thursdays, Jim took the train to Houston and spent the day there, making contacts and getting office work done . . . Thursday afternoons after class several DTS men would drive Jim's car down to Houston (two hundred forty miles to the south), meet Jim for dinner, and spread out around the city to lead the city's Miracle Book Club chapters. After their clubs, Jim and the men would drive back to Dallas together. They would spend the several-hour drive reporting on their club meetings, discussing things they were learning about reaching non-Christian high school students, and praying. They would arrive back at the seminary in the early hours of Friday morning."

ON BOARD

With the ministry expanding, many supportive adults felt it would be wise to incorporate the movement. This provided Rayburn (and every subsequent president of the mission) with the collective wisdom of a board of directors who could help direct the work and further legitimize the campaign. Furthermore, they would support the vision and integrity of Young Life by helping to set policy, approving the budget and fulfilling other assignments related to the governance of the mission. While they undertook these responsibilities with little fanfare, the importance of the board could not be overstated.

On Christmas Eve 1940, the Young Life Campaign Board of Directors was officially formed, comprised of John E. Mitchell (chair), Ted Benson (secretary-treasurer) and Rayburn's favorite professor, Dr. Chafer. This was an important moment in an historic year; yet, as critical as 1940 proved to be, 1941 would be the year that truly launched the mission.

THE FIRST FIVE

As the work continued to explode, God called four men to come alongside Rayburn. George Cowan, Wally Howard, Add Sewell, and Gordon Whitelock enthusiastically joined Rayburn to become the first five Young Life staff.

This quintet followed the blueprint laid out in Acts 1:8, "But you will receive power when the Holy Spirit comes on you; and you will be my witnesses in Jerusalem, and in all Judea and Samaria, and to the ends of the earth." The men already had a presence in Dallas, their "Jerusalem"; from there they spread out to "Judea." Rayburn continued his work up north

in Gainesville; Sewell went east to Tyler, Texas; Howard traveled west to Wichita Falls, while Cowan and Whitelock traveled south to the Houston area.

Just as the first-century apostles didn't peddle the Word of God for profit, neither did these twentieth-century missionaries. The entire budget for the fledgling band was $893 a month, each man received a monthly paycheck of $100.

When God places a call on any man or woman's life, He ignites a passion deep within to follow single-mindedly this specific task. Rayburn knew this well and impressed this upon anyone interested in coming on Young Life staff.

Tom Raley, who met Christ in Add Sewell's club and would join the staff in 1949, recalled the process Rayburn employed. "If you were going to be around him, you were going to be involved in Young Life; you either bought in or you bought out. You could go do something else. When you would come to Young Life for a job, Rayburn's standard interview technique was to ask, 'Well, is there anything else you can do?'

"If you said, 'Well, yeah, I guess I could be a youth director in a church,' he'd say, 'Why don't you go and do that, and come back when this is all you can do?' He was that excited and committed to what Young Life was all about. He really believed you needed to think, 'This is all I can do. I feel compelled to preach the Gospel,' picking up on Paul's great statement to the Corinthian church."

BECOMING YOUNG LIFE

By the spring of 1941, change was in the air. Working under the dual banners of Miracle Book Club and the Young Life Campaign was no longer tenable. As the men grew in their wisdom and understanding on how to care for unreached teenagers, so grew their dissatisfaction with the methods and materials of the MBC, which seemed too flowery and effeminate when dealing with kids (especially the boys!). In a way, it had been like trying to put new wine into old wineskins.

Rayburn acknowledged the assistance the MBC had provided him in getting started, but he also knew to achieve the impact he desired, he must make a clean break. While the disentanglement from the MBC lasted longer than

Addison Sewell, Wally Howard, Jim Rayburn, George Cowan, and Gordon Whitelock.

he would have liked, Rayburn felt a load lift when the decision was finally made. In his diary entry of March 19, 1941, Rayburn wrote, "A great day. 'Young Life Clubs' came into being—unanimously voted by twenty-three fellows of the teaching force—the name—the motto (Christ is Life)—the verse (1 John 5:12)."

Over time the name "Young Life Campaign" was shortened to "Young Life." "The reason 'campaign' was there, of course, is that Young Life started as an evangelistic campaign," Bob Mitchell said. "But then as we moved more into the relational style of ministry, the word 'campaign' didn't fit. The whole feel of the word 'campaign' sounded of high pressure and we were definitely low pressure. So it was dropped because it conveyed mass meetings and that kind of approach."

Later in the year, Rayburn and the board set in motion the process of establishing Young Life as a separate, legally recognized organization. The process was completed on October 16, 1941, the official date of Young Life's incorporation in the state of Texas. Only fifty-two days after this happy occasion, however, came the "date which will live in infamy."

A WORLD AT WAR

On December 7, 1941, a place previously unknown to most Americans captured the attention of the world. The Japanese attack upon Pearl Harbor catapulted America into the war and, in the process, uprooted the lives of countless teenagers. Mitchell, being too young to enlist, remembered how the war impacted the Dallas club he attended:

"You could see the influence of the Second World War on a lot of the songs we sang. We sang songs like, 'What though wars may come / with marching feet and beat of the drum / for I have Christ in my heart'—songs inspired by the war. All these songs had a national as well as a Christian overtone to them—that was the atmosphere. It was a very different time and a lot of the kids in that club were drafted and didn't make it. They didn't come back."

Back home, the Young Life work faced other unique challenges. Churches were suspicious of this upstart group who came into town and, without much fanfare, began working with the high school crowd. In West Texas, Wally Howard bore the brunt of this interrogation. "Where I was, there was a lot of suspicion about Young Life. Who are you? On what authority are you here? Who sent you? They thought we were Nazis!" Howard experienced the first taste of what the rest of the mission would soon discover: It was imperative staff build relationships with the church in order to educate, define, and explain Young Life's calling and place in the kingdom.

As the Great Depression hung over the early days in Gainesville, World War II cast its own shadow through the first four years of the mission's work. Many of the men who would have served as staff were fighting across the world. As the allies helped bring about V-E Day in May and then V-J Day in August, countries around the world celebrated the return of their finest men and women. Meanwhile, the mission welcomed many veterans like Arnie Jacobs (Marines), Van Nall (Army), and Bill Starr (Navy) onto Young Life staff.

SAY GANG

While the tragic events of war played out across the nation's newspapers, another publication filled with good news arrived on the scene. In March of 1944, the mission began publishing *Young Life*, a "real live-wire monthly magazine designed especially for the high school gang." The magazine ran for the next twenty years, aimed at presenting the same message kids were hearing in club, through articles and pictures. Like Young Life club, each issue featured humor ("The Silo" featured "corny" jokes), updates ("Cross Country" told of the goings-on in Young Life throughout the country), and spiritual insights ("Say, Gang" was Rayburn's own column, where he challenged and encouraged his high school readers).

Rocky Morgan and Bobby McKenzie, club kids from Tonkawa, Oklahoma.

"I got the *YOUNG LIFE* magazines and I sat down and read them from cover to cover just as soon as they came. They really took me back to the swell times of fellowship we used to have in the Lord."

Part of a 1945 letter from Rocky Morgan, stationed in France, to his Young Life leader back in Oklahoma.

"THE PRINCIPAL OF THE THING"

In the early days, the staff concentrated on meetings as the way to reach kids. To help the work spread, Rayburn and the men traveled from city to city to reach kids through high school assembly meetings. Here, Rayburn would spend the first half of the assembly winning kids over with eye-rolling lines like these:

"High school isn't so bad, is it? It's just the principal of the thing."

"Did you hear about the cross-eyed teacher they had to fire? She couldn't see eye to eye with her pupils."

"I was talking with the principal this morning and he told me he just had to do something about all this kissing going on right under his nose."

When he had drawn kids in with the humor, he could then share with them about the Christian faith and the foundation it played in the forming of the United States. He'd challenge them to consider this faith for themselves and come out to the Young Life club they'd be holding that night. Sometimes the men would repeat this approach five or six times in one day in schools throughout the city.

The results at the night meetings were staggering, as many kids responded to the invitation to follow Jesus. This success encouraged the men, but they also worried about forging on to repeat the process in the next city, while leaving these new believers without follow-up. In regard to long-term effects, these assemblies left much to be desired.

MAKING CONTACT

Meanwhile, Add Sewell moved to Tyler, Texas, where he made perhaps one of the greatest "discoveries" in the history of the mission simply by doing what came naturally. He was well aware the work there must run differently than the earlier "appearances" he and his fellow seminarians made in their weekly commutes to Houston. "You can't have a Young Life club like that," he said. "We had no contact with kids prior to or after those clubs."

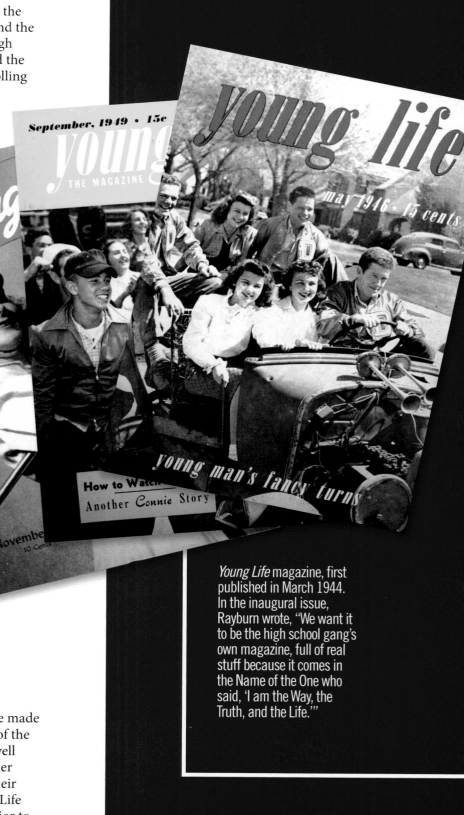

Young Life magazine, first published in March 1944. In the inaugural issue, Rayburn wrote, "We want it to be the high school gang's own magazine, full of real stuff because it comes in the Name of the One who said, 'I am the Way, the Truth, and the Life.'"

Roy Riviere in full "contact work" action.

Sewell knew the missing ingredient was time. Club meetings, while filled with energy, could never be the lifeblood of outreach work to kids. They needed adults who cared enough to come alongside them and spend time learning what was important to them. Looking for a better approach with the ministry in Tyler, Sewell started showing up at football practices, where he simply hung out and kicked the football around with the kids. In the process, he developed relationships with kids— exactly what he saw missing in the weekly trips to Houston.

Sewell's simple "discovery," which came to be known as "contact work," helped enlarge the staff's vision of what kids (and adults) needed.

Souvenir copy of Campaigners song book, 1943.

As Wally Howard would later reflect, contact work was actually a very old concept. "Our message is a person. God made Himself known to us through a person. And He still makes Himself known through people. And that's what Young Life's all about."

The slow, patient practice of hanging out with kids in order to build relationships ultimately became the very fiber of the ministry. Of course at the time, Sewell was just doing what came naturally. "I think I was the first one to do it in Young Life, and to do it pretty intensively, but that was my strength. I was not a great speaker in the Young Life club."

This sentiment is a profound encouragement to all Young Life leaders who've ever felt their greatest abilities lay in the simple (but essential) task of earning the right to be heard.

GOING DEEP WITH "CAMPAIGNERS"

One of the more important friendships in Jim Rayburn's life was the one he shared with Dawson Trotman, who in 1933 had formed the Navigators ministry.

Having seen Rayburn lead many kids into relationships with Christ, Trotman implored him to follow up with these newborn believers. Trotman shared his emphasis on discipleship with Rayburn, who then used the Navigators materials in Bible studies with his high school friends.

"The early leaders started meeting with kids who had become followers of Jesus," Mitchell said. "They called these groups 'Campaigners,' from the early tent meetings which were called the 'Young Life Campaign.' Our group of boys met at Jim Rayburn's home on Sunday afternoons. There were no refreshments. The meetings had a 'down to business' feel about them. For two hours we each gave a weekly report on our assignments, studied Scripture, memorized Bible verses, and learned to pray.

"The same things went on in the girls' Campaigners groups, led by Gladys Roche, Ollie Dustin, Kay McDonald, Wanda Ann Mercer, or Anne Cheairs, some of the first women to join the Young Life staff. These women, and many others, would be legendary in their contribution to the mission."

The sudden growth of staff was exciting, but what was about happen in Wheaton, Illinois, would multiply the young mission exponentially.

In the early forties, Rayburn traveled frequently to Wheaton College to teach interested students on Young Life methodology. (One of these students was Billy Graham.) When Add Sewell moved to Chicago in 1946, he deployed those students to serve the growing ministry throughout the city. With that simple step, Young Life received perhaps the greatest gift it has ever received—the introduction of volunteer leaders, who would give of their time, energy, and resources to reach kids, all the while studying and taking classes. Before long, volunteer leaders would also come to include young professionals.

Sewell had only just begun. After serving three and a half years in Chicago, he and his wife, Loveta, moved to Seattle, where he enjoyed yet another first. Sewell started a Young Life leadership program at the University of Washington, the first such program connected with a public school.

RAISING UP LABORERS

Because of the mission's appeal to both kids and adults, it didn't take long for the staff to grow in size and expand outside the borders of Texas. Within two years of incorporating, the staff had grown from the original five men to sixteen men and five women. In Bellingham, Washington, Grant Whipple, a graduate from Dallas Theological Seminary, oversaw the first Young Life work on the West Coast. In a few years the East Coast would likewise have its first clubs in Chester, Pennsylvania, and at Baltimore's Towson High School. In-between the coasts, the mission field in 1945 included Dallas, Tyler, Houston, Memphis, Little Rock, Tulsa, Chicago, Seattle, Portland, Yakima, and even Mexico.

Staff Conference—Star Ranch, 1946.

The staff were thrilled with the idea of volunteer leaders. In those days, staff were expected to run a minimum of two clubs, meaning they were ministering to students from at least two high schools throughout the week. At one point Wally Howard spent two years ministering at five different clubs a week, from Memphis to Little Rock and then (overnight by train) to St. Louis. By his own admission, Wally Howard knew spreading himself so thin left him little chance to follow up with the kids, as Sewell had learned in Tyler.

More leaders meant more quality time invested in kids after school and on the weekends (not just on the night of club). Across the U.S., the advent of volunteers and the increased ministry they could provide surpassed the wildest dreams of the Young Life staff; by the beginning of the 1950s, only four years removed from Wheaton's inaugural group, volunteers outnumbered staff almost nine to one.

EARLY CAMPING AND THE FIRST SKIT

Jim Rayburn loved introducing kids to the rugged outdoors so they could marvel at its beauty and fall in love with the One who created it all. In the early days of the mission, Rayburn would take several boys, like Mitchell, out to the East Texas hills where the camping was primitive. The day's activities revolved around armadillo and rattlesnake hunts, hiking, and sitting by the campfire at night, Mitchell remembered.

Mitchell is fond of telling another story from those camping adventures: "I guess Jim gave the first Young Life skit that ever was. As we were sitting around the campfire, he acted out all the parts of the story of Little Red Riding Hood. He got about halfway through the story, when he tripped and fell into the fire (which was an unplanned event). It was really great. It couldn't have been better. We thought he was the funniest guy we ever saw. So midway through Little Red Riding Hood, he's climbing out of the fire and fortunately he doesn't get burned. That was the very first camp skit, and it ended up in disaster. Of course, years later a lot of our skits ended up in disaster!"

At that same campfire, Rayburn would open his New Testament and share the Gospel stories. These sacred times paved the way for Rayburn's larger dream of a Young Life camp for kids. Until this dream could be realized, Rayburn rented camp properties in the summers. The camps were nothing to write home about, but Mitchell said, "It wasn't the property itself that brought camping alive for us, but the way Jim gave us things to do and took us on all kinds of hikes. We got to know a man whom we knew had a special touch with God. Many of us opened our lives to Christ in these primitive camps."

KINDRED SPIRITS

Understandably, much has been written about Rayburn and the other leaders who helped forge a path to the door of teenagers. Their vision, dogged determination, and love helped draw kids to the feet of Jesus. These staff and volunteers would be quick to proclaim, though, that their efforts might not have endured without the quiet, behind-the-scenes support of people like Herb and Gloria Taylor.

Knowing the Taylors and Rayburn shared a love for Christ and kids, Ted Benson introduced them. After hearing Rayburn's novel ideas on how to reach unchurched teenagers, Taylor, the president of Club Aluminum, decided to underwrite the expenses for the 1940 summer campaign. When Young Life was incorporated, it was Taylor and the Christian Workers Foundation who largely funded the first five staff salaries.

Taylor's vision for the work was equal to (and sometimes even ahead of) Rayburn's. Seeing the campaign surge in popularity throughout Texas, Taylor knew they had to think bigger. He gave Rayburn the ultimatum, "You'll have to go national, Rayburn, or I'll not give you another dime."

Taylor's ability to see was clearly matched by his willingness to hear. Char Meredith, whose book *It's a Sin to Bore a Kid*, focused on Young Life's early history, wrote about a time in 1945 when Taylor listened intently to the Lord:

"There was not enough money to meet the budget as the fiscal year ended. The policy at that time was simply to wipe out the deficit if salaries were not paid up, and start with a clean slate October 1.

Gloria and Herb Taylor

'We needed $2,500, as I recall,' Kay [McDonald] continued. 'We all spent the day praying. We'd read something, then get down on our knees and pray, then read some more and pray some more. At one point the phone rang. It was H. J. Taylor in Chicago. 'I couldn't get away from the feeling that I should call and let you know I'm sending $2,500 to you today.' "

Herb and Gloria Taylor served as forerunners to thousands of donors who have supported the work throughout the world. If possible to choose the grandest among their many contributions to the mission, in Taylor's mind at least, it would be the purchase of the first Young Life camp.

"THE BEST INVESTMENT I EVER MADE"

Rayburn dreamed of having a place for kids where he could share the great love story that consumed him. He was fond of sharing this vision with anyone who would listen. Maxine recalled a time in 1935 when he said, "Maxie, I have a dream of a real camp for kids. A camp that'll be so great that when they get out of the bus and they walk onto the camp, they'll know somebody was thinking about them before they got there."

As Rayburn dreamed of a camp, he thought of the Colorado Rockies, where he had vacationed with his family as a child. In 1946, after a failed attempt to land Crystal Park, a property a few miles east of Pikes Peak, an excited Rayburn notified Taylor of another opportunity.

"I know now why the Lord didn't want us to have Crystal Park," Rayburn explained to Taylor. "We've found something better. It's all complete, ready to move into. It's a beautiful spot. I want you and Mrs. Taylor to fly out here and take a look at Star Ranch."

The Taylors flew into Colorado Springs and, discovering Rayburn was not there, proceeded to survey the property on their own. A discouraged Rayburn, whose plane had been delayed six hours, met the couple for dinner at the Broadmoor Hotel, where they were staying. Years later he recounted their conversation over dinner . . .

> "[Mr. Taylor] said, 'Well, Jim, I've got a surprise for you. The Mrs. and I have been out to Star Ranch . . . Sorry you couldn't make it.'
>
> I said, 'I'm sorry, too.'
>
> 'Beautiful place.'

Star Ranch
— Acquired 1946, Sold 1972.

The log cabin at Star Ranch, which served as Young Life's headquarters.

'Yeah.'

I went on slurping my soup, disheartened. Things just hadn't gone right. Nothing was right that didn't turn out according to my calculations . . . We weren't very long in the meal until this eminent gentleman turned to me and said, 'Do you think you could use Star Ranch for Young Life work? Is it the kind of thing you want?'

I told him I'd never seen anything in my life like that. It was a dream spot! I never imagined there could be anything so wonderful. Then he looked at his wife and said, 'We've decided to buy it for you.'

Half of the crew of the Broadmoor waiters dug me out!"

A month later, Star Ranch became Young Life's first camp; Taylor had purchased the camp for $50,000 and would lease the camp to Young Life for one dollar a year. Not only did this beloved camp host kids for the next twenty-six years, but Star Ranch also served as the headquarters for the mission from 1947 until 1961. Over the years, the camp miraculously survived two forest fires as God's hand protected the camp from the destruction that came upon all the surrounding areas.

Years later, when he stopped to calculate what his purchase had produced, Taylor couldn't help but laugh. "Best investment I ever made," he proclaimed. "Probably thirty thousand kids heard the Gospel at Star since we bought it. That's about a dollar and a half apiece."

"LET THE REDEEMED OF THE LORD SAY SO"

One of the traditions carried over to Star Ranch from the early "rental camping days" was what came to be known as the "Say-So," named after the biblical exhortation found in Psalm 107:2, "Let the redeemed of the Lord say so" (KJV). After a week or weekend of being challenged by the claims of the Gospel, kids were invited to publicly proclaim their decision to begin a personal relationship with Jesus.

Longtime staff member Roy Riviere explained the reasoning, "We weren't asking youngsters to sign a pledge, we didn't have some formula they needed to follow through, nobody told them what words to use, but we let it be known that we thought it was extremely appropriate if you had done eternal business with Jesus Christ, to stand up and say so." In the early days, this happened around the campfire as kids threw a stick onto the fire and shared their decisions with the other campers.

One such boy went by the name of Frog Sullivan. On a weekend camp, Sullivan did his best to disrupt the proceedings. Murray Smoot, who shared speaking duties with Rayburn on this particular weekend, remembered Sullivan's strategy. "Every night when I would bring the message, Frog would wait until he knew I really had the gang, when they were listening. Then he would get up and yell some dirty thing and just wreck the whole club meeting. Time after time, he did that."

The boy's rebellion came out of a troubled place. As a young teen growing up in a hard part of Memphis, he struggled with feeling loved. It was at this moment he met a Young Life leader named Howard Kee. "Howard came and sat on my steps in front of my high school and said, 'I'm Howard Kee,' " Sullivan said. "He knew me. He knew every kid in that high school. That's what made the difference, because when he met somebody he knew them.

"He knew if he could change my life, he could change the school. I was drawn to him. He was a very warm and caring person and I didn't have that. That didn't exist in my neighborhood. My mother was probably the only person in my life who really loved me."

After enduring a weekend of Sullivan's outbursts, Smoot recalled the Say-So on the last night. Kids were throwing sticks into the fire and sharing their newfound faith in Christ, he said, "and Frog Sullivan gets up, and you could just sense it all around. Oh no. Not again! This is going too well and here he's going to . . . And he got up, and he said, almost word for word, 'You guys know me. You know what I've been doing all weekend long. There's one thing you don't know, and that is, I just gave my heart to Jesus.' "

Howard Kee and the others' love for Sullivan hadn't escaped the teenager's notice. Nor did Rayburn's message. "He said there was a guy who lived in his town who was a half-wit, and he could cuss for thirty minutes without using the same word twice," said Sullivan. "That was me. He nailed me that night.

"After that was over I went out by myself and opened my heart to Christ. I had never gone to church. I didn't know anything about Jesus. It wasn't emotional, there wasn't anything incredible about it, no lights went off, but from that moment on, my life was totally different."

Over time the campfires went away, but the Say-So never would. One of the most poignant moments of a camp trip

Silver Cliff Ranch

By the end of the 1948 camping season, only two short years after its purchase, Star Ranch was already packed beyond capacity. Rayburn was on the hunt for another camp so no kid would ever have to be turned away. Located one hundred miles west of Colorado Springs near the little town of Buena Vista, Colorado, sat a vacation resort known as Chalk Cliff Lodge.

In the late fall of 1949, the Board of Directors agreed to purchase the property for $70,000, and the first camp was held over Christmas break of that year. The following summer, staff arrived to work on bringing it up to the high standards they expected.

George Sheffer, who would serve with Young Life through five decades, was the first summer director there. "I called it the 'world's leading dust bowl,' but its potential was boundless. Now it has been realized. The first summers were replete with digging (with picks and shovels) adequate sewage facilities, etc., and at the same time carrying on an exciting camp program for the kids who had come for a thrilling adventure in the Colorado mountains. Our great and loving heavenly Father worked miracles in kids' lives through the love He displayed in the work crew and staff of Silver Cliff. As we would climb Mt. Princeton (14,197 feet) each week, we passed through another camp—one of the most exclusive dude ranches for boys in the U.S.A."

(That dude ranch, by the way, would also come to play a prominent role in the mission in the following decade.)

Silver Cliff Ranch, Acquired 1949, Sold 1983.

Going Where They Are

A Reflection by Denny Rydberg, president

One of the great distinctives in our mission and one of the reasons Young Life has had integrity and results after seventy-five years is that we go where kids are and we win the right to be heard. That was Jim Rayburn's passion and it still exists today. We are incarnational and relational. We learn the names of kids, we care about them as individuals, and we want them to meet and accept Jesus as their Savior and Lord because we know personally the difference He can make in a person's life.

Early in my tenure as president, we did a survey and discovered Young Life staff and volunteers spent two million hours in a year's time hanging out with kids! That was and is absolutely incredible. But what makes it even more amazing is we have more than doubled in our outreach to kids since that survey was taken. My guess is that our leaders currently invest over five million hours per year in going where kids are and winning the right to be heard.

And, because of that priority, you can talk to adults from the forties, fifties, sixties, and up to the present who met Christ as kids in Young Life through a passionate, pursuing and caring leader. They will tell you about this significant leader (staff or volunteer) who loved Christ so much that he or she was not afraid to step onto a school campus or enter a neighborhood and get to know them and spend time with them over and over again.

One of my favorite examples is Norman Larson. He was forty-four years old when he emailed us in 2000. He had been stationed aboard the USS Cole when it was bombed by terrorists in Yemen. Seventeen U.S. sailors were killed and thirty-nine injured; he wrote about Young Life and his leaders and what he had experienced aboard the ship.

"I was active in Young Life from late 1970 to 1977, when I joined the Navy. I had many memorable experiences: attended Saranac, Hilltop, Windy Gap, Virginia Beach; visited Frontier, Silver Cliff, Trail West Lodge; did work crew for three weeks at Windy Gap, and more. In addition to the fellowship and exposure to Jesus Christ, we sang songs, lots of songs, and I remember so many songs to this day. Just a month ago, I was on the USS Cole in Aden, Yemen, when it was bombed. Throughout the turmoil and uncertainty of the next few days, before we got the ship stabilized and the flooding stopped, I recalled the many lessons learned from Scott and Marilyn Dimmock at the meetings in Annandale High School. I also found solace and comfort in the songs I remembered. Thank you, Young Life, for putting a song in my heart."

That's what happened to Norm. And that's what millions of others have experienced. What they heard at Young Life was absolute Truth. What they experienced was Rock Solid. And it was because two leaders (in Norm's case, Scott and Marilyn) went to where Norm was (Annandale High School), won the right to be heard, shared Jesus with him, and "put a song in his heart."

Going where kids are. It's what we do.

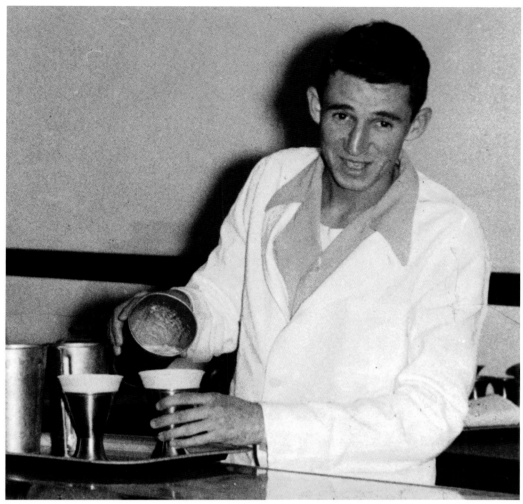

Frog Sullivan pours malts for teens in Memphis, 1946.

and the hearts of the kids and adults we contacted. The response wasn't any cleverness of ours. Somehow, it just blossomed and came to fruition and real change. Man, I can't get over it. It was incredible."

When reflecting on the history of Young Life, many personalities may spring to mind—Rayburn and the succeeding presidents of the mission, funny program directors, and dynamic speakers, to name a few. But the list probably doesn't include Mrs. Frasher and her unnamed friends who asked the Lord to rescue those lost Gainesville teenagers who "don't know where they're going." These dear praying women would embody a vital contingent of Young Life men and women: those who pray for things that the Lord, in His kindness, has allowed them to see.

Frog Sullivan enjoyed telling the story of how Rayburn eventually learned of Clara Frasher's efforts. Once Rayburn had the Gainesville club up and running, he proudly shared his success from the pulpit

(not to mention the campers' lives) still generally occurs at the last club of the week.

Reflecting on one such Say-So at Frontier Ranch, Roy Riviere remarked to the other staff, "I really don't know when kids are saved. But, if hearing them speak in a Say-So meeting ever ceases to thrill me, I hope one of you will throw a little dirt on me and maybe put a lily on my chest."

AN INCREDIBLE, IMPERISHABLE MONUMENT

As the sun set on the forties, a vibrant mission had formed, and the glory, as in all things, belonged to the Lord. In His timing, He brought about a perfect convergence of need, opportunity, and calling that produced an atmosphere where ministries like Young Life, The Navigators, and Youth for Christ flourished.

In looking back on these amazing years, George Cowan remarked, "The whole business is evidence to me that the Holy Spirit was in it, because He was working in our hearts

one Sunday morning. After the service, he met a group of ladies waiting for him at the back of the church. According to Sullivan, the ladies calmly informed him, "Mr. Rayburn, we are so glad you came to town and you have a club going here and you're reaching our kids in our town for Jesus Christ. But we've been praying for that high school for years!"

In a message given much later in life, Rayburn said, "I was there a year before I heard about that prayer meeting. I used to go over there with those five or six old ladies and get down on my knees with them after that club started to roll. That was the thing the Lord used to start it."

If you travel to Gainesville, Texas, today, you will not find Mrs. Frasher's house—it is no more. Thankfully, though, Mrs. Frasher's legacy is an imperishable one—for it lives on in the hearts of the millions of kids who've since encountered Jesus Christ through the mission of Young Life.

Rayburn-isms

As a communicator, Jim Rayburn spoke like no other. His impassioned pronouncements on Christ, kids, camps, and many other subjects revealed a man who longed for excellence in himself and others. Below are but a few of his gems . . .

"JESUS IS THE ONLY ONE WE CAN TALK ABOUT WITHOUT FEAR OF EXAGGERATION."

"THE BEST YOUNG LIFE WORK HAS YET TO BE DONE."

"JESUS DID SOMETHIN' TREMENDOUS FOR ME, SO MUCH THAT WHEN I THINK OF IT THE TEARDROPS START; SO MUCH THAT I'LL NEVER BE ABLE TO THANK HIM; SO MUCH THAT IT WOULDN'T MAKE ANY DIFFERENCE IF I NEVER HAD ANOTHER HAPPY MOMENT, IF I COULD JUST PLEASE HIM AND HONOR HIM, AND SHOW HIM HOW THANKFUL I AM. HE SUFFERED FOR ME, THE JUST FOR THE UNJUST, TO FREE ME FROM THE CURSE OF DEATH, AND GIVE ME A NEW LIFE."

"YOU KNOW, GANG, IF YOU DON'T BELIEVE THE CHRISTIAN FAITH, YOU'VE GOTTA DREAM UP A WHOLE LOT OF OTHER STUFF TO EXPLAIN WHAT'S ALL AROUND US—I MEAN A WHOLE LOT OF STUFF."

"YOUNG LIFE IS A GROUP OF PEOPLE COMMITTED TO THE IDEA OF WINNING A HEARING WITH KIDS FOR THE GREATEST STORY EVER TOLD."

"WHO STARTED THE IDEA THAT CHRISTIANS OUGHT TO HAVE THE SEAT OF THEIR PANTS IN PATCHES, OR THAT WE OUGHT TO HOLD CAMP IN TENTS? WE TALK ABOUT THE KING OF KINGS; LET'S ACT LIKE HE'S IN CHARGE! WE'RE GOING TO HAVE THE CLASSIEST CAMPS IN THIS COUNTRY."

"I DO NOT WANT ANYTHING IN MY LIFE THAT IS NOT OF THE LORD JESUS."

"MOST KIDS HAVEN'T TRUSTED JESUS CHRIST SIMPLY BECAUSE THEY DON'T KNOW WHO HE IS, AND WHAT HE HAS DONE FOR THEM."

"THAT'S NOT JUST WHAT YOUNG LIFE'S ALL ABOUT; THAT'S *ALL* YOUNG LIFE'S ABOUT— JESUS CHRIST."

"CHRIST IS THE STRONGEST, GRANDEST, MOST ATTRACTIVE PERSONALITY EVER TO GRACE THE EARTH. BUT A CARELESS MESSENGER WITH THE WRONG APPROACH CAN REDUCE ALL THIS MAGNIFICENCE TO THE LEVEL OF BOREDOM . . . IT IS A CRIME TO BORE ANYONE WITH THE GOSPEL."

"**THERE ARE THOUSANDS OF PEOPLE IN THIS COUNTRY THAT NO CHRISTIAN HAS EVER SAID A KIND WORD TO. MOST OF THE KIDS IN THIS NATION ARE LIKE THAT. A FEW MILLION MORE OF THEM WILL GRADUATE FROM HIGH SCHOOL THIS YEAR . . . AND THEY'VE NEVER HEARD THE STORY. AND I CAN'T STAND THAT.**"

"EVERYONE HAS THE RIGHT TO KNOW THE TRUTH ABOUT JESUS CHRIST. THEY HAVE A RIGHT TO KNOW WHO HE IS, A RIGHT TO KNOW WHAT HE'S DONE FOR THEM, A RIGHT TO KNOW HOW THEY RELATE TO THAT, A RIGHT TO MAKE THEIR OWN CHOICE OF HIM."

"I'VE ALWAYS FELT A LITTLE TWINGE OR SOMETHING WHEN I WAS INTRODUCED AS THE FOUNDER OF THIS OUTFIT. I AM THE FOUNDER, DON'T GET ME WRONG! BUT THE REASON FOR MY EMBARRASSMENT IS THAT I ALWAYS FELT LIKE A FELLA WHO FOUNDED SOMETHING SHOULD AT LEAST KNOW HE WAS FOUNDING SOMETHING. I DIDN'T HAVE THE SLIGHTEST IDEA I WAS FOUNDING SOMETHING . . ."

"WHEN YOU TALK TO KIDS ABOUT THE SOVEREIGN OF ALL THAT IS, THE ONE WHO MADE YOU AND EVERYTHING ELSE, THE ONE WHO BECAME ONE OF US, THE ONE WHO DIED FOR US, AND THE ONE WHO IS ALIVE FOR US TODAY—DON'T YOU DARE BORE ANYONE WITH THAT. IF YOU CAN'T DO THIS, THEN YOU NEED TO GET BETTER ACQUAINTED WITH THE ONE YOU'RE TALKING ABOUT."

"IT'S A SIN TO BORE A KID WITH THE GOSPEL."

"WE'RE NEVER GOING TO JUSTIFY YOUNG LIFE WITH NUMBERS BECAUSE OUR COUNT MAY NOT MATCH HEAVEN'S."

"DON'T EVER LET 'EM QUIT TALKING ABOUT JESUS!"

FRONTIER RAN

VISTA, COLORADO

the
1950s

An Absolute Dream

When thoughts drift to the 1950s, wholesome images of America often come to mind. Children of this era might remember playing with hula hoops, Silly Putty, or Mr. Potato Head while watching *The Lone Ranger*, *The Howdy Doody Show*, and *The Mickey Mouse Club* on the family's first television set. At night, their parents enjoyed such fare as *I Love Lucy*, *The Honeymooners*, and *Gunsmoke*.

For the 1950s teenager, the latter half of the decade must have seemed a dream. The youth subculture was now a permanent fixture, and their fashions, slang, and entertainment created a brand-new consumer market. By the middle of the decade, a new style of music had emerged, and it was coined "rock 'n' roll." Deemed by many parents as dangerous, the jumpy sounds of Elvis Presley, Chuck Berry, and Little Richard could be heard blaring out of car radios and on the new national TV show, *American Bandstand*. Cruising in cars to the local hamburger joint or school sock hop became all the rage.

That doesn't mean, of course, everything was fine. In between the history-defining Second World War of the 1940s and the cultural overhaul of the 1960s sat the decade where tensions seemed to bubble just below the surface. War, both hot and cold, still permeated the world, as did the painful presence of racism.

Young Life, meanwhile, continued to faithfully meet and walk alongside kids in the midst of a culture that blended innocence and danger. If the forties were marked by a pioneering spirit, then the fifties would be remembered as a time of expansion. The mission grew up alongside the teenagers of the 1950s, and as Young Life reached its own "teenage years," it truly hit its stride.

"For a Young Life staff person, the 1950s were an absolute dream," said Bill Starr. "There was such a response; the middle class was becoming prominent and we moved with it."

In 1958, Tom Raley, who oversaw the work in Seattle, Washington, came up with a plan to double the city's already impressive number of ten Young Life clubs. "We named the plan 'Operation Flex,' " Raley said. "We selected ten schools where Young Life had never been. We encouraged everyone to begin to pray for those ten schools. We put ten leadership teams together, and they began to get to know some kids from those schools. They also tried to meet some adults in those communities."

In late March, Raley and the leaders hosted a banquet for the new kids at the Olympic Hotel in downtown Seattle. "We invited ten kids from each of the new schools and ten kids from the existing Young Life clubs plus the leadership from all twenty clubs." The banquet itself was a success, but there was still more to be revealed.

Opposite: Just one of the many busloads of kids that rolled into Frontier Ranch in the 1950s.

the **1950s** | 23

Because clubs had outgrown homes, staff had to become creative in finding new locations, like this one—the Swan Funeral Home. Pictured here is Jim Rayburn (top left) with 467 kids at the Colorado Springs club (obviously not everyone fit into the picture!).

The leaders asked the crowd of two hundred kids and leaders to move to the main ballroom, where they were surprised by more than one thousand kids from the existing clubs waiting for them. "The new kids loved it and saw that Young Life was something a lot of kids were into," Raley remembered. "It was a great evening all the way around. Leaders and committee people were excited." Just two weeks later, on April 4, 1958, ten brand-new clubs formed in Seattle.

"We had huge clubs in the fifties," Raley said. "The largest Young Life club in the country, at one point, was in Salem, Oregon." That club, led by Doug Coe, witnessed more than four hundred kids coming out every week. It was evident that throughout the country, the Lord was opening doors and drawing kids to Himself.

"A MIRACLE BEYOND BELIEF"

In 1950, while serving on work crew at Silver Cliff, Cy Burress and Jerry Kirk would often hike up the mountain behind camp to read the Bible and pray. On one such trip they saw another camp directly above them, the Round-Up Lodge for Boys.

"They actually prayed Young Life would someday have that camp," explained Bob Mitchell, who was their work crew boss that summer. "When we heard what those kids were doing, we counseled them to pray more appropriately and not ask God for stupid things like that—especially right after He'd

given us Silver Cliff. It's a wonder we didn't ruin their prayer life. Instead they strengthened ours."

Undeterred, Cy and Jerry continued to pray. Meanwhile, Rayburn was also aware of the ranch, and carried a passion for it that matched the boys' prayers. At the end of the summer, Rayburn served as guest speaker at Round-Up Lodge's banquet. Driving out of the camp that night, he confided to Maxine, "Max, these folks don't know it yet, but this place doesn't belong to them anymore. I asked our Father for it this evening."

In October, Ted Benson came across an ad in the back of *The New Yorker* magazine, which touted a half-million-dollar boys' camp for sale "in the high Continental Divide country of Colorado." Benson gave the ad to Rayburn as a joke, suggesting the two go in 50-50 on the price.

To Rayburn, however, it was no joke; it was, in fact, a confirmation from the Lord. While the ad never mentioned the camp's name, Rayburn knew this had to be Round-Up Lodge. After some investigation, it was indeed confirmed to be the camp just up the mountain from Silver Cliff, now listed at an asking price of $350,000. Rayburn approached the board in January about the unbelievable opportunity that lay before them. They approved the purchase, as long as Rayburn could raise the money from foundations and donors (preferably new ones). Rayburn's first meeting was with the owner of

Round-Up Lodge, Dr. E. Alfred Marquard. As a result of their meeting, Marquard dropped the asking price down to $250,000.

Rayburn crisscrossed the country via train to find the funds, and "two months and many miracles later," he raised the entire amount from nine donors. Later, Rayburn took staff up to the newly named Frontier Ranch, where they dedicated it to the Lord. "We prayed in every building in that place," said Roy Riviere. "We were overwhelmed with what God had given us!"

Frontier Ranch hosted its first campers a mere six months later, in July 1951. As Emile Cailliet wrote in his book, *Young Life*, "From beginning to end it was all 'a miracle beyond belief.' "

"THE GREATEST KIDS' CHEF IN THE WORLD"

While speaking on a Young Life weekend in Harvey Cedars, New Jersey, in May 1951, Rayburn met Andy "Goldbrick" Delaney and his wife, Jerry, who worked for a Philadelphia catering company. "Next thing you know," Jerry said, "he's asking us if we'd come work for him at a big kids' camp out in Colorado. We said 'no,' so he said he was going to put us on his prayer list. Andy and I looked at each other, both knowing what the other was thinking. 'This guy is crazy. Put us on a prayer list?' "

"Well, we didn't know what it was like to be in Jim's prayers!" Within a month the Delaneys were working at Frontier Ranch.

Frog Sullivan remembered an early conversation between Rayburn and his new cook. "Jim, Goldbrick, and I had a meeting one day up in Frontier's dining room. Jim said, 'Camp travels on its stomach. You can have the best program in the world, but if you don't have good food, the program isn't going to be any good.' Goldbrick looked at him and said, 'Boss, it'll be good.' And it was."

The entrance to Frontier Ranch.

The couple brought far more than good cooking to Frontier. As the first black Young Life staff, their commitment to excellence, love for people, and humble service helped usher in a new era in the mission.

"Goldbrick and Jerry had a profound influence on my life concerning racial issues," Mal McSwain, longtime staff member, said. "Their attitude and love changed an awful lot of impressions ingrained in so many kids who came out to Frontier from the South in the fifties. It was a powerful thing to see young men and women from these southern states actually fall in love with Goldbrick and Jerry and realize these people not only loved them, but were committed to being their friends for the rest of their lives."

"Oh, I loved Goldbrick to death," Frog Sullivan said. "He knew I was a southern white kid and I'm sure he knew the feelings I had, just from growing up in Memphis, but the first time I met him, he said, 'I know you and I love you,' and he hugged me."

It became tradition on the first night of camp for Rayburn to introduce a packed dining hall to "the greatest kids' chef in the world." Cheers of "Hurrah for Goldbrick" rang out when the conquering hero entered, replete in tall white chef's hat and coat.

"There will never be another Goldbrick," Roy Riviere proclaimed. "With a perfectly straight face, he told me once, 'Roy, don't ever trust a skinny cook.' And he lived up to that!"

For more than a quarter of a century, Goldbrick and Jerry joyfully served thousands of campers, as they served their Lord—whom they both met as a result of their early days in Young Life.

Goldbrick greets the campers.

EXCELLENT CAMPING REFLECTS AN EXCELLENT SAVIOR

Along with delicious food, Rayburn always stressed excellence in every aspect of the weeklong experience. Kids, he reasoned, must experience the best in setting, humor, adventure, and message, to make the connection with "life to the full." The founder once told his staff, "When you're talking to kids about the Sovereign of the Universe, the King of kings, the Lord of lords, do it in a place that speaks well of Him."

Throughout the fifties, the camps provided the staff an opportunity to determine what worked and what should be discarded. "We didn't learn all about camping and then do it," Bill Starr said. "We didn't have a great idea about researching camp properties and then plot out how we could buy the right ones. All that gradually occurred. The same with the clubs, the same with communicating the Christian message, the same with training. I really sense we were Spirit-led to do what we were doing."

LEADERSHIP WAS KEY

Lessons learned in the local field ministry often made their way to camp. Take, for example, leadership. A Young Life leader, explained Starr, was always a driving force in the life of a kid. He or she led kids "in fun, at mealtimes, into competition, even in music. Leadership needs to take place in all we do. If it's authentic, kids will follow. As I think back about the ideas that moved me, it wasn't about being a hot shot with kids. It was the willingness to be vulnerable, to befriend and let the Spirit of God do what He wanted. That's a person who kids remember."

In most summer camping programs, the "camp counselor" was traditionally someone the kids met upon arriving at camp. In the early days of the mission, when there were very few volunteer leaders to accompany staff to camp, Young Life also used adults and college students as counselors. Relationally, however, the ideal leader for a kid at camp would always be that kid's leader from back home.

By the late 1950s, as more volunteer leaders joined the work, Young Life turned the corner from camp counselors to homegrown leaders. The same leader who had invited kids to camp now sat beside them on the bus ride and experienced everything together with them during the week. It was their leader from back home who helped the kids participate in the activities, articulated the Gospel in cabin times, and listened as their young friends processed what they were hearing. Best of all, leaders accompanied kids back to their shared hometown where their friendship continued and discipleship could begin.

ACCEPTING KIDS WHERE THEY ARE

How do leaders invite non-Christian kids into a Christian environment like Young Life camp? From the early days the staff wrestled with issues like these as they sought to provide a welcoming atmosphere where kids could experience the message of God's love.

"I remember," Starr said, "seeing a counselor watch kids smoke at the Ranch, and just absolutely die inside—because this was a 'Christian' camp. That left a real impression on me because we were trying to act out the biblical idea of 'Don't judge people.' I thought, 'How can we change their lifestyle unless some new life inside makes them want to change their lifestyle? Could we trust God to get to kids if we just let them be themselves—even smoking and stuff?' "

1950s
BEST PICTURES

1950
All About Eve

1951
An American in Paris

1952
The Greatest Show on Earth

1953
From Here to Eternity

1954
On the Waterfront

1955
Marty

1956
Around the World in 80 Days

1957
The Bridge on the River Kwai

1958
Gigi

1959
Ben Hur

This thinking led to the creation of the smoking pit, a designated area where kids of age who arrive at camp with a smoking habit could hang out. This place, made especially for them, was an outward expression of the desire to meet these kids exactly where they were.

"We didn't talk against smoking," the thirty-five-year staff veteran John Miller reasoned. "We didn't have to. [The kids who smoked] weren't picked at, pointed at, or anything, because that's not the issue. When you make negatives the issue, you drive people from Christ."

AN ATMOSPHERE OF JOY

From the start of the mission, humor was essential in working with teenagers. Humor relaxed kids, broke down walls, showed the kids their leaders didn't take themselves too seriously, and subtly pointed kids to the abundant life they craved.

Bob Mitchell explained, "Jim and the early staff believed the proclamation of the Gospel has to be done in an atmosphere of joy, so humor and entertainment have been a hallmark of Young Life. We always did quality stuff, not just slapstick, yelling, or screaming. We made up a lot of the skits; 'The King and Queen,' for instance. And we stole a lot of it, too, like, 'The Movie Skit'—that was a Sid Caesar and Imogene Coco production. The operas [hilarious musical shows featuring program characters from the camp week] were created to be funny, but with real quality.

"We had talented people like the Rary Mountain Boys, the Sylte Sisters, who sang on the radio, Phil McDonald, and Jay Grimstead. We sang crazy songs. I pray Young Life will always be quality in what it does and will think through its forms of entertainment so they're professionally done. When Jesus changed water into wine, He made it into the best there was and when we do program, it's got to be quality. Whatever's worth doing is worth doing well."

Mal McSwain remembered another gifted performer in the camping pantheon, Tom Bade. "Tom was an entertainment phenom. He was offered a TV contract to go on his own show by Spike Jones and some others back in the fifties, when TV was brand new, but he turned it down. He was a great influence in my life."

The entire weeklong program at camp was thoroughly prayed for and thought through far in advance. There was a special progression as the week went along and each day had its own unique schedule. Starr explained, "Program was the way to get kids involved and to build this sense of oneness. In the beginning of the week you start at a high level and gradually diminish the place of program. Meanwhile, the Gospel has a chance to ascend as the week progresses. Program is a vehicle to launch the message."

The Rary Mountain Boys (Jay Grimstead, Dick Lowey, and Phil McDonald) and the Sylte Sisters (Deanna, Joan, and Deanda).

CLUB TALKS

Like the program, the Gospel message at camp was divided up by days, with a purposeful sequence of talks planned.

"The progression of talks was pretty much the same back then," Mitchell recalled. Speakers began the week by pointing kids to the person of Jesus, and in following days, addressed the need of humankind and the redemptive work of the cross and resurrection. By week's end they would talk about what it meant to follow Jesus, the implications of the Christian faith, and its impact on their relationships with family and friends.

THE "TWENTY MINUTES"

By the mid-1950s, a new idea arose that helped kids have more "space" to process the Gospel message at camp. Immediately following a message on the cross, where a speaker not only explained what Jesus endured but why, kids were given the gift of silence. For twenty minutes, they went off on their own to think, process, pray, or simply "be," in an environment of absolute solitude. During that time, in a camp filled with hundreds of teenagers, not a sound was heard.

Mitchell explained the thinking behind the twenty minutes, which originally followed the message on sin. "Well, those of us who had the privilege of speaking to kids at the camps were looking for ways we could help kids take that initial step of faith to Jesus. And we kind of stumbled onto this, I think, by the grace of God. We thought, 'You know, kids are never quiet, never alone.' And it's very important to have some period of time in their lives when they're just still. And so we would give them twenty minutes to go and be alone, and we found that was so powerful, and kids didn't have much of that in their lives, where they sat somewhere alone in reflection and in prayer."

TAKING CARE OF BUSINESS

As Young Life grew in size and complexity, it was evident Rayburn must find a strong individual to oversee the mission's financial and business administration. As it happened, Rayburn needn't worry because Roy Riviere had the matter well under control.

"One of the early things the good Lord let my bride, Doris, and me do for Young Life was get John Carter in here," Riviere said. "This mission would not have gone where it was without the skilled business manager it had for years and years."

Carter's career consisted of making improvements in the mission's various departments—during his four-plus decades of service, he worked in areas as varied as development, insurance, human resources, camp purchasing, and funding.

"John had a wonderful humility about his life," Tom Raley said. "I never once remember feeling, nor do I know anyone who did, that John was out of line, demanding, pompous, or power-happy. He handled his roles in the mission over a long period of time more gracefully than almost anybody else I know."

The mission needed Carter because the operation continued to expand. The "business model," which consisted of Rayburn flying across the country to raise the entire mission's budget on his own, was becoming less feasible. Three camps and a growing staff inevitably led to a growing budget. Rayburn could no longer be the sole means of raising support for each person.

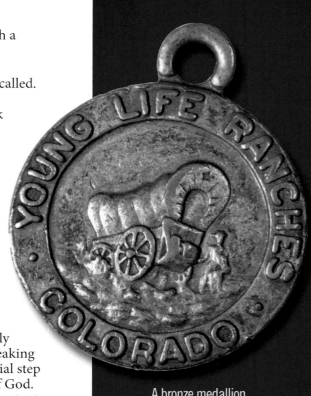

A bronze medallion commemorating the Young Life camps in Colorado (Silver Cliff and Frontier Ranch in Buena Vista, and Star Ranch in Colorado Springs).

It would be wiser to have each staff person responsible for raising his or her own support. While this would certainly make life easier on Rayburn, it would place an added responsibility on every staff person. In Portland, Oregon, Bill Starr found a solution.

A COMMITTEE IS BORN
Starr felt acutely the disconnect between Young Life and the local church. Possessed with a strong church background himself, he wanted to make sure Young Life was "not simply outside the church, but a part of the ministry of the church. I wanted us to have a representative body out of the congregations. So it forced me to go to pastors, explain who we were, what the goal was, and how we wanted to participate with them rather than outside what they were doing."

Starr visited local churches and asked for someone from each congregation to become a part of the area ministry. And thus was born the local Young Life committee.

"None of these people had any Young Life connection,"

he said. "There were a couple of things motivating me: I wanted them to be part of the overall ministry taking place in Portland at that time. I also thought this could help decentralize fiscal responsibility.

"Jim took it all on himself; he'd go out and raise money and distribute it. Well that seemed to me to be unfair to him and to us. We needed to assume and accept our responsibility, and the move really freed us up to grow."

Rayburn's reaction? Starr laughed, "I think he was thrilled!"

LEARNING "ON THE GO"
As the years passed, Rayburn recognized a need in his staff. Wanting the men and women on staff to grow in their understanding of the Word of God, he came up with a novel approach. In September 1951, seven students climbed into a station wagon to travel around the country for the next ten months, so they might be better trained in the Gospel message. The students visited seminary professors and theologians in Los Angeles, Chicago, Philadelphia, New York,

Bob Mitchell hanging with kids at the local soda fountain.

Station Wagon Grad School, 1951.

Portland, Seattle, Colorado Springs, and Denver. The "Station Wagon Grad School" was ultimately deemed impractical, and shelved after the trial year.

In 1954, Rayburn told Wally Howard, "We're going to start an institute and we want you to be the dean. Larry Culp will be the president." Howard remembered, "Larry was still on the faculty at Columbia University, and also in private business. The two of us sat down and started putting together a faculty. In 1954 we took over Star Ranch and held the first year's class."

The summer school at Star Ranch helped the staff develop a solid biblical identity for who they were and what they were doing. "The institute had such an impact on teaching Young Life staff to think theologically," said Mary Stam, longtime staff member. "We were being given tools to 'rightly divide the word of truth.' "

Within two years, the institute had outgrown Star Ranch's facilities and summer classes were moved to Fountain Valley School, located south of Colorado Springs, where it remained until the mid-1980s.

"THEY WERE OUR MISSIONARIES"

As the staff plunged deeper into theology, the work ventured outward. God continued to open doors for His Gospel, and for the first time, Young Life would have staff working outside the United States. In 1953, Rod and Fran Johnston, former leaders in Chicago, answered the call to go overseas and help begin Young Life's international work in Paris, France. Rod's brother, Art, was already there leading a club as a volunteer when the Johnstons arrived.

" THE INSTITUTE HAD SUCH AN IMPACT ON TEACHING YOUNG LIFE STAFF TO THINK THEOLOGICALLY. WE WERE BEING GIVEN TOOLS TO 'RIGHTLY DIVIDE THE WORD OF TRUTH.' "

—MARY STAM

Rod and Fran Johnston, with son David, on their way to Paris in 1953.

Paris was a perfect fit for the couple. "Rod was a driver," said Chris Cook, who served alongside the Johnstons during her early days on staff. "He was called 'the bulldozer.' He had lots of vision, strength, and energy to get things done."

Writing about their first days in France for *Young Life* magazine, Fran said, "What has saddened us most is to see the conspicuous lack of God-consciousness. Thousands of French teenagers have never had a chance to hear about the Lord Jesus Christ and the wonderful way in which He can bring peace and joy into their lonely, grasping hearts."

The Johnstons were an inspiration to stateside staff and kids. Bob Reeverts, who would go on to lead the mission's international work in the 1980s and 1990s, had fond memories of the couple. "They were pioneers who really raised the bar for us. At Campaigners, there would be the 'Rod and Fran fund.' If you had an extra nickel or quarter you'd put it in that bank for their ministry in France. Campaigners kids from all over the country supported them—they were our missionaries. Rod and Fran were models of incredible faithfulness, toughness, and courage."

The couple stayed actively involved with French teenagers until their retirement in 1990. Meanwhile, another country much closer to the United States was also calling with an opportunity of a lifetime.

MALIBU CLUB

By 1952 the mission had a wonderful "problem": all three ranches were filled beyond capacity. Rayburn recognized the need to have a camp in the Northwest, since so many of the kids coming to Colorado were from Washington and Oregon.

The challenge of finding yet another camp didn't deter the man, who simply laid the need at the Lord's feet. In fact, it seemed no request was ever too big for Jim Rayburn.

"One hymn the staff sang constantly," Recie Raley said, "was John Newton's 'Come, My Soul, Thy Suit Prepare.' The second verse says, 'Thou art coming to a King/Large petitions with thee bring/For His grace and power are such/None can ever ask too much.' And Jim believed that with all of his heart. This was a God who delighted in His children asking for the impossible."

"And I think from Rayburn's perspective," Tom Raley added, "the more far out it was, the more excited he got about it. It's a little bit like somebody who rises to the occasion, a golfer who feels 'the more pressure, the better.'"

As Rayburn pursued the possibility of a camp in the Northwest, the Lord again was working behind the scenes in a way much grander than even Rayburn's wildest dreams. While visiting Seattle in January 1952, Rayburn met Jim and Elsie Campbell, who mentioned, in passing, a resort for sale named Malibu Club in British Columbia. Jim fully expected Rayburn would lose all interest when he informed him the asking price was $1 million. "Little did we know," Elsie said, "the tenacity of Jim Rayburn and how once an idea was planted in his head, only God could control him."

The Campbells flew Rayburn, Add Sewell, and Bill Starr out to see the resort that once served such Hollywood luminaries as John Wayne, Barbara Stanwyck, Walt Disney, Bing Crosby, and Bob Hope. As the plane flew over the breathtaking site resting beside the Princess Louisa Inlet, Rayburn calmly stated, "There is Young Life's next camp."

The five toured the grounds with Rayburn declaring what Young Life would do with each building "when" not "if" the mission had Malibu. Elsie recounted the conversation after several of these "when" declarations: "After clearing his throat, my Jim timidly and half-jokingly said to Mr. Rayburn, 'It sounds like you think Young Life is going to get this place. They only want one million dollars for it, you know.' [Mr. Rayburn] turned toward Jim, pulled himself up to his full height, and looked him up and down. If looks could have knocked Jim down, he would have fallen flat. Rayburn very slowly, in his Texan drawl said, 'If the Boss wants us to have it, we will have it!'"

The resort was magnificent, but so was the cost. "There was no way we could even think of it," Bob Mitchell said. "But Jim was so persistent at times like this, and he trusted God. So we invited Tom Hamilton, the owner of Malibu, to come to Frontier Ranch and see what we were doing there. He came on a wonderful week. He saw all those kids and he dropped the price from $1 million to $700,000, and Jim told

The flags of Canada, the U.S., and British Columbia greet visitors at Malibu Club.

Malibu Club

Malibu Princess, 1950s.

Jim Rayburn, Bill Starr, Bob Mitchell, and Tom Raley waterskiing at Malibu, August 5, 1955.

him he was headed in the right direction but it was still way too much."

Over the course of the fall, the dominoes continued to fall and by November momentum was on Young Life's side. "Tom Hamilton and his associates sold a well-known California hotel," Elsie Campbell explained, "and the amount of the sale was such that the capital gains tax would be exorbitant. He needed a tax break to offset it. There was Malibu standing unused—deteriorating and useless to him. However, if it were sold at a considerable loss, that would compensate for the profit on the hotel sale. How beautifully God takes care of His own."

Hamilton lowered the asking price of the 645-acre property to $300,000 and even contributed a sizable amount himself. Rayburn needed to raise a down payment of $150,000 by the end of the year and spent the next seven weeks traveling twenty-three thousand miles and visiting twenty-five cities in the U.S. and Eastern Canada. With the down payment raised, Rayburn signed the purchase contract on December 21, 1953.

Young Life now possessed a camp nestled in one of the most beautiful places in the world. The staff recognized the potential in Malibu and its most unique attribute: offering kids a water-themed program.

The camp was not without its unique challenges, however. The housing, Starr said, "was configured for adults, just two to a room. We needed to house eight to ten to a room. Now Malibu was located in the midst of many logging camps. We hoped that they had bunks we could purchase. We were right. We secured about three dozen, and piled them on the raft we were pulling back to Malibu." After four days using this approach, Mitchell and Starr had enough bunks to ready Malibu for kids.

The purchase also brought another benefit which only the Lord knew about at the time. "In order to own property in Canada," Char Meredith explained, "it was necessary to form a Canadian corporation to hold Malibu in trust, so they set up Young Life of Canada for that purpose in 1954." "We never planned to be an international mission," Starr explained. "Here was another point where I can look back and see God leading, even though at the time we did not understand."

Young Life was now in Canada and the first staff arrived in 1957. While the U.S. leadership maintained operation of Malibu Club, a Canadian organization with its own board assumed operation and oversight of field ministry throughout Canada in 1978.

INVESTIGATED BY THE FBI!
The 1950s, while an era of growth and prosperity, were by no means trouble free. With the end of World War II came a new threat to world peace: the Cold War. "McCarthyism," named after Senator Joe McCarthy's obsessive desire to rid the country of any subversive communist threat, inflamed fears

throughout the country toward any unknown movement. Young Life was not exempt. The success of the ministry raised its profile and many wondered, "What's the story on this mysterious organization working with our local young people? Is Young Life communist?"

"The church looked, at that point, at any parachurch ministry as being suspect," Raley explained. "Young Life coming on the scene when it did in 1941 was not exactly warmly received by the denominational church. They just didn't understand."

Mitchell remembered clearly his own experience. While a student at Wheaton College, he would drive to Downer's Grove High School in his old '36 Chevy. "It had no windows and it was really cold," Mitchell said. "By the time I'd get to the high school I would just be frozen. So, I'd get out of my old car and go into the high school to do contact work, wearing an overcoat because I was freezing. I'd have the collar turned up and some teacher saw me with my overcoat on and turned me in as a communist and some kind of subversive drug dealer or something. I found myself in the principal's office trying to explain who I was and that I was not a communist!"

Suspicions of the mission, ironically, often helped further the relationship between Young Life and the local church. "I'll never forget one touching moment," Riviere said, "when we had a good work going in Topeka, Kansas. Some man, who was a McCarthyite at heart, got it in his mind that Young Life was bound to be communistic. He really was effective at propagating that idea.

"There was one Baptist preacher in Topeka who heard that charge and took the time to look carefully into the leadership and backing and history of Young Life. He presented a sermon entitled 'A Baptist and His Brethren,' and he lined himself up 100 percent square on the side of Young Life. He said he would be delighted if people who absolutely had to shoot at Young Life would shoot at him instead. They wanted young people to know the Savior and he did too. That one man and that one sermon kept Young Life alive in Topeka in that era. I couldn't wait to get out there and thank him in person."

Around this time, Don Jones, an FBI agent in Seattle, came into contact with Young Life because of these types of rumors. Jones said, "The Special Agent in Charge threw a letter down on my desk and said, 'Some lady has written about an outfit called Young Life and thinks they're a communist group and her kids are going. I want you to go and find out what's going on with this outfit called Young Life.' "

Jones, a Christian, had never heard of Young Life. "I went out and started digging around a little bit and met Add Sewell. And I went and interviewed this parent who had written that letter. Wonderful lady with a wonderful family. She was just concerned her kids were getting involved in something that must be communistic. Because everything was 'communistic' if you loved kids and wanted to work with kids in those days.

"The next thing I knew, Jim Rayburn was at my door. I had no idea who Jim Rayburn was. But Jim, in his slow Texas drawl, introduced himself, kind of invited himself into our little apartment and I got acquainted with Jim Rayburn and we became good friends."

In 1958, Jones was invited onto Young Life's National Board. Bob Stover, an early board member who would go on to serve alongside each of Young Life's first five presidents, remarked, "Don went to [then FBI director] J. Edgar Hoover. The FBI in those days was not allowed to be on boards, because they didn't want to do anything to damage the work of the FBI.

"But, Hoover gave Don special permission to be on the board. And that was marvelous because—Young Life is so well known now, it's hard to imagine this—but, in those early days when you'd say 'Young Life,' the next question was, 'Well, what's that?' All the organizations that were subversive had 'youth,' 'young,' 'America,' or something like that in their name. So, when Don came on the board, it was great because the first thing we'd say is, 'Well we have an FBI man on the board.' That solved it!"

A TALE OF TWO CITIES

Along with accusations of communism, the mission faced another threat to its identity. In the 1950s racial separation was the rule and Young Life, like many organizations of the day, struggled with the implications.

In 1955, John Miller began pioneering the work in Leland, Mississippi. After he returned from taking kids to camp, their parents confronted him. They were outraged to discover black kids attended camp the same week, and to make matters worse, these kids were in the pool at the same time as their own children. The committee made their feelings on segregation quite plain to the young area director and to Rayburn. It would be fine if black kids attended camp during other weeks, but their kids would not be going if black campers were also there, nor would they continue to support the ministry.

"They didn't want to tell us what to do in other parts of the country," Wally Howard, the Southern regional director, said. "But when their kids went to Frontier, they wanted a guarantee that there would be no black campers there. And second, they wanted a guarantee that there would be no pictures or stories about blacks in any Young Life publications."

This mentality was a sad sign of the times and went against everything Young Life was trying to accomplish. It quickly became evident John and his wife, Beverly, would need to leave Leland, and the Young Life work in Mississippi was shut down.

Not too long after, twelve hundred miles to the north, a new work began in the city of Newark, New Jersey. At the time, Young Life was still primarily a suburban ministry. "We were building a doughnut organization," said Starr. "In the middle of the doughnut was the inner city, and we were building our ministries around it."

At the time, Harv Oostdyk was serving on Young Life staff in Morristown, New Jersey. Starr remembered Oostdyk as one of a kind. "Harv was a genius, a risk taker, and probably the most charismatic guy I've met in my life. For a white Christian, he was way ahead of his time in his thinking about the inner city."

The "risk taker" often drove the streets of Newark and witnessed the overwhelming masses of kids hanging out with nothing to do. Burdened by the sight of these lost young people, he began to reach out to four in particular.

That summer Oostdyk packed these young men in his car and drove west to Frontier Ranch. The four were members of the Romans, the largest gang on the East Coast. Their leader was twenty-three-year-old Vinnie Di Pasquale, a recovering heroin addict who had twenty-five arrests and fifteen imprisonments to this point.

The week at Frontier proved life-changing for the gang leader, who was also known as "Diablo" or the Devil. Sitting in the club room, he heard the story of Christ's crucifixion for the first time in his life. After the talk, he went outside to pray and invite Jesus into his heart. Diablo now belonged to the Savior.

Vinnie's conversion in 1956 set the stage for the further blossoming of Young Life's urban ministry, in which he would continue to play a pivotal role for years to come.

AN ATMOSPHERE OF FRIENDLY INFORMALITY

When Dr. John A. Mackay, then-president of Princeton Theological Seminary, learned of Young Life's distinctive strategy to spend time with kids, he coined the phrase "winning the right to be heard." The willingness to patiently invest in kids and get to know them was the key to winning a hearing in their presence. That hearing often came at club.

Young Life exploded in the 1950s in part because club was a place where kids felt like honored guests. Like camp, it was tailored to kids and their needs. John Miller remembered Rayburn's admonition about the importance of meeting

Harv Oostdyk speaking in club.

length. "Jim said, 'Don't ever let a club be over fifty-nine minutes and fifty-nine seconds. Never. No reason. Have your hay baled so you can give it out. You want to turn those kids loose when they want to hear more.'

"You see," Miller continued, "we have to develop our skills in how to talk about the Lord in an attractive, true, honest way, to the point where kids are engrossed. You want to shut it off when they want to hear something more. And that's an art."

Music was also important. In the early days of the mission, songs in club were mainly hymns. Many adults found it astonishing that kids outside the church would come out to a meeting and join hundreds of other teenagers in singing hymns. How this was achieved, though, was no mystery to Martie Sheffer, an early Young Life pioneer along with her husband, George. It was simply an issue of leadership. "Pagan kids would sing hymns," she explained, "because they trusted their leaders. That was so significant to us."

"WHO'S PRAYING FOR THEM?"

Most importantly, the entire work was to be undergirded by prayer. Rayburn's insistence on the importance of prayer never wavered, as Annie Cheairs and others would testify.

Cheairs recalled, "I heard Jim say, 'If we don't pray for these kids, who's praying for them? We may be the only person in that child's life that breathes their name in prayer.' "

McSwain had his own Rayburn prayer story. While working at Frontier one summer in the mid-1950s, he was sent to Denver to pick up Rayburn from the airport.

"All of us just craved being around Jim, especially the young college kids," he said. "I couldn't wait to get all the inside scoop, so I could get back and say, 'Jim and I were talking about this . . . ' "

As the pair left the airport, Rayburn asked, "What staff are at Frontier? Where are they from?"

After McSwain answered the questions, Rayburn replied, "Well, why don't we pray for them?" The young man patiently held his questions as Rayburn started praying. "He prayed for everybody I'd mentioned plus all their wives and especially the ones he knew were not getting paid."

When Rayburn finished, the college student was ready to hit him with questions, but realized "the boss" was giving him the chance to pray. "I prayed a real short

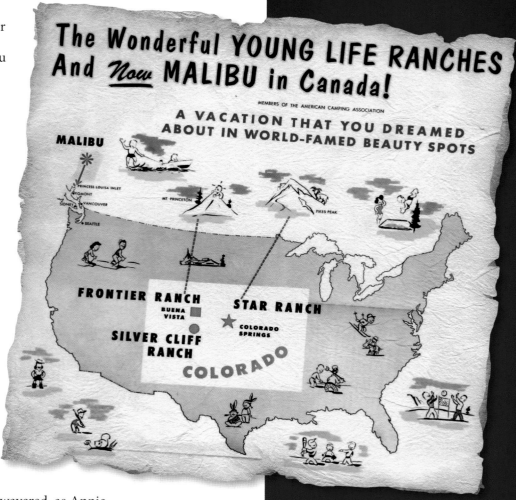

A 1954 brochure telling kids about Young Life camps. Incidentally, the price for a week at camp was $35 and horseback riding was $1 per hour.

prayer," he said. "I was intimidated to pray in front of Jim, and I was ready to get into another agenda."

McSwain wrapped up his prayer and Rayburn started praying again. "This went back and forth," he said, "until, all of a sudden, we were over the hill coming down into Buena Vista. I was really disappointed because I thought, 'What am I going to say to all the guys about Jim and me?'

"I realized later I wanted to talk to Jim, but Jim wanted to talk to God. I don't know if he did that for my benefit, but it left a lasting impression on me of how important prayer was to him. It was a life-changing experience. I didn't have any great gossip to tell my buddies, but it was good."

JOY AND PAIN
Besides his passion for prayer, Rayburn loved to laugh. From his early one-man skits around the campfire to the pun-ishing humor he doled out at high school assemblies, the man embodied life to the full. Mitchell fondly remembered the Boss's natural use of humor—both spontaneous and planned. "He liked his jokes better than anybody else did and one of the reasons we laughed at him was because he thought it was so funny. Frankly, I didn't think some of his jokes were all that funny, but the way he told them was, and he'd get so tickled halfway through these stories and jokes that we were rolling off our chairs just watching and enjoying him."

Perhaps Rayburn's joy was so profound because he was also a man in chronic pain. Both he and Maxine endured various illnesses throughout their lives and this pain intensified in the 1950s. For Maxine the most common conditions were severe depression, anxiety attacks, and lower back pain; meanwhile, Jim suffered debilitating migraines. Surgeries were common in the Rayburn household, as were medications, which often led to worse side effects than the symptoms themselves. Jim's reactions to his prescribed medications continually plagued him—and one day would alter the course of his life's work, not to mention the mission of Young Life.

EXPANSION, EXPERIENCE, AND EXCITEMENT
From committees to city work to communism, Young Life seemed to experience a little bit of everything in the 1950s. Whether doubling the number of camp properties, or holding clubs in the hundreds, or pioneering ministry in France, the era was marked by expansion and expectation.

"When I think of the fifties," Mitchell said, "I think of tremendous growth in Young Life and the excitement of an emerging ministry; the excitement of an acquisition of a camp. Whoever would have thought we could have Round-Up Lodge for Boys, this beautiful property? And then shortly thereafter, the fabulous Malibu Club and all that went with that acquisition?"

But no matter how large the ministry became, no matter the club attendance, the number of camps, or the size of the budget, Young Life was first and foremost about Christ and kids. And Rayburn made sure to remind the staff of this.

"These were the days of Jim's greatest effectiveness in

Rayburn and Millie (Sisco) Carter (far right), who served as Jim's secretary and as a local Young Life leader, enjoy doughnuts with kids atop Pike's Peak.

leadership in the mission," Mitchell said. "Young Life in the 1950s was a little organization that didn't take itself too seriously; we had a lot of laughs, a lot of fun, and good times. There was great camaraderie between the staff. It was just an exciting time to be involved in the ministry."

Throughout Young Life's second decade, the Lord continued to bless the "little organization" with His favor and protection. In many ways, the simplicity and innocence of the times proved the perfect soil in which the burgeoning young movement could take root. In retrospect, this turned out to be an important time of strengthening and preparation. As the mission turned the corner from the glory days of the 1950s to the unknown of the 1960s, Young Life would need the Lord's presence in ways the mission could never foresee.

Webster High cheerleaders from Tulsa, Oklahoma, 1950.

A Mission That Camps

A Reflection by Denny Rydberg, president

Before Jim and Maxine Rayburn ever dreamed of an organization like Young Life, they were committed to camping. In January 1935, they took an assignment in Arizona as part of a mission with the Presbyterian Church. Immediately, in their desire to reach kids, they began a primitive camping ministry. With open fires, sleeping bags, and tents, Jim and Maxine realized the benefits of camping.

Later, when Young Life began, camping became a special part of the ministry. George Sheffer, who joined the staff in 1942, wrote about those first camps. "Since Young Life was new, small, lacked finances, owned no camp of its own . . . most of the staff would travel by car to some rented facility . . . Immediately upon arrival all would participate in preparing the camp to be the best possible. We wanted the facility to be as attractive as possible for the kids when they arrived. Sometimes the camp facilities were painfully inadequate—both the leaders and the kids knew it. Nevertheless, in the midst of some of those situations, the Lord performed amazing acts of love and redemption. At the end of each camp, all the leaders tried to make sure the entire camp was left 'spic and span' to fulfill Young Life's policy: Always leave a camp cleaner than it was when you arrived."

Jim dreamed of a first-class camp in Colorado owned by Young Life. He asked two primary questions: "Why should we not present the beautiful Gospel of the magnificent Jesus Christ in an equally beautiful and first-class surrounding? Also, why not locate a camp where the program could offer new and exciting adventures for the campers?"

God answered both of his questions. In 1946, the first Young Life camp was opened—Star Ranch. In 1949, Silver Cliff Ranch became a Young Life property. In 1951, Round-Up Lodge was transformed as Frontier Ranch. In 1954, Malibu was added. And now, as I write this, we have thirty-five camps around the world and we are in the planning stages for more!

Camping has exploded for one reason: When given the opportunity to get away for a week in the beauty of God's grandeur and hear a clear presentation of the Gospel in an atmosphere of love and fun without the distractions they normally encounter, kids meet Christ. It's as simple as that. And year after year, about 30-40 percent of the kids who go to camp make a commitment to the Lord. And in some places, like Africa (where our camps are more like the ones George Sheffer described) the number of kids responding is even more significant!

With deep gratitude, I honor Jim and Maxine and George and the others who began our camping ministry. And with profound thankfulness, I applaud the efforts of our staff and volunteers in training leaders, building and operating quality camps, inviting kids to come, helping them raise the funds to go, and sharing the Gospel every minute of the camping day. Through serving kids extravagantly (kudos to our work crew, summer staff, and camp personnel), participating with them in adventure and activities, talking with them one on one, proclaiming clearly the love of Christ, and introducing kids to a relationship with Jesus, our camps are a platform for changing lives!

Young Life CAMPAIGN

JIM RAYBURN • FIELD DIRECTOR • STAR RANCH • COLORADO SPRINGS, COLO.

January 1952

I want you to read this letter!

I am going to try to tell you something about Young Life's strategy for reaching high school young people for the Saviour.

It is easy for me to assume that you know more about the work of Young Life Campaign than you actually do. I am so close to it. I have watched the progress and the changes that the Lord has indicated from the very start. Some of you who receive this letter know of these matters perhaps as well as I do, but many friends have suggested that they would like to have me tell them a little more about the inside working of Young Life. We do have a very unique approach to the problem of reaching young people.

You see, we are after the UNREACHED. From the very beginning, the burden that the Lord placed upon us was to reach young people who were not being touched by any other methods. The vast majority of young people are not in a church and never hear the truth about the Savior's love, so we are after them particularly. To reach them, we have had to break with some traditional methods and, I am sorry to say, we have had to sometimes be misunderstood.

For example, take our "contact work." By that we mean the hours and hours that our leaders find it necessary to spend with kids, meeting them where they are, going along with them, living with them. Now this is a recognized procedure on any foreign mission field, but many well-meaning Christians have felt that we are wasting time. And yet it is this time spent with the youngster, before and after his confession of Christ, that has made Young Life something far more than the ordinary youth movement. Not only do we win a hearing among the most difficult and hardest to reach, but after reaching them, we stay with them as a true missionary should. The winning and establishing of a soul for Jesus Christ cannot be done on a hit-and-run basis.

The Lord Jesus Himself is our example in this. His heart was tender toward sinners. He longed for them. He was not ashamed to be with them. His compassionate approach to the lost is what we are after. We try to be kind in our approach to the lost. We insist that gentleness is essential if we are to properly represent Him. I am afraid we are oftentimes criticized for no other reason than that we are honestly seeking, under the Lord's guidance, to be as He was, the "friend of publicans and sinners."

Many people ask us about our "Bible Clubs." We do not have any! In Young Life, we have given years of prayerful study to this matter of the right kind of a Christian meeting for kids. What we call a Young Life club is actually a Gospel meeting for high school young people. It is perhaps different from any meeting you have ever been in. But the differences are in small things. We sing and pray and preach the Gospel in an atmosphere of friendly informality. The meeting is deliberately placed at their level. The language is that which will be understood and impressive to a modern adolescent. We avoid the clichés of evangelical terminology and present the sweet story of how Christ died for our sins in simple terms which young people can understand and appreciate.

The Young Life club is but a phase of this work. There are weekend camps, parties, rallies, high school assemblies and our intensive Bible study units. Then there is our summer ranch program conducted on our three nationally famous Colorado ranches, where more than one thousand young people are winsomely challenged with the Saviour's claim on their lives.

Then there are the leaders. We maintain a high standard for our leadership; all of them are carefully trained in our own approach to evangelism. These men and women are not selected because of some personal charm or magnetism. There is a deeper quality that makes for a successful Young Life worker. It is a sincerity, a warmth, a personal walk with the Lord Jesus Christ, a desire to see this hard job done for His glory!

There you have the three important phases of the Young Life strategy.

1. The emphasis on the direct and friendly contact with the high schooler. The emphasis on follow-up, follow-up, and more follow-up. 2. The leaders; trained, skilled, dedicated people willing to put up with kids, to live and play with them. 3. The gracious, informal Gospel meetings featured especially in our Young Life clubs, our camps, and summer ranch program.

There is much more to be said about Young Life strategy, but this much leads me to emphasize that the most significant thing is not the techniques or the people. It is, instead, this true compassion that comes from above. Much of the Gospel work today is hindered by the severity of its attitude toward the lost. In Young Life, we try never to forget that Jesus "looked on the multitude and had compassion on them." We keep always before our minds that when He mingled with sinners, He did not condemn and judge. He treated them as friends. He longed for them to be His friends.

We do too!! He has led us that way. That is why a Young Life leader knows more young people than anybody in town. That is why he or she spends hours and hours sitting around soda fountains, going to ball games, wandering around the campus—doing things that may look kind of silly! But they are not silly, they are essential. We go where young people are. That is where they can come to understand a Christian leader and love him and respect him and want to listen to him.

Because we are dedicated to such principles, we will never become a statistically prominent movement, but we know of no other way to reach young people for the Lord and get results in lives that will stand the test of time. Already, in the first eleven years of work, the Lord has honored us with an outstanding host of young men and women who have been reached in high school and are taking a prominent place in Christian circles. Most of these would not even have heard the Gospel if the Young Life leader had not deliberately gone after them. The quality of these young witnesses across the nation is sufficient demonstration that God is doing a unique work through Young Life. Scores of these young people are vitally associated with us as staff and volunteer leaders, going after more kids like they were when they were in high school.

We feel no sense of superiority, nor do we feel that we have a patent on a special kind of evangelizing. We know that the Lord used these methods in every age and throughout the world. But we also know that these truly Scriptural methods for reaching the lost are sadly neglected in America today. We trust that more and more of God's people will rediscover how basic and important it is to "walk in wisdom toward them that are without" making friends and helping people for the glory of God and for the purpose of making known the Saviour and His love.

While we are speaking of the Young Life work, I should, perhaps, say a word to you about our financial policy. All of our staff works on a very modest allowance based on each individual's needs. The staff understands that this allowance comes to them only if the money is available after all bills and current obligations have been fully met. We have no guaranteed source of income. We seek to trust the Lord to supply our needs. Our salary budget for this fiscal year—$108,000.00—will provide salaries for 52 staff workers. Our total budget of $203,000.00 will take care of all salaries, expenses, and an extensive program of training more leaders for this work.

I hope that this very brief review of some of Young Life's methods and policies will help you to understand better our work and explain it to others. Pray for us.

Sincerely in Him,

Jim Rayburn

Jim Rayburn

JR:bd

the 1960s

Warning: Contents Under Pressure

There are eras, which, by the mere mention of the name, conjure certain images. The 1960s are just such a decade. Vietnam, demonstrations, race riots, crime, poverty, drug use, the sexual revolution—as well as the assassinations of President Kennedy, Martin Luther King Jr., and Senator Kennedy heightened the sense of uneasiness, fear, and confusion the world was feeling.

The word that best defines the decade is change. It was an uncertain era, where traditional mores, beliefs, and attitudes were challenged. "Authority" became a suspect word. Revolution was in the air. Music and dress, mirroring the times, broke away from earlier conservative styles.

Because much of this upheaval was coming from the younger generation, Young Life found itself in the middle of it all. The cultural forces outside the mission, as well as unprecedented events within, would change Young Life forever.

A LITERAL BRIDGE INTO THE CITY

On the surface, the sixties appeared to begin the way the fifties ended for Young Life—with successful ministry growing in many areas across the United States, Canada, and France. The model of reaching teenagers through contact work, club, and camping was successfully replicated in high schools throughout the United States.

The once fledgling mission now enjoyed a firm foundation. The ministry was robust and finding tremendous response among high school kids. At this point, it would have been easy to ride the status quo and continue doing what had always worked.

But, as He often does, the Lord was doing a work behind the scenes. The urban work begun with little fanfare on the East Coast was slowly building and would soon trigger the entire mission to reexamine itself. The seemingly small seeds Harv Oostdyk planted in 1956 with the kids in Newark, New Jersey, were starting to bear fruit. Vinnie Di Pasquale was now Oostdyk's right-hand man, with a heart for city kids that rivaled his mentor's.

By this time, others like Bill Milliken, a college freshman who had met Christ at Frontier Ranch, wanted to get in on the act. Milliken drove from his hometown of Pittsburgh to Newark to visit with Oostdyk and Di Pasquale. The three men talked throughout the night about their vision for kids in the city. The next morning,

posite: Former gang leader turned Young Life leader, nie Di Pasquale, with kids in New York City.

the 1960s | 45

June 18, 1960, as they left Newark, the men could be spotted dribbling a basketball across the George Washington Bridge in the hopes of meeting New York City kids who wanted to shoot hoops.

From these humble beginnings, the work in New York City was born.

"When Vinnie and I moved to the city," Milliken said, "we had one gift between us: Like me, Vinnie could have earned a degree in hanging out. But that was exactly what was missing in the lives of those young people. Nobody was out on the streets with them, walking with them, talking with them, shooting hoops . . . Being there was what it was all about."

By the early sixties, Oostdyk's team now included Di Pasquale, Milliken, and Dean Borgman, a doctoral student at Columbia University. Throughout the United States other teams would soon follow the lead of these four men, who were simply finding their way in reaching lost kids.

IN THE NEIGHBORHOOD

One of those kids was Bo Nixon, president of the Centurions, a local gang on the Lower East Side.

As Milliken became a frequent presence in their neighborhood, Nixon and his friends grew suspicious of the white man hanging out every day at the basketball court. Was he an undercover cop? The kids simply didn't know what to make of Milliken.

Playing hoops in Harlem.

- 1960 *The Sound of Music*—Original Cast
- 1961 *Camelot*—Original Cast
- 1962 *West Side Story*—Soundtrack
- 1963 *West Side Story*—Soundtrack
- 1964 *Hello Dolly!*—Original Cast
- 1965 *Mary Poppins*—Soundtrack
- 1966 *Whipped Cream and Other Delights*—Herb Alpert and the Tijuana Brass
- 1967 *More of the Monkees*—The Monkees
- 1968 *Are you Experienced?*—The Jimi Hendrix Experience
- 1969 *In-A-Gadda-Da-Vida*—Iron Butterfly

"I was leery of him," Nixon admitted. "He hung out, just watching and getting to know the names of kids."

Milliken invited Nixon and his friends to Frontier that summer. Many took Milliken up on his offer—even Nixon's brother "Tap"—but a cautious Nixon did not. When the group returned, Nixon learned that Milliken was true to his word. Camp was amazing. Nixon vowed that if invited again, he would go the next summer.

Sure enough, in 1962 Nixon was sitting in Star Ranch's club room, mesmerized by George Sheffer's talks. "He wanted to know where you were from and who you were," Nixon said. "He was a great storyteller."

"The thing that really impressed me about camp was you could just feel God's love there. It was such a different place than where I came from." After the message on the crucifixion, during the twenty minutes of silence, the city kid sat outside and wrestled with the amazing story of the cross. "I had never talked to God before," Nixon said, "but they said you could talk to Him and He would listen. I said, 'Lord, if you can do anything with this life, you can have it.'"

When he told Bill about his decision to follow Christ, Nixon said, "Bill acted like it was his birthday! He was so excited. There were twelve of us in our cabin and he told us we could change our community if we stuck together."

A NEW "GANG"

Sticking together was a concept Milliken had been working on for the past year. He witnessed many gang kids embrace the Gospel, only to be choked out by the temptations of everyday life in the city. It was devastating.

"Christ made me realize," Milliken remembered, "that if gang activity was to be broken up because certain individuals met Christ, a structure as dynamic as the gang would need to be set up to fulfill the needs of these 'new creatures in Christ.' For as long as they fought the battle as individuals only, they became easy prey to the great forces of sin around them."

> "THE THING THAT REALLY IMPRESSED ME ABOUT CAMP WAS YOU COULD JUST FEEL GOD'S LOVE THERE. IT WAS SUCH A DIFFERENT PLACE THAN WHERE I CAME FROM.
>
> —BO NIXON

Bo Nixon

"THE MEN DISCOVERED THE LIFE-GIVING MESSAGE OF THE GOSPEL, WHICH HAD BEEN SO SUCCESSFUL IN THE SUBURBAN SETTING, WOULD BE SUCCESSFUL IN THE CITY TOO, ESPECIALLY WHEN KIDS' PHYSICAL NEEDS WERE ALSO BEING MET."

Bill Milliken shares life with the Cross Carriers.

Milliken laid out an idea with the guys closest to him: the Christian life is a battlefield and to follow Jesus for the long run would require they walk in their faith as a team. They would live under the banner of Luke 9:23, "Whoever wants to be my disciple must deny themselves and take up their cross daily and follow me." They named themselves the Cross Carriers, wrote up a constitution to live out, and met regularly to support each other.

Nixon joined the group after coming home from Star Ranch. The group dynamics were eye-opening to the new believer. "If you did something wrong, you had to come back and share it with the group. Some guys did drugs, some were gamblers—my thing was fighting. I had a bad temper. I saw guys I respected coming back and pouring out their hearts, crying, and talking about what they had done. It was just a different group."

Taking up his cross, though, meant Nixon would have to lay down a "crown." "One of the things I didn't want to do

with my commitment to Christ was to be phony about it," he said. "Bill said I couldn't stay president of the gang and be a Christian. Once I got involved in that group, I decided it was okay to let the gang go."

Gang involvement was one of the many challenges Oostdyk, Milliken, Di Pasquale, and Borgman faced in the city. Their openness to meeting kids where they were meant the men would do whatever they could to offer kids hope and break down the barriers that kept kids from Christ. Oostdyk, for example, concerned about the rampancy of illiteracy, began "Street Academies" held in churches and storefronts, where kids could come and learn to read. Meanwhile, Borgman concentrated on the problem of drug addiction, especially prevalent among the Puerto Rican kids there.

The men discovered the life-giving message of the Gospel, which had been so successful in the suburban setting, would be successful in the city too, especially when kids' physical needs were also being met.

MOUNTING TENSION

While lives were changing as a result of Young Life's efforts, the life of the man God used to bring the mission into existence was also about to turn upside down. For more than two decades, Jim Rayburn had led the charge. Known lovingly as "the boss" to the staff, he was the face of Young Life. Through those early years, the mission relied heavily upon Rayburn for vision-casting, fundraising, decision-making, and all-around leadership. What worked in the forties and fifties, however, could not continue, as the mission continued to explode in growth.

Visionaries, by their very nature, often cannot focus on the minutiae of the day-to-day operations of an organization. Delegation may not come naturally—it's hard to create something and hand it off to others.

This was evident in the growing tension between Rayburn and the Board of Directors over a proposed new property: Trail West in Buena Vista, Colorado. As with every other camp acquisition, Rayburn needed the board's approval to move forward. The man who had the vision to pursue camps such as Star Ranch, Frontier, and Malibu was now emboldened to open a new kind of property—one tailored to give interested adults a window into the ministry.

Money was never a deterrent for Rayburn when a dream was involved, but the board had strong misgivings as to where to find the funding for this latest idea. This was nothing new—year in and year out, the board had wrestled with supporting Rayburn's big dreams while responsibly handling the mission's fiscal problems.

In the end, the board approved the construction of Trail West, which ultimately proved to be another important piece of Rayburn's legacy. This camp came to be one of the crown jewels in leading many souls (young and old) to Jesus.

CHALLENGING THE CHURCH

While Rayburn was engaged in battles like this with the board, he also encountered exterior conflict with the organized church. Unlike today, where so many churches excel in their outreach to kids, the church at that time was still wrestling with how to care for the kids outside its doors.

Rayburn's desire to spur on the church in its outreach to kids would lead him to make hurtful statements like, "Bringing our kids into the church is like putting live chicks under a dead hen." Any deposits of goodwill the mission may have built up with church leaders would then be wiped out, and Young Life would once again have to rebuild relationships with local churches.

In fact, the first press the mission received in a national publication was on the topic of the church's view of Young Life . . . and it was not positive. The January 4, 1960, edition of *Time* magazine covered the controversy Young Life was facing in New Canaan, Connecticut, where five ministers publicly denounced the mission.

The article stated:

> "Nub of the ministers' charge: 'Young Life is, in effect, a separate teen-age church, financed and directed by adults who are not answerable to any local group. We believe its outlook is too narrow, and that its emotional effect is eventually damaging to the young people most attracted by its appeal.'

> "Founder Rayburn snapped back at once: 'There is professional jealousy in the ministry as well as in other fields. Young Life is not a teen-age church at all. It's a recruiting program for the church. I am sure we are not narrow unless the Apostles' Creed is narrow. Some of our critics want to drag us into the old static framework. If that were done the Young Life Campaign wouldn't work any better than what they are doing. Far too many pastors talk about daffodils and robin redbreast. We believe it is sinful to bore kids [with the Gospel].' "

Stung for years by criticism from the church, Rayburn put together the "Chicago Fellowship" in May 1962 to discuss Young Life's relationship with the church and their mutual desire to reach unchurched kids. The gathering consisted of Rayburn, twenty-two leaders of various denominations from around the country, and Young Life regional directors. The two days of give-and-take went extremely well, and the church leaders left the meeting with a higher regard for the mission, as witnessed by their signed statement endorsing Young Life and commending the movement to their fellow clergy.

Rayburn longed for a better relationship between the mission and the local church and also wanted the church to recognize the Spirit-led movement of Young Life in reaching out to non-churched kids. And while the Chicago meetings were a feather in Rayburn's cap, his love/hate relationship with the church continued to make life harder for the mission.

PAINFUL TIMES

Adding to these contentious issues were concerns with Rayburn's health, which continued to decline. The burden of Maxine's long emotional and physical health issues was weighing on him greatly. Further, his personal struggles

Trail West Lodge

By 1959 there was a growing need to find more land for the one hundred twenty horses used at Frontier Ranch, Silver Cliff, and Star Ranch. Dale Kaiser, who oversaw Young Life's expanding horse program, learned of the sale of a ranch just west of Buena Vista.

"There was just one problem," Stacy Windahl wrote in *Build it Here: Celebrating 50 Years at Trail West Lodge.* "Jim Rayburn was out of the country and could not be reached to approve its purchase. Kaiser and John Carter, Young Life's first business manager, acted anyway. On April 4, 1959, Young Life purchased the 640-acre ranch for a price of $38,500.

"When Rayburn returned later that April, Kaiser recalled that 'The Boss' was none too pleased. 'You didn't do anything without telling Jim Rayburn. So I took him in a jeep and we drove up into that country. As we were coming off the ridge where the Lodge now sits, down in that little valley were about 50 elk laying down there. Jim just came unglued. "This is it!' Rayburn quickly realized that this land could be the extravagant answer to his prayer for Young Life's first adult guest lodge."

The lodge would provide adults with a window to see the goings on at Frontier Ranch and Silver Cliff. After the purchase of the land, Rayburn often hiked through the aspen grove there, Char Meredith wrote. "It was a small piece of heaven that he wanted to share. As he was sitting on a lichen-spattered boulder in the middle of the rocky hillside, God said, 'Build it here.'"

A lodge was designed and completed in 1964, and Trail West became a luxury vacation place for people from coast to coast. Now, as they peered through this "window" and witnessed kids processing the Gospel message in the friendly confines of camp, adults could see for themselves why such significant changes were taking place in their children's lives.

Ultimately, Trail West became what John Miller referred to as "Jim Rayburn's last big dream for the mission."

Trail West today.

with migraines, insomnia, and the surgical procedure to remove a stomach ulcer were increasing. On rare but important occasions, side effects from medications needed to combat these conditions resulted in slurred speech, disjointed comments, and an inability to function normally. These problems came to a breaking point on February 13, 1963, when Rayburn was speaking at the Park Avenue Methodist Church in Minnesota.

Accompanied by Roy Riviere, Phil McDonald, and Bill Starr, Rayburn stood up to address the five hundred in attendance. It became quickly apparent, however, something was wrong. As he walked to the podium, he stumbled. Once there, instead of living up to his reputation as a master communicator, he "mumbled incoherently." Try as he might, he could not regain his composure. Riviere apologized to the stunned crowd that Rayburn could not continue; as Starr helped Rayburn away from the podium and into a chair, Riviere did his best to finish the message.

"It was very, very difficult for the man and it was hard for all of us," Starr said. "We had to consult quickly in the front row and do something before it was utter disaster. It was disaster enough."

In her book *It's a Sin to Bore a Kid*, Char Meredith wrote, "Until then, no one had been willing to suggest that Jim be replaced as chief executive officer of Young Life. He and the mission he had founded seemed inseparable. His early leadership had been brilliant and far-sighted. Even when he had rammed camp projects through, the directors eventually knew they were right to yield to his enthusiasms."

Confronted with the events in Minnesota as well as other similar reports, many of Rayburn's friends on staff and the board realized the Boss and his beloved mission were now on different trajectories. Seeing that Rayburn no longer had the capacity to direct the mission he'd begun, the board reluctantly decided it was time for a change in the leadership of Young Life.

On May 8, 1964, Rayburn was informed that due to health reasons, he must take a leave of absence for one year. If he were able to come back to work after that time, he would be reinstated in the position. In the meantime, he would hold the position of director emeritus. The board appointed Starr as the interim associate executive director and general manager.

The board tried its best to set the mission up for success while honoring the revered founder, but by any account the transition was a painful one. The decision shocked Rayburn, who felt both misunderstood and wounded by the way he was removed from his post.

In 1963, *Young Life* was published. The book's author, Emile Cailliet, was a professor at Princeton Theological Seminary, and a dear friend of Jim Rayburn. The book was a strong affirmation of the work and gave the public its first clear look into the ministry. In March 1964, *Christianity Today* praised the book. "Anyone who wants to know how thousands of non-church-going young people have been reached with the Message should read this book. It is hopeful, inspiring, and informing. And it is an honest book, recording distressing failures as well as heart-warming successes."

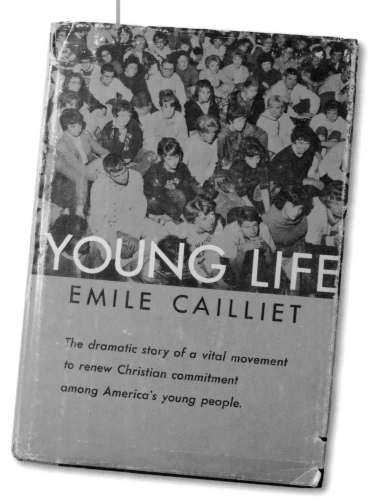

YOUNG LIFE
EMILE CAILLIET
The dramatic story of a vital movement to renew Christian commitment among America's young people.

In April 1961 Young Life moved its headquarters from Star Ranch on Cheyenne Mountain down into the city of Colorado Springs. Located at 720 West Monument Street, the brand-new 10,600 square-foot building was a vast improvement for the growing staff. Mirroring the growth of field staff in the late sixties and early seventies, the headquarters staff numbered fifteen when they moved to the new building; in a little more than a decade that number would more than triple in size. Pictured above is the headquarters staff in the late sixties; Bill Taylor, who played an important role in advancing business operations at the headquarters, is on the far right.

Starr recognized that the board's decision was "an accumulation of things." He said, "Any one of us as individuals were not privy to all of them, but the board knew the accumulation. When they made their move to relieve Jim for all those personal reasons plus organizational reasons, I think most of us [on the staff] came along quite reluctantly. I was personally not ready to see that happen. I think we needed a more objective view from the outside and the board provided that. And I think at a very judicious point."

Bob Mitchell agreed. "It was real hard to know all that was going on. Jim felt like many of us betrayed him, and we had to ask ourselves, 'Did we desert the man?' As I look back I don't think we did. Some of us were confused and hurt by what was going on, but we could no longer follow Jim as we had before."

The move and subsequent estrangement from Young Life was devastating for Rayburn. The founder of the mission now found himself on an island: All his contemporaries from the forties had by now left staff, his health was fragile as was Maxine's, and his life's work was no longer available to him. In the end, Rayburn would never return to lead the mission he had founded.

A STARR FOLLOWS A STAR

To follow a charismatic leader is one challenge. To follow the founder of the mission and the only "boss" the staff had ever known, was quite another.

Bill Starr knew this. "Of course, it's daunting, following a man like Jim Rayburn. Here's a man who I had the utmost admiration for; he was like a father to me. In that sense, it was a very daunting and awesome responsibility."

But, like Joshua before him, Starr followed the Moses-sized footprints of Rayburn with a firm belief that it was God who had placed him in this position.

Starr, husband of Ruth and a father of three, was a World War II veteran who had served on Young Life staff for fifteen years. Even though he was only thirty-eight when the Board of Directors asked him to assume the role of associate executive director and general manager of Young Life, the age factor did not deter him. "Leadership was natural to me. God had, for some reason, put that gift in my life; because it was natural, it seemed to me 'if that's what God wanted, then that's right.' "

Bill Starr

Along with all the cultural pressures the mission was addressing at the national and local levels, Starr also faced the much-needed task of steering and stabilizing the mission. In 1964, the mission had outgrown the organizational structure that had been in effect since 1941.

Starr and the board set about to transform Young Life from a pioneering model, based on one man's vision of management, to a corporate one, a challenging transition to say the least. The new president understood the growing pains that might ensue. "I think there's a constant tension—in the 'freewheeling, allow the Spirit of God to direct' (whatever that looks like), over against 'how do we organize for mission effectiveness?' "

TAYLOR MADE

To accomplish this, Starr immediately surrounded himself with the right people. Starr brought in Bill Taylor, a businessman and committee member from Chicago, who would help build on the strong foundation John Carter had already laid, by revitalizing the headquarters and its many moving parts.

Right away Taylor saw what Starr had known. "The real question was," Taylor suggested, "Is this a professional business or a mission? Well, it's both. You can't have a mission without both."

"There was a need to grow from a first-generation to second-generation company," Taylor said. "This was a very critical stage in the mission. The mission would not have lasted if it hadn't changed."

Castaway Club

In 1915, Mr. and Mrs. Sidney Smith from Winnipeg, Canada, purchased a piece of property on Pelican Lake in Minnesota and built their summer home on its spacious lawns. Smith and his sons would often take kids from around the Pelican Lake area on boat rides. During these outings, Smith and his sons would share Bible stories with their young friends, foreshadowing many more Bible stories to be told on the property.

Smith and Jim Rayburn had been friends since 1945, when Rayburn came and spoke at Smith's Elim Chapel in Winnipeg, Manitoba. Their mutual admiration was unmistakable. Smith once wrote, "Rayburn is a very lovable person and I was drawn to him at once." Years later upon Smith's passing, Rayburn journaled, "SID went HOME to-day . . . OF all the sweet memories that I shall carry thru life of this dearest friend GOD ever gave me—this is paramount. SID LOVED JESUS! . . . I want to love Jesus like SID did."

As time passed, the Smith family spent less and less time at their summer home. One of the sons, C. Gordon Smith, was on Young Life's Canadian Board of Trustees and had helped with the acquisition of Malibu. Believing the property was "too valuable to sell," Smith said he and his wife, Isabel, "felt that giving the property to Young Life would allow it to be used in ways similar to how Sidney Smith and the rest of their family had used it."

Phil McDonald, on staff in Minneapolis, recalled that in September 1963, "Bill [Starr] and I returned along with Jim Rayburn, and C. Gordon Smith met us at the property. We had a meal together and talked about what we would do to make it into a camp. After a while, Mr. Smith had to leave, so he tossed keys onto the table, shook hands with us, and walked out. The three of us just looked at each other. We owned a new camp."

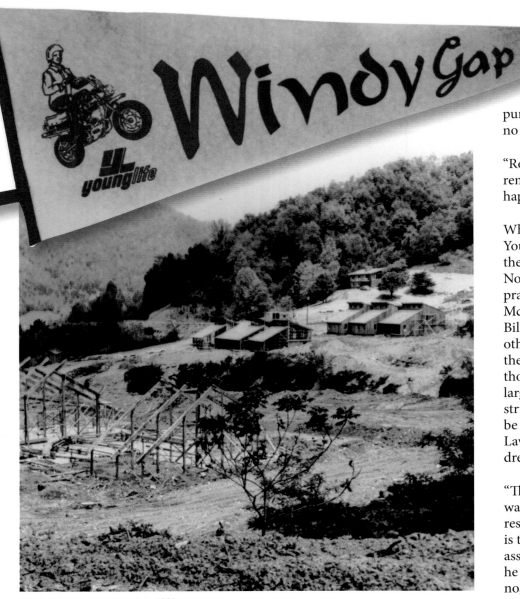

Windy Gap under construction, 1968.

due diligence, Roy Riviere, Southeast regional director, had pursued every lead he could find, but to no avail. Even so, he wasn't deterred.

"Roy had vision," Mal McSwain remembered. "He saw things that hadn't happened as if they already had."

When Lawrence and Sara learned of Young Life's search, they wondered if their dairy farm outside Weaverville, North Carolina, might fit the bill. They prayed for several days and called McDougal, who suggested they contact Bill Starr. Soon Riviere, McSwain, and others went to visit. They discovered the land to be magnificent, but at two thousand acres (more than twice as large as Frontier), and with no existing structures, the price tag would no doubt be too steep. Walking the property with Lawrence Douglas, Riviere could feel the dream slipping away.

"Then in one of the most humble-spirited ways I have ever seen in any man I respected, Lawrence asked kind of politely, is there any chance we could use it? I assumed he wanted us to buy it. And when he realized that, he laughed and said, 'Oh, no, we'd like to give it to you.'

SPEECHLESS!

While the mission owed much to Starr and Taylor, when it comes to its camps, Young Life owed much to work crew kids. Just as God honored the prayers of two boys to bring Frontier Ranch to the mission, so He would use one Florida girl's work crew experience at Frontier to provide a new camp in the southeastern part of the United States.

Ilene Douglas grew up in a believing family and her parents, Lawrence and Sara, were friends with Bouton McDougal, a member of the national board. McDougal suggested Ilene serve on work crew, and the next summer she came back from Frontier Ranch on fire, excitedly telling her family all about her experience.

During this time Young Life had indeed been looking for a property in the Southeast. Through much prayer and

"There comes a time when you just haven't got any words. That was one of them!" laughed Riviere.

The generous gift allowed Young Life to build the camp from the ground up—a first for the mission. With twenty-five years of camping experience, the mission could now tailor a camp to its own specifications. The property was developed largely by funds raised by Riviere in the Southeast Region, and when Windy Gap hosted its first campers in the summer of 1970, the man who stood up to tell them about Jesus was, of course, Roy Riviere.

"THIS IS IT! I'VE FOUND IT!"

While the expanding U.S. ministry necessitated more camps like Windy Gap, the mission also rejoiced over progress in other parts of the world. The work in France continued to blossom, and in 1963, Rod and Fran Johnston hired Marc

"THEN IN ONE OF THE MOST HUMBLE-SPIRITED
WAYS I HAVE EVER SEEN IN ANY MAN I
RESPECTED, LAWRENCE ASKED KIND OF POLITELY,
IS THERE ANY CHANCE WE COULD USE IT?
I ASSUMED HE WANTED US TO BUY IT. AND WHEN
HE REALIZED THAT, HE LAUGHED AND SAID, 'OH,
NO, WE'D LIKE TO GIVE IT TO YOU.' "

—ROY RIVIERE

Praz de Lys

Located in the beautiful French Alps, Praz de Lys's main building, a hotel, was built in 1900 as a summer resort. The grandson of the original owner, John Chardonnens, and his wife, Mitsy, sold the property to Young Life in 1965. Their desire was that the hotel be used for kids to hear about Jesus, a vision shared by Young Life's first overseas staff, Rod and Fran Johnston, who served in France from 1953 to 1992.

For the next five years, Young Life used the hotel for ski camps. Restrictions on wooden structures in France, however, shut down the hotel during the seventies. In the early 1980s, the C. Everett Koop family built the Koop dorm in memory of their son, David. U.S. Young Life gave the site to the French Young Life entity, Jeunesse Ardente ("Youth Aglow") in 1985, and today Young Life and Jeunesse Ardente have an affiliation agreement to partner in revitalizing Young Life in France.

Atger, the first national employed with Young Life outside the United States. Within a matter of years, Young Life enjoyed similar growth in new countries like Brazil, Bermuda, the Philippines, and Peru.

● Brazil

Harry and Hope MacDonald went to Brazil in 1963 and, with Brazilian nationals, started Alvo da Mocidade ("Target for Youth"). "Harry found out he could give the Young Life message and methods to the Brazilians who wanted it," Char Meredith explained. "That was the secret. If the Brazilians wanted it, then they would utilize it in their own culture."

Hal and Judy Merwald and family came in 1967 and Hal took over the directorship for Brazil in 1968. A few years earlier, Merwald received a commissioning from Jim Rayburn unlike anyone else in the mission. "Jim said we should have a prayer of dedication," Merwald recalled. "This is what he said word for word: 'Lord, we were hoping for a lot more, but would have settled for a lot less, but take him and bless him in Jesus' name. Amen.' That was my calling, dedication, training program, you name it!"

Working outside the States, Merwald was able to see the mission through new eyes. "When you're thrust into another culture," he said, "it filters out what maybe shouldn't be there. For example, a lot of my traditions had to go when I pushed my Christianity through the Brazilian culture. Being in these other cultures helps you see what is essential, what is real. I had to push Young Life through the sieve of another culture to see what's unique about Young Life."

When the Merwalds left Brazil in 1976, Brazilian leadership selected Iberê Meirelles, a national, to be the next director. The work continued to be indigenous and autonomous from that day on.

● Bermuda

Francis "Goose" Gosling was a World War II veteran who served in the Royal Air Force and a springboard diver who participated in the 1948 and 1952 Olympics. In 1964, the beloved Bermudan brought sixteen soccer players on a tour throughout the United States. The trip ended with a week of camp at Frontier Ranch that changed the lives of those boys and thousands of other kids in the decades to come. "We went into camp with three Christians that week," Gosling said, "and came out with eleven."

After the trip, the boys helped Gosling start the first Young Life club in Bermuda. Within a year, more than one hundred kids were attending club and eventually Young Life spread across the island to five clubs reaching more than three hundred kids weekly. Gosling volunteered with the mission for nearly four decades, until he passed away in 2001 at eighty-three years of age.

The Philippines

In 1965, a young Filipino named Eli Yasi traveled to the United States as the coordinator for the Philippines Crusades. He was looking to adapt a program for those Filipino youth who were difficult to reach. He visited many youth programs across the nation, but always concluded, "This isn't right." Everything changed when Yasi arrived at his first Young Life club.

"When I saw kids smoking cigarettes and deflating tires of the cars parked outside I said, 'This is it! I've found it! These are the ones I want to reach!' Then we went inside. The kids sang songs and shouted, and then the leader, Jim Shelton, told the story about the Good Samaritan. And the kids listened. After that I said, 'This is the concept that's been in my mind.' "

Yasi returned to the island of Mindanao, and after two months of contact work, witnessed three hundred kids pack out the first Young Life club in the Philippines.

Peru

Having met Jim Rayburn and his family on their 1959 trip to Germany, Diether Koerner, a young German student, followed Rayburn (or perhaps more accurately, Rayburn's daughter Sue!) back to the United States, where he began a relationship with Christ. Over the years, Koerner grew in his faith and passion for those without Christ, eventually joining Jim Rayburn's newly formed organization, Youth Research International, which was pioneering Young Life-type work overseas. Koerner, along with Rayburn and Jim Rayburn III, responded to the Lord's call to start outreach work in Lima, Peru, in July 1968. In the seventies, the Lord used Koerner to develop a solid core of seven young Peruvian leaders, who assumed Young Life leadership of the work in their native country.

On Base!

During an overseas trip in 1959, Rayburn met Colonel Henry Amen, an American commander in charge of the Rhein-Main Air Force Base outside of Frankfurt, Germany. The colonel, with high school kids of his own, asked about initiating a ministry with American high school dependents on the military bases in West Germany. Intrigued, Rayburn undertook some "reconnaissance" of his own and in 1959, wrote enthusiastically about the potential for this ministry:

"There are eleven Air Force high schools in Germany alone! Six of them within easy two-hour drives from Frankfurt . . . Right now good prospect of enough volunteer leaders for the six. One good Young Life man and one good girl can handle the whole area! They are as American as Chicago—football and basketball league games, the works. And these kids are stranded. If we don't go after them, no one will."

Later that year, John O'Neil moved to Germany to begin the work, and Young Life staff have been serving almost continuously on military bases in Europe ever since. Years later, Young Life Military would thrive on many military bases around the world under the name "Club Beyond" with Military Community Youth Ministries (MCYM), a partnership with Young Life and Youth for Christ.

The Great Exchange

The mission of Young Life also grew internationally as foreign exchange students came to the United States. Longtime staff member Ken Wright played a critical role in helping bring these kids to camp and ensuring they would not return home the same. Upon their return, these students spread the word about Young Life throughout their home countries. These experiences were a precursor to Young Life's Amicus ministry, an outreach to exchange students visiting the United States.

> **" BEING IN THESE OTHER CULTURES HELPS YOU SEE WHAT IS ESSENTIAL, WHAT IS REAL. I HAD TO PUSH YOUNG LIFE THROUGH THE SIEVE OF ANOTHER CULTURE TO SEE WHAT'S UNIQUE ABOUT YOUNG LIFE."**
>
> **—HAL MERWALD**

VOLUME 2 NUMBER 2 JULY 1968

focus
ON YOUTH

I'm not a problem. I'm a man.

Focus on Youth magazine, July 1968—a defining moment in the mission's history.

THE ISSUE

For Young Life, the sixties would end on the same issue that ushered in the decade. As lives changed in the cities of New York, Pittsburgh, Dallas, Chicago, Kansas City, Jacksonville, Atlanta, and Orlando, minds were challenged in Colorado Springs. The Board of Directors was trying to come to a consensus on this question: Was the work going on in the cities really Young Life?

This was no mere philosophical question. These were challenges facing the foundational beliefs and tenets of the mission: What is the Gospel and who is it for? Would Young Life be willing (and able) to adapt its methods, while not compromising the message, to reach these dear lost kids? Was the mission ready, by embracing every race, to receive the pushback that would inevitably come?

These questions, particularly the last one, would be answered before the decade came to a close in an issue of Young Life's magazine, *Focus on Youth*. No Young Life publication, before or since, has received the response the July 1968 issue did. Bill Starr reflected on this critical event in the history of the mission:

"Dr. Martin Luther King appeared on the American scene in a big way in the sixties, preaching about the sin of racism. Many white churches and leaders from all walks of life joined in to be a part of the marches and demonstrations led by Dr. King and other black leaders. Many Christian organizations were shamefully quiet. Young Life was working in a number of urban areas out east with some very outstanding black leaders. We decided it was past time to declare our position. Young Life had needed a vehicle to express our convictions on a number of issues, so we developed a magazine called *Focus on Youth*. A group of us gathered in Colorado Springs to put together a focus issue on our support of the Civil Rights Movement. We titled this issue "I'm Not a Problem, I'm a Man." It created quite a stir—eight Young Life areas closed and let their staff go. We, at the same time, grew twelve new areas and raised thousands more dollars. It was another learning experience. If we do what our Lord asks us to do, He blesses us way beyond what we might expect Him to do! From that experience, we were able to add another whole division—Urban Ministries."

Bob Mitchell agreed, "That issue was a defining moment. When Young Life published something like that, it made a statement about what we believed about humankind, what we believed about racism. That whole magazine was about racism. We grew into an understanding that the Gospel was inclusive and we had to be the same in the mission of Young Life."

As Starr wrote in his editorial in the magazine:

"Young Life has always sought to be involved in the doing and the being, as well as in the telling of the Gospel. But it has always sought the right to be heard. In the racial dilemma we can do no less . . .

"Young Life is committed to searching out the human resources that are buried in kids of any color. It is our job to enter the high schools of our day to give young people the best news we know about living. In the great cities, we are learning we must go beyond the schools and walk the streets to get to the people. In New York, Chicago, Jacksonville, Dallas, and other urban areas, we are making a deliberate effort to help young men and women find dignity and worth by fitting into God's big plan."

The issue was an important step in letting the public know the course Young Life was taking in the race issue. There was still a long way to go for this belief to become reality, however, as the tensions between the races were spilling over into the staff itself.

A MAN FOR ALL SEASONS

As the urban work grew throughout the country, Starr recognized the need for leadership in Young Life's new mission field. In 1964, he appointed George Sheffer to the position of director of Inner-City Young Life.

Few in the history of the mission have sought change (and adapted to it) as well as Sheffer and his wife, Martie. From the early 1940s until 1961, Sheffer worked in the suburban schools of Tyler, Texas, Oklahoma City, and Chicago. In 1961, he began to reach out to kids in Dallas's inner city and later moved back north to the Southside of Chicago, where his ministry in the midst of violence and mistrust was legendary. In the seventies, he was instrumental in starting the Dale House, a refuge for hurting kids, in Colorado Springs, and then became the mission's director of training. And after "retirement" in the 1980s, he served as a missionary in Nairobi, Kenya, and helped start the Young Life work there.

Rudy Howard, longtime staff member, recalled the reputation Sheffer held in the city of Chicago. "George earned the right to be heard by all kinds of folks, but particularly the inner-city kids. He came to track meets when no one would come. He came to see our fencing team. He'd show up at places. He'd knock on the door and ask my momma, 'Do you need anything?' He'd sit in meetings when he was the only white person there, representing all-white America, and let these people scream and yell at him. But after a while they knew he was for real. People would tell you, 'George is for real.' Martie told me he would come home some nights and just lay across his bed and cry, because sometimes he wasn't understood by African-American people and he sure wasn't understood by a lot of white people."

"If there wasn't a George Sheffer, there might not be an urban Young Life," Bo Nixon said. "There might not be a Bo Nixon sitting here along with thousands of other kids."

Sheffer's wisdom and leadership would prove to be a critical stabilizer in a time of tumult.

George Sheffer

ONE GOSPEL

As racial tensions in the nation increased after the assassination of Dr. King, so did tensions within the mission. Many on the urban staff felt they were on the outside looking in, when it came to having a place in Young Life. They were tired of feeling ignored by the all-white leadership, yet still having to take orders from the top down.

The tipping point came in 1969 at an urban staff conference in Chicago. A group of black staff walked out, boycotting the final one and a half days. Later they held a "minority leader only" conference at Frontier Ranch, where they composed "The Black Manifesto." The group also selected Joe White, an African-American, to represent the urban ministry at the Young Life headquarters. He was appointed executive assistant specializing in the field of Urban Affairs in October 1969.

Because of the divisiveness and ensuing pain, Starr recalled, "There was a push by many in the mission to make urban and suburban two separate organizations. They thought, 'Well, God taught us how to work with middle-class kids. Why not just do that—we know how to do that.' That to me was a denial of the Gospel; the oneness of Christ's body. How could we talk about the Gospel and talk separation like this? To me it was incompatible theologically. We had to fight to keep it all together; it was not right to separate it. America was becoming more pluralistic all the time. It's one mission. It's one Gospel."

Starr was proven right. The one Gospel would ultimately hold the mission together in this, its time of greatest testing, and bind the mission during the rough patches that lay ahead.

A HEART SET FREE

Meanwhile, the mission continued to make tremendous strides in the suburban work. Kids flooded into clubs where they found community and a message that spoke to them where they were. One such kid was a sophomore named Joni Eareckson, who attended Woodlawn High School in Baltimore, Maryland. On a fall weekend in 1965, Eareckson experienced the message of God's love in a way she never had heard before.

"Carl Nelson was speaking," Eareckson said. "I remember sitting there, hugging my knees on the hardwood floor, and listening to Carl tell us we needed to measure our lives against [the impossibly high bar of] the Ten Commandments. And I thought, 'I'm not going to make it.'

"Later, my counselor in cabin time explained that's why Jesus came, and it was like a giant light bulb came on. That's what my parents were hinting around about all those years? That's what all those years of going to church meant? It struck me afresh and anew. I happily and readily embraced Him. I felt a change immediately.

"I remember singing, 'And Can It Be That I Should Gain?' in club that weekend. When we got to the line 'My chains fell off, my heart was free, I rose, went forth, and followed Thee,' I remember literally feeling my chains fall off. There wasn't any major sin in my life, but I knew I was free."

That newfound freedom in Christ would change Eareckson, and so many others around the world, in more ways than she could ever imagine. Two years later the teenager was involved in a diving accident, which left her a quadriplegic. Her faith, and the support of her family and Young Life community, sustained her in the early years when she questioned if God could ever use her again.

"It was my Young Life friends who came to the hospital. They were my most faithful visitors," Eareckson said. "They brought their guitars, *Seventeen* magazines, and Bingo, and didn't treat me like an invalid or a cripple or sick. They treated me like Joni. They related to me as though I were still whole and complete. I didn't sense an ounce of pity from my Young Life friends, and I loved that."

Over the next five decades, God would indeed use Eareckson (Tada) to minister with people with disabilities. Through

Joni Eareckson Tada

Woodleaf

Nestled in the forests of Challenge, California, you'll find Woodleaf, Young Life's fifth camp. In the 1800s this two-hundred-and-forty-acre plot of land was a stopping point for stagecoach passengers during the gold rush era. By the early twentieth century, it became home to a world-renowned hotel, which hosted guests as varied as President Ulysses S. Grant and the infamous stagecoach robber Black Bart.

While its history is interesting, it can't hold a candle to the story of how the Lord enabled Young Life to purchase it . . .

In 1966, as California's population was exploding, Young Life was in dire need of a West Coast camping facility. Vern Pynn, the district attorney for Walnut Creek, California, and a friend of Young Life, persuaded a local official to consider selling the land that would become Young Life's next camp. "Have you considered maybe giving your rights to it to another group?" Pynn asked the official. "I'll tell you what I'll do, Vern," the man replied. "You give me three thousand, and I'll give you a week to look at it and see if it's any value to your people."

Pynn immediately called Bob Stover, who would go on to become the longest serving board member in Young Life's history and a key financial contributor to Woodleaf through the years, and said, "There is a piece of property in Central California up in the Mother Lode Country that I thought might have some interest for you."

Stover, along with the chairman of the Young Life board, Frank Muncie, and Ernie Romine each contributed $1,000 to the "holding fee." Alongside Bob Mitchell, the men assessed the land and knew it was a place the mission could use. The next step was a big one: finding the necessary funds.

"Young Life had signed the papers to purchase Woodleaf for $100,000," explained John Miller, camp director at Trail West. "Everything was wonderful except for one item: We were short $100,000."

A few months later on a Saturday afternoon at Trail West, two guests, Jack and Arlene Kough, being led by the Holy Spirit, informed Miller they would buy him a lot at Trail West where the property director and his family could live. Over the moon with this unexpected news, Miller could hardly fathom what the Koughs would tell him the next day.

After a time of prayer on Sunday morning, Jack Kough informed Miller, "God told me to buy Woodleaf." Miller recounts Bill Starr's reaction when he heard the news:

"Being president of Young Life, it was Bill's responsibility to raise the needed funds. This naturally was of great concern to him. You can't imagine the excitement, gratitude, and relief that Bill had just experienced. I'm sure his hope was that Jack would do something to help meet that need—then to hear Jack say, 'Bill, I feel the Lord has led me to give Young Life the $100,000 for Woodleaf.'"

Starr and Miller promptly rejoiced over this newly realized dream—Young Life now owned Woodleaf, where generations of kids would also see their own dreams realized.

movies, novels, music, art, and her ministry called Joni and Friends, the Young Life alum went on to give hope to lives around the world—the same hope she encountered as a high school kid in Young Life.

THE BEST MEDICINE

The sixties served as a kind of mirror for the mission, but this is not to suggest the whole decade was comprised of serious introspection. Humor was still an integral part of Young Life's DNA. The following story illustrates how even a world-famous comedian/entertainer recognized Young Life's gift of humor.

"When I was serving on committee in the early sixties, I got snookered into leading a Young Life club," Ted Johnson, who promoted committee health on a national level, said. "I took that club from forty-four kids to four kids in four weeks—I'm the all-time charisma bypass! That was tough stuff. But one kid kept coming, Dave Siegle. I got Dave a summer job in the boathouse at Malibu, because I felt I owed it to him.

"Later on, in August of that year, I've got the *Jack Paar Show* on, and Dick Van Dyke comes on. Paar told him, 'Without a doubt, you've got to be the most naturally funny and talented guy I've ever met.' Of course the audience applauded. Then Van Dyke said, 'Hey, look, Jack, sometimes it takes your kids to remind you who you really are. My kid came home last Monday and said, "Dad, I just met the funniest guy in the whole world." '

"And Van Dyke pantomimed as if to say, 'Well, who could that be other than me?' And his kid said it was Dave Siegle! And the audience roared. He said, 'My kid just came from a camp up in Canada, at this thing called Young Life, and had the time of his life, where he met this Dave Siegle, the funniest guy in the whole world.'

"Well, Dave Siegle was the kid who came to club the night we had four. He came every Tuesday night. And he befriended Dick Van Dyke's son at Malibu. I didn't even know Dave was funny! But I found out after the fact that the program manager didn't show up at Malibu, and Dave filled in, and in fact was probably one of the funniest guys they ever had. He ended up being program manager for three years.

"I love to tell that story, because sometimes people get discouraged. They think, 'I really wasn't any good.' But, God makes things work."

Dick Van Dyke on the set of *Mary Poppins*, 1964.

A BETTER VERSION OF ITSELF

God used the turmoil of the sixties to prune and shape the mission into a better version of itself. As with individuals, when a movement faces a crisis point, it can go one of two ways. It can shrink back into the safe shadows of what's always been done or take the painful steps of being open to how the Lord might disrupt the careful confines of the present.

Changes in leadership, organization, and church relations enabled the mission to re-examine every facet of its ministry. Furthermore, it is no exaggeration to say that because Young Life accepted the need to change, particularly the need to go beyond the norm of reaching white, suburban American teenagers, the mission more fully realized God's call to reach many kids with the Gospel.

The 1960s changed the world, and as the combustible decade came to a close, the changes that had rocked Young Life ensured the mission would no longer limit its scope to only certain kids with certain means in certain places. Young Life had expanded into eight countries, with inroads to many more, and would truly reach out to every kid—regardless of income, geography, culture, disability, or race. The mission would never be the same. And neither would the world of millions of teenagers.

All Kinds of Kids

A Reflection by Denny Rydberg, president

Jim Rayburn's prayer, shown to the right, sounds very contemporary, doesn't it? "Our hearts ache for the [millions of] young people who remain untouched by the Gospel and for the tragically large proportion of those who have dropped by the wayside and now find themselves without spiritual guidance."

Does that sound like today? Of course. "Oh, thou Holy Spirit, give us the teenagers. For we love them and know them to be awfully lonely." Are kids lonely and alienated today? Are they looking for relationships with people who truly care about them? You bet.

Jim's desire to reach teenagers was the motivation behind his life and the reason Young Life was created. And this same focus propels Young Life forward today. It's the reason for our being. And because of that desire and commitment, literally millions of kids have heard the Gospel clearly presented by loving, caring adults, and many of these young people have said "yes" to Jesus.

That's the good news.

The sad and bad news is that, despite all our efforts—yours, mine, and thousands of staff and volunteers before us—there are still millions of kids across this country and around the world who have never heard the Good News.

And our job is not done. We want to reach more kids. All kinds of kids. We have several taglines we like to use in Young Life. "Every kid, everywhere, for eternity" is one. "Reaching a World of Kids" is another.

So we pursue kids everywhere.

We are on middle school, high school, and college campuses. We are in rural, suburban, urban, and international locations. Some kids are lost in the midst of a crime-infested housing project in an inner city. Some are lost in the midst of an affluent suburb. Some are lost in a small town where they are bored and disconnected in the same way their urban counterparts are. Some are Anglo and some are Hispanic and some are African-American. Some are African or Asian. Some are from the Former Soviet Union, or Latin America; others from Europe. Some are from two-parent homes and some are from one-parent homes and some are living by their wits on the street. Some have an unlimited future because of their talent or where they are from. But until they give their lives to Jesus, they too are lost.

So we are involved with all kids—including kids with special needs who overcome disabilities, and adolescent single moms (kids with kids), and military brats (that's what they call themselves). Wherever kids are, we want to be there.

We continue to pray Jim's prayer:

"Good Lord, give us the teenagers that we may lead them to Thee . . . "

"GOOD LORD, GIVE US THE TEENAGERS THAT WE MAY LEAD THEM TO THEE. OUR HEARTS ACHE FOR THE NINE MILLION YOUNG PEOPLE WHO REMAIN UNTOUCHED BY THY GOSPEL, AND FOR THE TRAGICALLY LARGE PROPORTION OF THOSE WHO, HAVING ONCE BEEN LED TO ATTEND SUNDAY SCHOOL, HAVE DROPPED BY THE WAYSIDE AND NOW FIND THEMSELVES WITHOUT SPIRITUAL GUIDANCE. HELP US GIVE THEM A CHANCE, O FATHER, A CHANCE TO BECOME AWARE OF THY SON'S BEAUTY AND HEALING POWER IN THE MIGHT OF THE HOLY SPIRIT. O, LORD JESUS, GIVE US THE TEENAGERS, EACH ONE AT LEAST LONG ENOUGH FOR A MEANINGFUL CONFRONTATION WITH THEE. WE ARE AT BEST UNPROFITABLE SERVANTS, BUT THY GRACE IS SUFFICIENT. O, THOU, HOLY SPIRIT, GIVE US THE TEENAGERS, FOR WE LOVE THEM AND KNOW THEM TO BE AWFULLY LONELY . . . GOOD LORD, GIVE US THE TEENAGERS!"

—JIM RAYBURN, JULY 1962

Saranac Village

In the early 1900s, copper magnate Mr. Adolph Lewisohn built a summer home on Prospect Point in the Adirondacks of New York at a cost of $2.5 million. In those early years, his guests included United States President Calvin Coolidge and Mark Twain. After the Great Depression, the property became a hunting lodge, then, in 1952, began to serve as an exclusive girls' camp called Camp Navarac.

A major consideration for the 1968-70 Young Life Forward Fund (the mission's first professionally managed fundraising drive), was the urgent need for a camp in the east. After tirelessly looking at dozens of camps, Dr. Bill Keisewetter, a lifetime board member and a renowned physician from Pittsburgh, stumbled upon Camp Navarac.

This was Bill Starr's assessment to the staff about the potential new camp:

"Dr. Bill Keisewetter ran across a camp in upper New York State, not far from Lake Placid, that looks like a winner. It has the beautiful features of a complete water sports program with sailing, canoeing, small boating, waterskiing, and swimming coupled with a fabulous lawn recreation field which could accommodate a couple of football fields and lots more room left over. In addition to this, there are six hard-surface tennis courts. It would be a program director's dream. Up the trail from the waterfront are the housing units, which are large, hunting-type lodges. They would be most adequate for a total capacity of three hundred.

"Reid Carpenter, Dean Borgman, Tom Raley, and I have all seen it and believe you would agree it has the shots. This could be the answer to a lot of prayers and work."

Thanks to several generous donors, Young Life purchased the property for $400,000 in September 1969. One of these original donors has since admitted, "At that time in my life I invested in three major things: a jet, a yacht, and Saranac. The jet is rusting in a field somewhere, the yacht is transporting drugs off the coast of Cuba and Saranac is changing thousands of kids' lives for eternity . . . I should have donated to three Young Life camps."

FIT TO A TEE

Young Life is a pioneer in the proliferation of T-shirts. Literally. Millions of them.

Young Life's T-shirts are walking billboards. They say, *I've had the best week of my life at Woodleaf.* Or Saranac. Or Clearwater Cove. They tell passers-by, *I survived work crew.* Some say, *I'm part of Young Life Africa.* Or Young Life Anchorage. Others tell curious freshmen, *Young Life is TONIGHT. At 7:11 sharp.* They proclaim an affinity for teen moms and young people with disabilities. They promote runs, rides, and expeditions—and in cotton/poly blend, an interwoven love of Christ and kids.

Which is why fans around the world proudly wear their Young Life heart on their sleeves.

the 1970s

A Continuing Education

As the sun set on the 1960s, the upheaval that marked that decade gradually died down and other issues took center stage. The prolonged conflict in Vietnam and the Watergate scandal produced a variety of emotions, including feelings of cynicism and a longing to escape.

Sometimes coined "the 'me' decade," the seventies can be seen as a time when mass movements gave way to more specialized interests. Even popular music reflected the shift, as rock 'n' roll splintered into soft rock, punk rock, southern rock, heavy metal, and disco.

While the rebellion of the sixties subsided, in Young Life an interesting dynamic was at work. Clubs continued to flourish throughout the country, with large numbers of kids coming out every week. Some kids, however, didn't see the appeal in meeting together in big groups. In fact, there was a growing disinterest in things that seemed too organizational. Again the mission would need to consider how to pursue all kids in ways that met them where they were.

As the decade opened, Young Life staff gathered together to reflect on the past and look forward to what the Lord had in store for the next ten years.

ASILOMAR

The staff conference held at Asilomar, on the Monterey Peninsula in California in January 1970, was prophetic in its call for unity. There, the vision for the mission in the new decade was declared:

"To readily accept one another, with all our diversity, in love and in gratitude to God; to put to use our varied gifts in every way that will help young people come face to face with Christ; and to make Him the unifying center of our many faceted outreach."

Asilomar marked a symbolic turning point in the mission's history. Seven months prior to the conference, Jim Rayburn, already suffering from cancer throughout his body, had been diagnosed with inoperable prostate cancer and was now a shadow of his former self. Invited to speak to the crowd of roughly five hundred staff and spouses, Rayburn, knowing this would probably be the last time he stood before the mission, was at his most poignant.

After receiving a standing ovation, the mission's founder launched into what became known as "The Big Dream" speech, which included some of his most iconic statements . . .

Opposite: Greensboro, North Carolina, Young Lifers form one of the countless pyramids constructed throughout the history of Young Life.

1970s
#1 SINGLES OF THE YEAR

- 1970 "Bridge Over Troubled Water"—Simon and Garfunkel
- 1971 "Joy to the World"—Three Dog Night
- 1972 "The First Time Ever I Saw Your Face"—Roberta Flack
- 1973 "Tie a Yellow Ribbon 'Round the Old Oak Tree"—Tony Orlando and Dawn
- 1974 "The Way We Were"—Barbara Streisand
- 1975 "Love Will Keep Us Together"—The Captain and Tennille
- 1976 "Silly Love Songs"—Wings
- 1977 "Tonight's the Night (Gonna Be Alright)"—Rod Stewart
- 1978 "Shadow Dancing"—Andy Gibb
- 1979 "My Sharona"—The Knack

"I've always felt a little twinge or something when I was introduced as the founder of this outfit. I am the founder, don't get me wrong! But the reason for my embarrassment is that I always felt like a fella who founded something should at least know he was founding something. I didn't have the slightest idea I was founding something . . .

"I knew one thing, though—I knew that Jesus Christ was important. And I knew that anyone that didn't have a chance to know Him deserved a chance—and that's what Young Life is all about—and don't you forget it! . . . The Big Dream: that everyone has a right to know Jesus Christ, to know the facts concerning Him . . .

"They have a right to know who He is; they have a right to know what He's done for them. They have a right to know how they relate to that. They have a right to know Him personally. Furthermore, they have a right to make their own choice of Him. And if you got in here accidentally without realizing that that's what Young Life's all about, then you oughta get squared away or you oughta hunt the nearest telephone booth and ask for the bus schedule. That's not just what Young Life's all about; that's all that Young Life's all about—Jesus Christ . . ."

THE MOST POWERFUL ADMONITION

The time in Asilomar marked Rayburn's last January on this earth. His dear friend in the mission, Bob Mitchell, remembered one of his last visits with the man who had shown him so much of the Savior.

Jim Rayburn addresses the staff at Asilomar.

"He was dying of cancer yet his sense of humor was always there, even to the very last. So, we were laughing and talking and he got very serious. He made this statement to me. He said, 'Mitch, don't ever let them quit talking about Jesus.' And I've never forgotten the impact that had on me. I'll always remember that admonition, maybe the most powerful admonition I've ever heard in my life, but it's what has motivated me down through the years in Young Life."

When his time was drawing near, the family invited Rayburn's friend, pastor Harlan Harris, to be there. In her book, *It's a Sin to Bore a Kid*, Char Meredith chronicled what happened next. "Everyone thought Jim was unconscious as Harlan Harris opened the Bible and read from the Scripture; but Jim whispered, 'I know that one.' He never spoke after that."

The sixty-one-year-old Jim Rayburn passed from this world into the arms of his precious Savior on December 11, 1970.

PASSIONATE, POWERFUL, PRAYERFUL

What kind of man did God use to start the mission of Young Life? Who exactly was Jim Rayburn? Wally Howard, one of the first five Young Life staff, summed up the founder in three words.

"Jim was passionate, powerful, and prayerful," Howard said. "He was passionate about preaching the Gospel, about presenting the grace of God in Christ to kids. He was powerful. When he walked in the room, he made an impression; when he spoke, people listened; when he led, people followed. He was also prayerful. When he had that Gainesville club, he asked the rest of us to meet that night and to pray. And in those early years at camp, we'd be with the kids morning, noon, and night. We'd put them in their bunks, then we'd go into one of the cabins and pray for a couple of hours."

Mitchell, for his part, was careful to point others to the whole man. "Jim was a very human individual," Mitchell said. "Not in any sense to be deified. Sometimes we get these great images of people, and they're almost unrealistic. Jim had faults like we all do, but the one thing about Jim was a passion. He had a passion for Jesus. And I think that's the way the man should be remembered—that he was absolutely determined that every kid would have a chance to be exposed to the grace of Jesus Christ. And he devoted himself to that."

TRADITIONAL *AND* PROGRESSIVE

Entering its fourth decade, the mission continued to uphold the traditional Young Life club, while also adapting to needs of the 1970s teenager. By 1970 the U.S. work was divided up geographically into ten regions. As leaders from each region compared notes, they discovered similarities in how ministry was progressing around the country. These similarities included:

1) *Larger Young Life clubs*
2) *Greater number of Campaigners kids as a result of the program*
3) *"Team" concepts being developed for volunteer leadership of a club (more than just one male and one female leader)*
4) *Increased emphasis upon training both staff and volunteer leaders*
5) *More small-group camping as well as the large summer emphasis*
6) *Direct involvement with some of the apparent social problems of our day—drugs, racism, etc.*
7) *Deepening of relationships with committee people and friends*

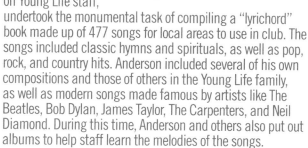

Music has been essential in Young Life ministry since the beginning. In the early seventies, the mission sought to help the staff become more proficient in leading and playing songs. Johan Anderson, a gifted musician on Young Life staff, undertook the monumental task of compiling a "lyrichord" book made up of 477 songs for local areas to use in club. The songs included classic hymns and spirituals, as well as pop, rock, and country hits. Anderson included several of his own compositions and those of others in the Young Life family, as well as modern songs made famous by artists like The Beatles, Bob Dylan, James Taylor, The Carpenters, and Neil Diamond. During this time, Anderson and others also put out albums to help staff learn the melodies of the songs.

Leaders also wisely modified the meetings to better reflect changes in the larger culture. In the *1971 Young Life Annual Report*, Bill Starr wrote, "Our staff have become flexible in such areas as music. It is rare to hear a piano in club. In some cases it has been traumatic for our people to switch over and try to find guitar pluckers, but the large majority have made the move in the direction of more contemporary music and are working hard at new ideas. There have been those who have printed their own songbooks and have gotten into difficulty where the copyright is concerned. Even this creates a healthy kind of activity and indicates a desire to be relevant."

The program used in club and at camp also changed with the times. Over the next decade or so, old-fashioned, vaudeville type humor that tended toward the negative (making fun of physical appearances, weight, stereotypes, etc.) gave way to more appropriate skits and characters. Leaders still found ways to make kids laugh hilariously, but in ways that were inclusive. "We discovered that we could get just as good a laugh if our skits and humor were of the 'slapstick variety,' " wrote longtime staff member Charlie Scott. "We began to 'make fools of ourselves for Christ's sake' rather than belittle someone else just to get a laugh. We also tried to do away with cynical or sarcastic humor."

Transitions in music and humor may appear insignificant on the surface, but for a mission intimately involved in the teenage culture, these changes were both necessary and revelatory. Kids who viewed piano playing as passé now had a club meeting where the instruments were the same as those they heard on their albums. Likewise, kids who felt insecure about their looks or background could come to Young Life club, a sanctuary from the harmful humor of the day.

OUTSIDE THE NORM

In the early seventies, there was growing interest in what was happening in the environment. Songs like John Denver's "Rocky Mountain High," Joni Mitchell's "Big Yellow Taxi," and Marvin Gaye's "Mercy Mercy Me (The Ecology)" reflected an expanding consciousness of the beauty and fragility of the natural world.

Sharing watermelon at camp.

Many young people yearned for the adventure offered in the great outdoors and Young Life's wilderness camping began as a response to this need. Unlike traditional camps with facilities, entertainment, and food prepared in kitchens, kids "roughed it" under the supervision of trained adult guides. These programs appealed to kids who, as Char Meredith explained, "would not respond to a club context, but would love to go off and live in the wilderness for a while."

The alternative camping approach began informally. An internal memo from 1970 reported that, "One group is operating out of Saranac Village, the other Malibu. The reports are mixed as to the success of the venture, which is designed after the Outward Bound™ program, but two things have become crystal clear—physical stress does open a young person to thinking of God; and, it also unites a group of young people. We will be doing more of this with our Christian fellows and girls as time goes on."

The operation outside Saranac Village was named "La Vida" ("life") and directed by George Sheffer III, son of Young Life pioneers George and Martie Sheffer. The young Sheffer could see the potential La Vida offered kids of that day. "Traditional Young Life camps were better for a proclamation approach; but wilderness and creative camping have a lot to offer kids who want to grow in their faith. La Vida was created more for discipleship."

While Sheffer was experiencing success on the East Coast, other programs also began to flourish. In 1970, Barney Dobson, a Vancouver, B.C., Young Life leader, started taking kids "beyond" the Malibu camp into the surrounding mountains. That year he led three experimental trips and Beyond Malibu was born. The Beyond Malibu program offered kids the opportunity to backpack through some of the most breathtaking scenery in the world.

In 1973, similar experiences took place as kids backpacked in the Rocky Mountains near Creede, Colorado. Three years earlier, Will and Betty Wyatt, who had decades of experience with Young Life, purchased the Lake Cliff Dude Ranch near Creede. As they visited with their friends Bob and Claudia

Backpacking at Young Life's Beyond Malibu.

Mitchell in 1972, the Wyatts dreamt aloud about introducing kids to wilderness camping, while also training them up in their faith. One year later, Young Life began adventure camping at the newly named Wilderness Ranch.

That same summer, the Lord led Jim and Sarah Hornsby, urban staff in Jacksonville, to create another program called Pioneer Plunge in the Great Smoky Mountains, near Windy Gap. *It's a Sin to Bore a Kid* chronicled the appeal: "Under experienced guides they shoved miles into the Smokies—built their own shelters, ground their own flour, baked bread, cut timber, drove mules, killed and cleaned small game and cooked it for supper, built rough furniture. And got lonesome, hungry and tired."

"My time spent at Pioneer Plunge," one Atlanta teen wrote, "was the greatest, most painful, joy-filled, cryingest, laughingest, into-it, out-of-it, concerned, indifferent, lovingest, hatingest time I ever personally spent! In other words, I'd do it again!"

Pushing themselves outside their physical comfort zones paved the way for kids to open themselves up spiritually. Like the twenty minutes of silence in a traditional camp, the

Wilderness Ranch

Rappelling in the seventies.

Discipleship camping in the mountains above Wilderness Ranch, Creede, Colorado.

Southwind

"I remember exactly when the turning point came, when we decided to begin a search for our own camp for Florida Young Life," Charlie Scott, longtime Young Life staff member, wrote in his book *The Story of Southwind*. "It was the fall of 1971, during a big weekend camp for over two hundred kids and leaders. We were using a large facility in central Florida we had rented many times. It was a bright Sunday morning, and I was in the camp manager's office, preparing to pay the weekend bill when I was stunned by a comment he made. 'Look out the window at that,' he said, 'you're bringing too many of them here. We can't have you bringing so many of them from now on.'

"When I looked out the window all I saw was a teenage couple, an African-American young man with his arm around a white girl, walking to the dining hall in the middle of a crowd of their friends. After what the manager said, I was in a state of shock. I distinctly remember thinking, as I wrote out the check, that this would be the last one I would ever write for this camp."

Within weeks, Scott, who would soon become the first Florida regional director, called his staff together to begin praying and looking for the next Young Life camp "where every kid would be welcomed and accepted." Four months later, the staff learned of a property for sale near Ocala, called the O.K. Dude Ranch. The owner was the father of a kid in Scott's Young Life club. The asking price was $175,000. For a mission with no money budgeted for another camp purchase, the only thing to do next was pray.

Within a week, a donor gave $5,000 toward a down payment. In fact, the owner himself—in response to the quick down payment— gave $3,600 toward the purchase! The rest of the down payment was provided by eleven people (including Lawrence and Sara Douglas, who had previously donated their North Carolina property to Young Life for Windy Gap).

The staff knew that "O.K. Dude Ranch" would never fly as the name of Young Life's newest camp, so they decided upon "Southwind," one of the early suggestions for Windy Gap. In April 1972, the camp hosted its first weekend for kids from Gainesville, Jacksonville, Orlando, Papano, and St. Augustine. The mission now had one more camp—and kids now had one more place where they would never be labeled as "them."

peacefulness found atop a mountain or under a sky of infinite stars provided space for receptivity to the Spirit's dealing in their lives. Having this play out alongside a small band of like-minded explorers also helped instill in kids their need for Christian community.

Throughout the decade, other ventures followed, as staff continued to explore creative experiences for their high school friends. In 1976, Sailing Beyond was born; the Vancouver program was "for the specific purpose of taking young Christians on weeklong saltwater excursions for fun and for a stretching, growing, concentrated time of fellowship with other young Christians and leaders." Meanwhile, leaders also took kids on white-water rafting, biking, and canoe trips to satisfy their hunger for adventure.

A GOOD RUN

While wilderness camping was booming, 1972 marked the end of the line for Young Life's Star Ranch. The mission's first camp, which had served thousands of kids throughout its twenty-six-year run, was no longer a viable location for what Young Life needed. "Star Ranch lost its isolation factor," Mitchell explained. "When we got the place in 1946, that's all there was up there on Cheyenne Mountain. But then over the years, real estate developments and private homes were built around that little forty-eight-acre piece. You can't operate a camp very well when you're right in the middle of a residential area."

The mission was also $600,000 in debt, which certainly didn't hurt the decision to sell when Young Life was approached—

completely unsolicited—with inquiries about the camp. So, in 1972, the mission sold Star Ranch to International Students, Inc., a Christian organization that also focused on relational ministry—but with foreign students studying in American colleges. Star Ranch would always be fondly remembered as the original Young Life camp and the place where so many first encountered the Savior.

LIGHTS, CAMERA, ACTION!

"What's so special about Young Life camp?" "Will it really be as fun as they say?" "Is it worth the time and money for me to go?" These were natural questions for kids to ask and leaders always did their best to convince kids that camp would exceed their expectations. Sometimes, though, seeing helped with believing. Over the previous two decades, Young Life had put together short films to sell kids on coming to the ranches. As the sixties ended, however, these films had become so dated that they often had the opposite effect. Leaders also attempted to sell the camps through their own personal slideshows from previous camp trips, but there was no uniformity in the promotion and the results were often subpar.

One of many staff to recognize the problem was Ken Parker, the property manager at Malibu; he had been a college classmate of Dave Vik and Ed Winkle, two film producers working in Los Angeles. Parker shared with them the need for a new camp film and one "small" detail: the mission had no money to fund it.

Vik and Winkle discussed the predicament and decided to produce the film for free. The men enlisted the help of

Video stills from *Time for Living*, 1971.

professional musicians and voice-over talent to make the product excellent. "It took about six months to edit the film at night after our regular jobs during the day," Winkle said. "Our production technique was new at the time and used a clever blend of high production values with documentary voice-over from actual Young Life campers."

Young Life's first professionally designed marketing piece for getting kids to camp was titled *Happiness Is Malibu* and its success was immediate. The film helped increase attendance at Malibu to more than 100 percent during the summer of 1970.

Fresh off the success of the Malibu film, Vik-Winkle Productions joined hands with Larry Entwistle, director of Properties, for an even more far-reaching approach: a film that would showcase all seven camps. The cost for the project was $40,000, "which for the mission in those days," Entwistle said, "might as well have been $400,000." Nevertheless, they went forward, knowing how important this film would be.

"This was a 'God moment,'" Entwistle said about the filming process. "We flew coast to coast and hit every camp in a ten-day period. We had perfect weather."

The cross-country sprint left the filmmakers at a distinct disadvantage, however, because they only had footage of those kids who were at camp when they were filming. When they were done, they had produced a film that showed no kids of color. Understandably, the urban staff made their feelings known, and the film was recut to more accurately represent the diversity of the ministry.

The end result was the twenty-two-minute-long presentation entitled *Time for Living.* The film was cutting edge for 1971—with "groovy" music and animated special effects that morphed into kids enjoying camp.

"It was a real watershed moment in Young Life," Entwistle said. "From the day that film came out, I don't think we seriously hurt for kids at camp again. It was a pivotal turning point in the marketing of camp."

Winkle remembered the excitement surrounding the new promotional tools. "Many Young Life leaders came up to me during the seventies and told me that the two films were the best tools any parachurch organization had at that time to reach young people for Christ. They told me only the Lord knows how many high school kids had accepted Jesus as Lord and Savior at camp as a result of our films. Praise the Lord!"

IN THE BUS-BUYING BUSINESS

For years, Young Life had rented or borrowed buses to transport kids to and from the camps. Because of tight budgets, the staff needed to find economical means of transportation, which often meant the buses were "lacking" in dependability. Joe Shelly, a mechanic who worked at Frontier, proposed Young Life purchase its own fleet of buses, which would give Young Life better control over the transportation process and costs. The mission agreed and purchased six forty-one-passenger buses, with Shelly presiding over the process.

Shelly built a network of drivers by hiring and training college students. A typical week might feature a team of two drivers picking up a Young Life group in Chicago and taking them to Frontier in Colorado. Once there, the drivers would pick up another group and take them back to Philadelphia. Then they would pick up yet another group to take them to Saranac. "Those buses covered about a million miles a year," said Entwistle.

By 1972, Young Life owned eighteen buses, which made up 40 percent of the total camp transportation. The program, however, proved to be too expensive to sustain, and by 1975 had to be discontinued. "In the end, we really couldn't continue because of liability issues," Entwistle said. "It was one of those wonderful eras in the mission where God, in His timing, took an idea and hundreds of thousands of kids ended up getting to camp because of it. In retrospect, it was an unbelievable deal."

Young Life buses ran from 1968 to 1975.

POSITIVE PRESS!

The Saturday Evening Post article,
October 1975

Like the *Time* magazine article fifteen years earlier, this piece, entitled "Tomorrow is In Their Hands," also touched on Young Life's presence in Connecticut. This story, however, couldn't have been more different in its portrayal of the mission. Below are some excerpts from the glowing article . . .

"Young Life is a process of pulling together the fragments of life around Jesus Christ as the permanent center. Young Life is a prophetic voice in a confused, depersonalized world, crying 'this is the way,' to teenagers who want to know what makes life good . . .

Take, as an example, a recent Young Life meeting at the home of a sixteen-year-old boy in Connecticut. If his parents were dumbfounded by what they saw, they could hardly be blamed. A week or so earlier the boy had asked permission to have the next Young Life club meeting at his home. His mother, knowing that these local teenagers met at different homes every week, readily agreed. Her son was new to the organization, and she had never witnessed a meeting. So she baked a cake, bought some hot dogs, and prepared soft drinks for what she assumed would be a dozen or so young people.

The shock came that evening. At seven o'clock she and her husband stood on the porch of their suburban home, open mouthed, watching scores of teenagers arrive in cars, on bicycles, on motorbikes, on foot. There seemed to be no end to the parade.

Before long the living room was so crowded that an adult representative of Young Life—a cheerful group leader in his late twenties—suggested that everybody go out to the front lawn. By seven-thirty on this moonlit spring evening, the lawn was thronged by more than sixty youngsters, all laughing, talking, having a noisy good time . . .

Presently a young fellow in jeans sat on a porch step, began strumming a guitar, and sixty young voices joined in a hand clapping chorus of 'He's Got the Whole World in His Hands.' That was the start. Other songs followed, contemporary spirituals mingling with popular rock. The neighbors must have enjoyed the concert they heard, for nobody complained . . .

Most of the youngsters sat down on the grass, cross-legged, looking up at the leader who had taken the top porch step as a rostrum. Like the boys, he wore jeans and an open collared sports shirt. Until now he had been merely another member of the crowd, drifting here and there, chatting with anyone who cared to talk. He had shared discussions about the local high school's baseball team, about the imminent senior prom, about the relative merits of certain male, female, and coed colleges.

Now from the top step, he launched into a brief talk, it took scarcely ten minutes and it was based on a Biblical theme in contemporary terms. What he said could not be characterized as a sermon. It was too colloquial, an easy conversation with friends. The manner in which he stressed the wisdom of the Bible's message sounded so practical, so rational, that any other attitude toward life seemed absurd. He spoke of trust: people trusting their friends, people trusting their parents, people trusting Jesus Christ.

When the leader sat down, there was no applause. The thoughtful silence indicated a meaningful message had been communicated . . .

Perhaps the most notable thing about this Connecticut gathering was that it was being repeated in almost a thousand places throughout the United States and in nine other countries."

THE DALE HOUSE PROJECT

By 1973, it was (conservatively) estimated there were one million runaways in the United States alone, and many of these were as young as eleven or twelve years of age.

Because Young Life had traditionally pursued kids in their neighborhoods and school activities, staff were at a loss with how to pursue kids who, in many ways, were "off the grid." "In the late sixties and early seventies," George Sheffer III explained, "there was a large population the traditional Young Life work wasn't coming into contact with—this whole 'hippie, troubled youth, counterculture thing.' "

It was Sheffer's family, in fact, who would become an answered prayer to these kids in crisis. George and Martie Sheffer instilled in George III the work ethic needed to care for troubled teenagers. "There was never any question of my parents' commitment to the Lord," he said. "They dedicated their lives to serving others. In Chicago, I saw my dad come home after being mugged and realized this wasn't a game to him. One thing that always influenced me was my parents would have a lot of urban kids in our home. I really became convinced of what a healthy and caring living situation could mean for kids."

Armed with this hospitality and concern for outcasts, George, Martie, and George III responded by establishing the Dale House Project in 1971. Located in Colorado Springs, the Dale House would provide "a home away from home" for hurting kids. The model had been successfully adopted in Pittsburgh by John and Christine Patak, who had begun the Circle C Project under the "umbrella of Young Life" in 1967.

From the beginning, it was clear the Lord was in this new venture, as the finances for staff and programs were initially funded by the Lilly Endowment and three houses (on Dale Street) were made available by a friend of the mission.

The Sheffers, knowing the program would need expertise beyond their own, enlisted the help of several other professionals including Dr. Jim Oraker, who became director of clinical services and staff psychologist.

The Dale House also provided a second service: training young leaders to help with these problems. College graduates would come to live in the houses and learn on the job how to work with residents. For fifteen months, they would be immersed in the fields of psychology, counseling, family systems, Bible, theology, and relational ministry. After this extensive training, graduates often went to other Young Life areas and replicated their experience, from establishing overnight and residential houses, to coordinating community services for kids with addictions.

Unlike his parents who, feeling called to pioneer new works never stayed in one place for too long, George Sheffer III would minister to kids through the Dale House for more than four decades. "I love it," he said. "You have the 'Peters' who stay in Jerusalem and the 'Pauls' who move around; maybe one of the reasons I stayed at the Dale House was because we did move around a lot when I was young and I felt like

The Dale House; inset, George Sheffer III.

I wanted to put down some roots in the community and be there over the long haul. I'm just kind of made that way and the kids we're working with need that kind of person."

YOUNG-ER LIFE!

With the cultural turbulence that rolled through the late sixties into the seventies, kids seemed to grow up faster and become less inclined to listen to the Gospel message. Sensing this growing trend, many staff began reaching out to the younger generation.

In 1969, Jay Grimstead, on staff in the San Francisco Bay area, trained his high school Campaigners kids to share their faith with junior high kids. Within two years, Doug Amidon, Grimstead's friend in San Diego, started "Younger Life" based on Grimstead's model. Soon small pockets of staff on both the East and West Coast were also reaching out to this new demographic.

Meanwhile, in Chicago and other urban centers, staff like Verley Sangster who witnessed firsthand the challenges urban middle school-aged kids faced, also began Young Life clubs for the younger set. In Philadelphia, Gene Wright started bringing middle schoolers to camp while facing ridicule from other staff over the decision. Les Comee, on staff in Jacksonville, Florida, said: "Our urban staff helped because they had been telling us to start earlier long before we listened to them. In the urban scene, kids always grew up faster."

Realizing the tremendous need to reach kids at an earlier age, Bill Starr, at divisional conferences in 1974, officially announced that Young Life as a mission would minister to middle school kids. Two years later, in Winter Park, Florida, a Young Life church partner named Jim Spencer began middle school ministry at All Saints Episcopal Church. He called the program "Wild Life," a name the mission would eventually adopt (and tweak) for its own middle school ministry.

EAST MEETS WEST

As the U.S. staff were exploring the frontiers of middle school ministry, the international work, under the leadership of Harry McDonald, also blazed new trails. During Young Life's fourth decade, the mission expanded into countries as diverse as Austria, India, and Switzerland. Meanwhile, ministry begun in the previous decade in Brazil and Peru continued to thrive, while the Lord allowed several new countries to open up, most notably in the east.

● Australia

How many Young Life ministries (not to mention friendships) have begun over a game of basketball? Just as urban ministry took off when Bill Milliken and Vinnie Di Pasquale dribbled a ball into New York City, nine years later and ten thousand miles away, the work in Australia would also be born from an idea involving basketball.

Like many men and women who have helped bring Young Life to a new place, Keith Swagerty was an unlikely pioneer. In 1969, Swagerty was a center for the Kentucky Colonels, a team in the American Basketball Association. The former club kid was coaching in his off-season in New Guinea when he met Jim Edson, a man working with youth in Brisbane. Swagerty shared about his experiences with Young Life and the two men arrived at an idea: What if they assembled a U.S. high school basketball team to bring over to Australia to run basketball camps? The next summer Swagerty, along with a few Young Life staff, put together the first-ever Young Life team, which in subsequent summers also toured in Melbourne and Sydney.

U.S. basketball team in Australia, 1979.

The tours were a hit with kids from both countries and helped sow the seeds for Young Life to begin in Australia. Americans Cliff and Liz Johnson, serving a two-year assignment teaching in Melbourne, started club there in 1973 and Arthur Ongley, eventual New South Wales director, began the work in Sydney.

In 1980, Young Life incorporated in Australia and became a separate national entity.

● South Korea

Surely the Lord must have smiled upon the bewildering events—at least from a human perspective—which led to Young Life's presence in South Korea. In 1970, two Korean gentlemen, Mr. Sun and Mr. Chung, traveled to the United States for ministry training. Accompanied by Mr. Kim Jong Dal, the group arrived speaking very little English.

Bruce Sundberg, on Young Life staff in St. Louis, met the men and because of the poor communication, assumed all three were Christians. He later discovered, in fact, that Mr. Kim was an anti-Christian, anti-American Buddhist and a high official in the South Korean government. Believing a trip to the United States would empower an even greater career in politics—his ultimate goal was to become president of South Korea—he came simply to gratify these aspirations.

Something funny happened on the way to his political dreams, however. Drawn in by the hospitality of Bruce and his wife, Beth, Mr. Kim gave his life to Christ. In 1971, Kim Jong Dal returned to Seoul, not as a rising Buddhist politician, but as a Christian missionary, starting Young Life for the teenagers in his homeland.

The Philippines

After their indirect influence on the work in Korea, the Sundbergs left the States in 1972 to minister in the Philippines and other parts of Asia. The country had begun Young Life seven years earlier and the Sundbergs were excited about the prospect of strengthening the country's leaders, like Eli Yasi, while expanding the work into Manila.

By 1975, Sundberg was meeting regularly with the president of the Philippine Senate.

"All that time I never mentioned anything about Young Life as I had a sense I was not to. However, I was praying all along about the kids of the Philippines."

One day, a senator's aide handed Sundberg a copy of the recent *Saturday Evening Post* article on Young Life. The senator (who had no knowledge of Young Life, much less Sundberg's involvement in it) wanted to hear Sundberg's thoughts on the article and how to reach kids in the Philippines!

All Kinds of Leaders

A Reflection by Denny Rydberg, president

I love the quote from A.B. Simpson, one of the founders of the Christian Missionary Alliance movement: "God is preparing His heroes. And when the opportunity comes, He can fit them in their places in a moment. And the world will wonder where they came from."

In Young Life that's been the story for seventy-five years. God has prepared heroes and placed them in this mission. If we're going to reach lost kids around the world, we desperately need these hero-leaders. And if we're going to try and reach every kind of kid, we need every kind of leader. That's diversity.

Leadership diversity is required at every level of our mission. Volunteer leaders need to be diverse. Currently, we have more than sixty thousand volunteers who serve Young Life in direct ministry with kids and/or as committee members shepherding local areas. We know from our experience that at a Young Life club, with some exceptions, of course, kids like to see someone who looks like them involved in leadership. So we recruit men and women. We need African-Americans, Latinos, Asians, Native Americans, and Pacific Islanders to reach the kids of the U.S., and we pray for, recruit, and train indigenous leaders for our global initiatives. We need diversity in other ways as well. We now have leaders with disabilities ministering to kids. On our area teams, we're blessed when we have the energy of the young adult volunteer with the experience and wisdom of the seasoned veteran. We need area directors who can cross cultures—all united in loving and pursuing kids for the sake of Christ. Every year we hold Area Director School, and I'm so impressed with the way God keeps sending us absolute stars!

At the regional, divisional, and "missionwide" levels—including the Board of Trustees—we also need a wide variety of skilled, committed, passionate followers of Jesus with the ability to manage and lead. I'm pleased that God has blessed the President's Cabinet with a rich montage of people: men and women, African-Americans, Latinos, the younger and the older. As we have moved into the international arena, we have developed leaders in country who are making a huge difference in how we impact kids. Do the names Mungai Kamau, Moges Berassa, James Davis, Alexis Kwamy, Simon Okiria, and Martin Wamalwa sound familiar? They are the current regional directors in Africa from the countries of Kenya, Ethiopia, Liberia, Tanzania, and Uganda. And there are more being prepared to step up as we move into new countries (we are in over twenty African countries now) and reach more kids. How about Stepa Velilyayev, Sergie Romanyuk, Zhenya Pustoshkina, and Sasha Utkin? They are our first four regional directors in the Former Soviet Union. And we have indigenous leaders in every one of the more than ninety countries where we're pursuing kids.

In the mission of Young Life, do we need to be more diverse? Of course. Will we ever be as diverse as we would like? Probably not. But I am thankful for the kaleidoscope of leaders God has placed on our team.

Two pioneers: Eli Yasi from the Philippines and Kim Jong Dal of South Korea.

> ## "
> **IN MY FONDEST DREAMS AND HOPES THAT WAS WHAT I HAD PRAYED WOULD HAPPEN, BECAUSE AS SOON AS THEY DID THAT, I KNEW THAT IT WAS THEIR WORK; IT WAS NO LONGER MINE."**
> —BRUCE SUNDBERG

"So the next morning, after the meal," Sundberg said, "the senator turned to me in the presence of all those leaders, and asked, 'Bruce, please share with us about the article on Young Life and your thoughts about reaching out to the youth of the Philippines.' Incredible!

"I shared with the Fellowship the Young Life article, including a few things, of course, that were not in the article. There was a very animated discussion that day and a common consensus reached by the end of the meeting that they wanted a Young Life-type outreach in their country. Then they turned to me and asked if I would implement it. In my fondest dreams and hopes that was what I had prayed would happen, because as soon as they did that I knew that it was their work; it was no longer mine."

Over time, Sundberg connected with Cardinal Jaime Sin, the Archbishop of Manila and spiritual leader of the country's thirty-eight million Roman Catholics, who gave the work his blessing. Soon the work there, which was called "Bigkis"—the Filipino word meaning "bind together"—was under way.

PARTNERING WITH THE CHURCH

Always eager for Young Life to have a robust relationship with the church, Starr felt it critical to continue building bridges with church leaders wherever possible.

"During the early seventies," Starr said, "we in Young Life were asking: 'To whom can we be accountable? Who can we expect to ask us the hard questions?' I recognized that Young Life had a basic accountability problem. People were asking us, 'How does Young Life relate to the church?' "

In 1975, the mission began work on its third version of a magazine. *Focus on Youth,* the previous magazine that was aimed at parents and dealt with serious issues like materialism, war, rebellion, and authority, had run its course. The new magazine was simply titled *Young Life,* and like its namesake that ran from 1944 to 1964, was aimed at kids. The magazine was intentionally designed to be small enough for a kid to put in their back jeans pocket. According to the first edition, the magazine was "aimed to give you a 'club in covers' to go home with . . . to take you from where you are to where you gotta stretch to get."

Young Life magazine cover (Winter 1976 issue).

This emphasis on church relations was not simply limited to discussions among mission leadership, but encouraged at the local level as well. "Staff and leaders were asked to view themselves as part of the larger church," Mitchell explained, "and to relate in dialogue and cooperation with local Protestant and Catholic churches."

This "dialogue and cooperation" was happening both in the U.S. and beyond, most significantly in Württemberg, Germany. Dr. Darrell Guder, an American pastor teaching there, recognized strong similarities between the evangelical methods of the Württemberg church and Young Life, and invited mission leadership to begin building a relationship with the leaders there, for the purposes of mutual encouragement and learning. The experiment was a success, as the cordial give-and-take led both sides to grow in their understanding of the kingdom and the opportunities to serve one another.

TRAINING WHILE DOING

The German dialogues would not be Darrell Guder's sole contribution in the decade. He was also instrumental in the further development of the mission's training program. Young Life would never outgrow the need for serious theological and practical investment in its staff and volunteers. Every year more and more young men and women followed their calling onto Young Life staff; few, however, arrived with deep biblical training.

Just as it had since the fifties, the mission was committed to providing them with seminary instruction. Bob Mitchell, then director of Training, recognized that without intentional direction in this area, the mission could easily drift off course. "It's easy to get some soft things going here and there that don't look like us. Maybe it's a theological degeneration, or a club ministry that isn't reaching out, or where the strategies for reaching into the community are not thought out . . . just because somebody wasn't trained."

Realizing he would need help in developing a strong accredited program, Mitchell enlisted the aid of Guder, who helped form an academic partnership with Fuller Theological Seminary. The result was the Institute for Youth Ministries (IYM), Young Life's newest training program. Other institutions to participate included Gordon-Conwell near Boston, Luther Seminary in Minneapolis, North Park Theological in Chicago, and even a new program for undergraduates at Flagler College in St. Augustine, Florida.

Every summer, many staff would travel to Colorado Springs and hit the books. Donna McClellan, who would later

Engaging in meaningful conversations at camp.

become the national field associate for women, remembered fondly her time at the Fountain Valley campus. "Where else do you have an opportunity to live in community with people who want to grow in terms of their lives in Christ and come from all over the country, from a lot of different churches and traditions? That's an incredible gift. For one thing, your view of God is expanded. There's more than one way to sing a song, present Christ, and infiltrate a culture. I'll be eternally grateful that I could do my seminary along with the work of Young Life. It kept me in the real world. It kept me more real."

A NEW STATEMENT OF FAITH
Along with much of the Christian community in the 1970s, within Young Life circles there was considerable conversation over the issue of inerrancy (the belief that the Bible is free from error). This discussion over the reliability and accuracy of Scripture brought the mission to the point of needing to clarify its Statement of Faith. In an effort to reaffirm the mission's belief in the centrality and supremacy of God's Word, the first article in the new Statement of Faith read, "The Scriptures of the Old and New Testaments being given by divine inspiration, are the word of God, the final and supreme authority in all matters of faith and conduct."

A VOICE IN THE MISSION
In the mission's urban work, the seventies picked up where the previous decade left off—with growth in understanding how to reach kids of color. In 1973, at the National Urban Conference, the staff acknowledged the need to find an urban vice president. By the next year, there was a consensus by the urban staff, regional directors, and national leadership to elect Dr. John Porter to serve in the post. Porter was a pastor who understood leadership well, having worked side by side with his friend, Martin Luther King Jr., during the civil rights movement.

Verley Sangster, who would later serve in high-level capacities within Young Life, applauded the choice of Porter. "We did not have to define who we were and what we were about to John. He really tried to make some changes to the structure."

While changes were slowly occurring at the higher levels of leadership, the urban staff continued to feel underrepresented at the local level. Sangster and Bo Nixon knew the time was right to attack this problem head on. In 1977 the two men, along with Scott Shively, John Thomas, Bernard Thompkins, and Eddie Turner, helped create the Urban Primus Council

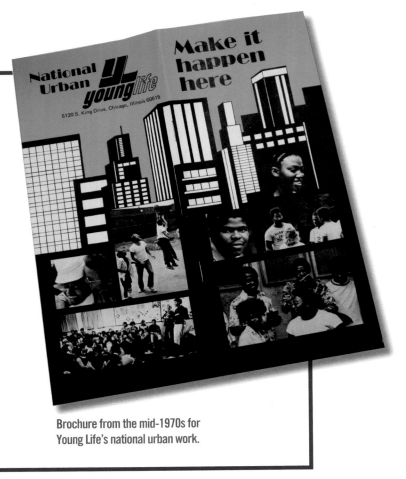

Brochure from the mid-1970s for Young Life's national urban work.

(UPC). The UPC was a place for urban leaders to come together and give voice to the needs of the staff. The group would then stand in the gap and communicate these needs to the larger mission. Sangster was soon voted the first UPC chairman.

"I thank God for the Urban Primus Council," said Rudy Howard, who would later become the mission's associate urban director. "The UPC was formed to pull us together, to organize us, not to go against Young Life."

In 1978 Porter decided it was time to move on and resigned from his post as Urban vice president. Sangster succeeded him in February 1979, and the UPC eventually initiated a new development called "the National Urban Office," which Sangster would also direct. The UPC continued to support the Urban Office, meeting twice a year with a national representation of urban staff.

Throughout the decade, there was strong give-and-take within the mission as the urban work grew. The staff learned valuable principles from each other. "When the Bible talks about 'every tribe and every nation,' " Nixon said, "that's something that urban leaders taught the rest of Young Life. That God is after every tribe and nation and He won't be satisfied until He has every tribe and nation.

"What urban staff learned from the suburban staff," he continued, "is that there must be excellence in all you do. There's an organized way to run an organization, a model to take and expand upon."

Rudy Howard added, "For a while, urban Young Life played the role of a prophet to hold the mission accountable. Without African-Americans, Young Life might not have the vibrancy it has. Without Young Life I wouldn't understand incarnational witness and be able to teach it to other African-Americans."

The 1970s saw urban work begun in the cities of Washington, D.C., Philadelphia, Boston, Canton, Cleveland, Indianapolis, Tacoma, Portland, Birmingham, Memphis, Houston, Minneapolis/St. Paul, and the San Francisco Bay Area. This growth in the urban ministry necessitated the addition of exclusive urban weeks of summer camp, where the message, music, and program were tailored specifically for kids from the city. The advancement of the work and the gains urban leadership made within the mission were evidence of God's hand strengthening Young Life for the new decade just around the corner.

EQUAL MEMBERS OF THE BODY OF CHRIST

Young Life was a mission born by a woman's private prayers as much as a man's public calling; what the Lord encouraged Clara Frasher to ignite, He inspired Jim Rayburn to fan into flame. And over the course of the next three decades, men and women both settled into these respective roles: men maintained their "up front" presence, while equally busy women worked "behind the scenes."

While men directed the area, raised the funds, led the clubs, and spoke at camp, women assisted with club and took a leadership role in the "girls' " Bible studies and groups, but rarely more than that.

This approach, of course, mirrored the times, when men were the predominant leaders and breadwinners at work, and women were in charge on the home front, where they cared for the needs of their families. Nevertheless, the questions of women's abilities and opportunities were a topic of consideration throughout society—and the mission.

"In the early days," Wally Howard remembered, "there was a good deal of unresolved tension about our respective roles—a lot of insecurity on the part of the men, not knowing how to relate to the obvious abilities of those women who worked so hard along with us. There was a lot of talk about how effective a woman could be as a club leader."

A significant step occurred in 1972. That spring, the Board of Directors elected Marge Peterson, a fifteen-year staff veteran, to be the first woman to serve on the board. Other changes were to come, but not until the latter half of the decade. There was still much wrestling and convincing—on both sides of the issue—to be done. The next major stride for the advancement of women would come six years later.

The year 1978 was historic for women in the mission. Leadership had by this time reconsidered its traditional view on what the Scriptures said about women. "During my tenure as president of Young Life," Mitchell said, "I became increasingly convicted, with some external prodding I confess, that there is no biblical basis for withholding women from positions of leadership.

"I began to get angry letters, from both men and women, including some staff, when I began to push for a more equal role for women. They didn't feel it was right for Young Life to open up any and all positions of leadership to women."

Despite the controversy, that year the first women's conference was convened. At the conference the attendees "emphasized that their purpose in reviewing the role of women in Young Life was not pro-liberation according to the doctrines of the Women's Lib movement, but to ensure that women in the ministry can relate as equal members of the Body of Christ."

The conference initiated many recommendations to mission leadership, the most prominent being the appointment of a woman to a national level position to work alongside Field Director Bob Reeverts. Mitchell agreed and appointed Mae Page to serve as the associate director of Field Ministries.

These changes represented the tip of the iceberg when it came to improving conditions for women serving in mission leadership and in the field. Throughout Young Life, women and men performing the same job were now offered the same salary and enjoyed the same benefits of training. While the progress made in the 1970s on the issue of women's leadership was profound, it was but the beginning of a conversation that would continue into subsequent decades.

STARR STEPS ASIDE

In January 1977, while the United States welcomed in Jimmy Carter as its thirty-ninth president, Young Life said goodbye to its second. After thirteen years faithfully executing the duties of president, Bill Starr sensed God calling him out of the role.

Enjoying field games at Windy Gap.

"By 1977," Starr said, "I was beginning to feel I had, by God's grace, made my contribution and it was time to do something else. I was experiencing frequent migraine headaches. My doctor, wanting to help, generously prescribed sleeping pills to help me sleep, and other pills to get me going in the morning. I had watched Jim Rayburn suffer from similar headaches and become dependent on pills also, so Ruth and I prayed about resigning.

"At a division conference in the South, I offered my resignation and made the announcement from the platform to a group of about five hundred. We said nothing before to anyone for fear someone would try to convince me to reconsider."

Starr, who played "Joshua" to Rayburn's "Moses," indeed led the mission into a land of new challenges. He bravely navigated the mission through the stormy sixties and seventies and stuck to his firmly held conviction, no matter the amount of opposition, that the mission must include both suburban and urban ministry. A man of vision, Starr also brought a new degree of organization and professionalism to the work, and did so in a quiet, confident manner. Within the first six years of his tenure, the mission enjoyed a 20 percent annual growth rate, necessitating the decentralization of field operations and leadership into three U.S. divisions: Northern, Southern, and Western. According to many who worked with him, when it came to modeling grace, truth, and thankfulness, the second president was always first class.

Bob Reeverts, Young Life's international director, was quick to recognize Starr's giftedness as a spiritual leader. "You had a natural respect for Bill. For many of us younger people coming up at that time, Bill could articulate the compassion of Christ in a new and different dimension than Jim had communicated, and that impacted our lives so much. He was another one in Young Life who, through his articulation of the Gospel, enlarged the mission's understanding of our Lord."

Starr also made major inroads outside the mission, most notably in his passion for building Young Life's relationship with the church. "People didn't know how to fit us into the mainstream of the church," Starr said. "My deep conviction was that Young Life is the church, but it needs to take its rightful place in order to make its contribution. We needed a body to which we were accountable."

Furthermore, Starr reasoned, "How do you make your staff feel like they are on par with other ministries, other parts of

Heartfelt joy at camp.

the body of Christ? I felt from early on we didn't have any theological self-awareness of who the mission was, and we needed that.

"Bill [hoped] Young Life would not just be some group out there doing its own thing," said Doug Burleigh, future Young Life president, "but that a lot of its importance would be defined in the context of a local church. He worked hard on building relationships with church leadership in various denominations. That season was a very important one for Young Life, to grow more laterally in its infrastructure and its relationships with the local church. And Bill was the person for that."

"The positions of leadership, in which I was placed, were not of my design," said Starr. "It seemed I found myself there and just did the best I could. I do not need to know my impact. Just to remember all these things, fills me with gratitude for a role that I could play; and I pray that God was glorified."

Although called out of the office of the presidency, Starr did not want to leave Young Life altogether. He knew he could help in some other facet, and the board demonstrated its wholehearted agreement by appointing him to the position of president of the Young Life Foundation.

A NATURAL PROGRESSION
With Starr's resignation from the role of president, the Board of Directors sought as his replacement a man with a long,

long history in Young Life. Few within the mission had held as many titles as Bob Mitchell. One of the first kids Rayburn ever met, Mitchell served in various roles: club kid, work crew, summer staff, volunteer leader, program director, camp speaker, area director, regional director, divisional director, and vice president of Training. Likewise, Mitchell's wife, Claudia, had a long history with the mission, having been involved since her high school days. It seemed only natural, then, to appoint him as the mission's third president.

A WALK WITH THE WISE

After accepting the board's invitation, Mitchell sought Billy Graham's counsel, to see what advice the famed evangelist would give him on leadership.

The two met in Toronto, where Graham was conducting a campaign. "He gave me most of the afternoon," Mitchell said, "and we sat in his room and talked about leadership, the Gospel, his experiences, and mutual friends.

"That's when he said, 'Of all the organizations, the one I hear the most about from people having met Christ is Young Life. Most of the people working in our campaigns met the Lord in Young Life.' That was a startling thing for me to hear him say. Then he said, 'I really wish you well and I will pray for you. In fact, let's pray now.'

Bob Mitchell

OF ALL THE ORGANIZATIONS, THE ONE I HEAR THE MOST ABOUT FROM PEOPLE HAVING MET CHRIST IS YOUNG LIFE. MOST OF THE PEOPLE WORKING IN OUR CAMPAIGNS MET THE LORD IN YOUNG LIFE."

—BILLY GRAHAM

"When Billy Graham prays, he kneels, and we're in his hotel room, kneeling there at the bed. We prayed for kids and I can remember about halfway through his prayer, he broke down and began to cry. I'm thinking, 'Wow, how powerful.' Here's a man that doesn't just work with kids, but his heart is broken for kids.

"He was praying about his own children, as well as the needs of all the kids we would be meeting. That endeared the man to me. He knows what it is to minister out of brokenness, his own sense of forgiveness. I think that's where he's so powerful. The man knows he's been forgiven and will proclaim that wherever he is."

WHAT'S IN A NAME?

During Mitchell's first year, mission leadership felt it appropriate to change some terminology. For one, the Board of Directors became the Board of Trustees, a designation deemed more in line with a nonprofit organization. A second change was more philosophical in nature. Because of Mitchell's long history on field staff, he knew the way staff responded to certain titles. He knew it was time for a new name for the mission's headquarters.

" 'Headquarters' sounded a little heavy-handed to me. I thought headquarters were 'out there' where the kids were. That's where God's headquarters are. We changed it from headquarters to the Service Center because I felt like these people were here to serve the Lord and keep people out there on the front lines getting to know hard-to-reach kids and leading them to Jesus. I thank God for each person at the Service Center."

By 1973, Emile Cailliet's book, *Young Life*, which shone the light on the philosophy and early workings of the mission, had been out for ten years. Bill Starr felt the complete Young Life history needed to be captured in written form, and commissioned Char Meredith to tell the story. The task proved to be monumental; between interviews, fact-gathering, writing, edits and a complete rewrite, the book took five years to complete. The response was equally monumental—the book sold out in its first printing.

"*It's a Sin* was more about the staff," Meredith said. "I wanted to write it like a novel. The stories are so amazing and truth is stranger than fiction. I have people say to me, 'Oh, I used that book when I was in seminary.' So, it seems to kind of have slipped into a lot of interesting niches and supplied materials for people's lives. I've always felt it had a special quality because I was totally dependent on the Lord."

It's a Sin to Bore a Kid

THE SILVER DOLLAR CITY DISCIPLESHIP EXPERIENCE

An area of growth for the mission was that of discipleship—how to take young leaders to a deeper level of faith and service. Will and Betty Wyatt, who had helped establish Wilderness Ranch, felt the Lord leading them to develop a program where students could live in community, study the Word, and live out their faith in a paid work setting. The Silver Dollar City amusement park in Missouri's Ozark Mountains proved to be the ideal location for such an undertaking.

In the summer of 1977, thirty college students began the inaugural program. Throughout the summer they sold ride tickets, performed in melodramas, served as wait staff, and did various maintenance jobs, while also learning deep biblical truths from the Wyatts and Terry and Suzette McGonigal. The results were obvious. "It is one of the best leadership training experiences I've ever seen," said Mitchell. "The best thing about it is that kids are working right out in the world; they have to relate to the public, and work right alongside the other non-Young Life college students."

RENEWING THE CALL

As the seventies drew to a close, Young Life again gathered the entire staff together for a time of renewal. For four days in April, leaders from around the world met at the Broadmoor Hotel in Colorado Springs for the "1979 Staff Congress." The choice of the word "congress" over "conference" implied active participation, not spectatorship, on the part of the attendees.

Their participation resulted in a "Covenant for Ministry" that identified the seven commitments of the mission: incarnational evangelism, incarnational community, spiritual disciplines, building healthy families, the church of Jesus Christ, personal stewardship, and social and political stewardship.

After a decade of heartfelt introspection, it seemed appropriate that the mission would again renew its call to

Young Life staff from around the world gather in 1979.

teenagers. After all, kids were still meeting Jesus because leaders and committees were faithfully serving in the local area. At the end of the day, Young Life did not want to be defined by the issues that divided, but by the cause that had always crystallized the movement.

Along with the 1970 Asilomar conference, the 1979 Staff Congress helped bookend a decade of numerous changes and challenges. And while the mission had learned much in regard to loving Christ and one another, the Asilomar vision still held true . . .

"To readily accept one another, with all our diversity, in love and in gratitude to God; to put to use our varied gifts in every way that will help young people come face to face with Christ; and to make Him the unifying center of our many-faceted outreach."

With the 1980s around the corner, the mission needed to continue in this teachable spirit as God would lead Young Life into even greater frontiers.

YOUNG LIFE CAMPS THROUGH THE YEARS

Star Ranch
Colorado • 1946-1972

Trail West Lodge
Colorado • 1964

Praz de Lys
France • 1965

Windy Gap
North Carolina • 1966

Woodleaf
California • 1966

Pioneer Plunge
North Carolina • 1973

Fazenda Salto
Brazil • 1974

Wilderness Ranch
Colorado • 1978

Trinity Ranch
Philippines • 1979

'90s

Rockbridge Alum Springs
Virginia • 1992

La Finca
Nicaragua • 1992

Crooked Creek Ranch
Colorado • 1994

Frontier Ranch
Philippines • 1997

'00s

Timber Wolf Lake
Michigan • 1999

Clearwater Cove
Missouri • 2000

Carolina Point
North Carolina • 2001

RockRidge Canyon
Canada • 2002

Silver Cliff Ranch
Colorado • 1949-1983

'50s
Frontier Ranch
Colorado • 1951

Malibu Club
Canada • 1953

'60s
Castaway Club
Minnesota • 1963

Breakaway Lodge
Oregon • 1969

Saranac Village
New York • 1969

'70s
Beyond Malibu
Canada • 1970

Southwind
Florida • 1972

'80s
Mountain Lodge
California • 1981

Oakbridge
California • 1982

Buttercreek Lodge
Washington • 1984

Lake Champion
New York • 1986

Lost Canyon
Arizona • 1997

SharpTop Cove
Georgia • 1997

Washington Family Ranch—Canyon
Oregon • 1997

Pico Escondido
Dominican Republic • 1998

Washington Family Ranch—Creekside
Oregon • 2009

'10s
RMR Backcountry
Colorado • 2010

Cairn Brae at Loch Monzievaird
Scotland • 2013

Armenia
2013

the 1980s

Branching Out

The 1980s were marked by "big-ness." For teenagers roaming the malls and skating rinks, big hair was in—from gravity-defying moussed-up bangs to feathered sides to high-top fades to mullets. Quite often this huge hair was accompanied by large lingo (see: "Totally!" and "Awesome!" and "Totally Awesome!").

The decade's soundtrack was populated by big, sweeping music by big artists. Multiple singles from best-selling albums like Michael Jackson's *Thriller*, Bruce Springsteen's *Born in the USA*, and U2's *The Joshua Tree* filled the airwaves, which also featured "consciousness-raising" hits like "Do They Know It's Christmas?" and "We Are the World." The music, in turn, helped spawn a variety of star-studded charity concerts, most notably Live Aid.

This was a time of substantial movements and changes in Young Life, too. From 1980 to 1989, two new ministries were formed, the mission's fourth president came on the scene, one camp was sold, two more were purchased, and ministry was begun in a country that had been the "archenemy" of the United States.

Young Life was branching out with new specialized ministries to kids who were, up until now, mostly out of reach. In the U.S., the mission officially recognized efforts to work with kids with disabilities; overseas, new kids were introduced to Christ through military and foreign exchange programs. In fact, while the suburban efforts continued and the urban ministry strengthened, Young Life's international ministry entered a new phase of expansion.

AMAZING REFLECTIONS OF JESUS

In 1980, Bob Mitchell introduced a familiar face as the mission's new International director. Bob Reeverts, who had served on staff since the early sixties, felt it important to raise awareness of the work. Despite his predecessor Harry McDonald's attempts to spotlight the international ministry, the work needed more attention. "I remember Harry's lonely voice in our national management meetings," Reeverts recalled, "because he would always be making this appeal for international and what God was doing, but it was like a voice crying in the wilderness."

To bring about a greater awareness, Reeverts began his new role by inviting anyone who might be interested to pray and consider how they could support the international work. A group of fifty emerged and met faithfully every quarter for two to three days, with the first day consisting of fasting and prayer.

Opposite: A beautiful sight—kids roaring with laughter at Young Life club.

the 1980s | 97

1980s
FASHIONS, FADS, AND PHRASES

Out of these faithful fifty, the new director looked for proven staff who could flourish in an overseas adventure. Reeverts encouraged veterans like George Sheffer and John Miller to consider new assignments, and they accepted, in Africa and Australia respectively. While moves like these grew the work, the work also grew the staff.

"It's incredible to see the face of Jesus Christ in the lives of men and women who have served in places like India or Bangladesh or Cambodia," Reeverts said, "or to see it through the charismatic church of Latin America or the Orthodox church of Russia—amazing reflections of Jesus."

Under Reeverts' leadership, new work began in Africa and Europe, while ministries were founded in the Latin American countries of the Dominican Republic, Costa Rica, and Nicaragua. Several specialized ministries that naturally fell under the umbrella of Young Life International were also developed—Amicus, Military Community Youth Ministries (MCYM), International Schools, and HELPERS all emerged in this decade. The growth overseas, in fact, created the need for a larger support staff and forced the International department to move from an already overcrowded Service Center to a separate facility a few miles away.

● England
By the early eighties only 4 percent of England's population was involved in any way with the church, and 95 percent of fifteen- to twenty-four-year-olds said church was "painfully irrelevant."

Arnie and Mary Lou Jacobs started ministry with kids as volunteers in 1953. A mere thirty years later, in June 1983, the staff couple began a new adventure—an outreach to the kids in England. Theirs was a unique approach; for three months every year the couple would stay in England, training church leaders in relational evangelism and helping establish models of youth ministry. Then they would return to the States, as the indigenous leaders owned the work in their home country.

In 1987 a milestone event occurred—the first outreach camp for Young Life England. Of the forty kids who attended, twelve made decisions to follow Jesus. The leaders, needless to say, were ecstatic.

The leaders in England were discovering one of Young Life's time-tested principles—as they took the time to forge relationships with kids, they found their young friends more willing to trust them. Arnie Jacobs recalled, "A kid in Oxford said to Pete Ward, one of my good friends [leading the work there], 'You are the safest person I know.' That's good. I would like to be called a safe person for anybody, but particularly high school kids."

● Switzerland
Young Life Switzerland owes much to France, their neighbor to the west, where the mission's international work originated. Likewise, the Swiss ministry is indebted to Chris Cook, who not only founded the work, but also continued it for more than thirty years.

After a 1969 Wheaton College mission trip, where she worked at Praz de Lys, Cook returned for a two-year commitment to serve with Rod and Fran Johnston and their ministry in France. As Cook grew in her love for kids and her ability to navigate the French culture, she realized her two-year commitment would be just the beginning. In 1977, Cook and the Johnstons moved to Annemasse, a French suburb of Geneva, where they ministered to both French and Swiss kids.

The ministry grew to the point where parents asked if a club could be formed just for Swiss kids. In 1983 their wish was granted, as Contact Jeunesse (the name under which Young Life would operate in Switzerland) was formed. Throughout her time in France and Geneva, Cook modeled to the rest of the international staff what it meant to commit to people of another culture.

FASHIONS
- Turned-Up Shirt Collars
- Feathered Hair
- Mullets and Rat Tails (long strip of hair down the back of neck)
- "Members Only" Jackets
- Adidas, Air Jordans, Chuck Taylors, Vans Shoes
- Jean Jackets
- Parachute Pants

FADS
- Atari
- Rubik's Cube
- John Hughes Movies (*Sixteen Candles, Breakfast Club, Pretty in Pink*, etc.)
- Pac Man
- Sony Walkman
- Break Dancing
- MTV

PHRASES
- "Word"
- "Where's the Beef?"
- "Totally" used alone or with the following . . .
- "Awesome"
- "Tubular"
- "Gnarly"
- "Rad"

Kenya

For three years, beginning in 1981, George Sheffer and Bill Taylor made several trips to Africa to explore possibilities for ministry. The seasoned staff veteran and the director of International Administration, respectively, were greatly encouraged in meeting so many African nationals with a heart for Christ and kids. In March 1984, Sheffer and his wife, Martie, moved to Nairobi, Kenya, for fifteen months to explore opportunities for ministry as well as lead the first Relevant Youth Ministry course at Daystar University, an affiliate of Wheaton College.

After the overwhelming response of the thirty youth workers who attended the class, the ministry opportunities came quickly. In 1985, the Sheffers invited longtime staff Nobie and Carol Hill to continue training youth workers in Kenya. By April 1986, ten Young Life staff gathered in Victoria Falls, Zimbabwe, for the first African Young Life Staff Conference. One year later, the Sheffers helped teach another Relevant Youth Ministry course alongside leaders from Youth for Christ, The Navigators, Scripture Union, and Daystar.

"Africa has the fastest-growing Christian population of any continent," Sheffer explained in 1987, "but outreach has been platform centered—getting a group of folks together and asking them to raise their hands to accept Jesus. There's no relationship building or follow-up. Our approach is new to Africa, and it's dynamic and powerful."

The response could not have been better, Sheffer said. "By the end of the course, we had become a real family. African men do not cry in public—it just isn't done—but on graduation day tears could be seen in the eyes of these strong, young, African youth workers."

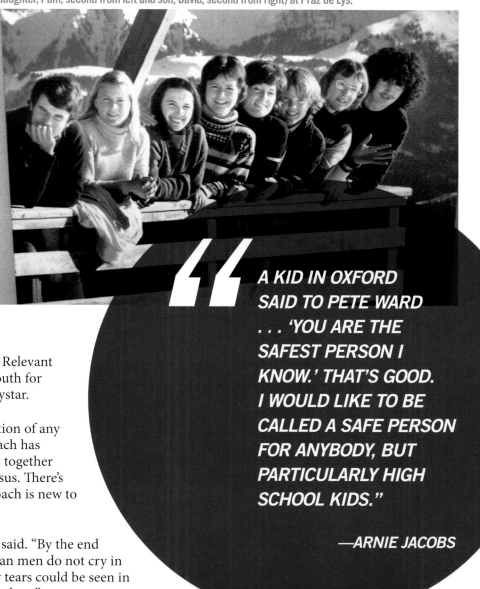

Chris Cook, third from right, with other leaders (including Fran Johnston, fourth from left, Johnston's daughter, Pam, second from left and son, David, second from right) at Praz de Lys.

" *A KID IN OXFORD SAID TO PETE WARD . . . 'YOU ARE THE SAFEST PERSON I KNOW.' THAT'S GOOD. I WOULD LIKE TO BE CALLED A SAFE PERSON FOR ANYBODY, BUT PARTICULARLY HIGH SCHOOL KIDS."*

—ARNIE JACOBS

Luke, an Amicus student from Kenya, 1985.

It was a fitting tribute to Sheffer in what would prove to be his last trip to Kenya. On November 15, 1987, George Sheffer Jr., a man who had meant so much to so many in the mission, went home to be with his Lord.

AMICUS

Since the early 1960s, foreign exchange students had frequented the U.S. Young Life camps on summer trips before returning to their home countries. Some came because they were invited by friends they met through Young Life club. Others came, maybe, because their student exchange organization was invited by a Young Life camp. For many, these camp weeks represented their first taste of the Gospel. As exciting as this exposure to the Savior was, the discouraging piece often came when they went back home without any support system to help them consider further the claims of the Christian faith. For two decades, the question lingered as to what Young Life could do to help them in their transition.

In 1980 Bob and Ann Reeverts instituted Young Life's own exchange student program, named Amicus (pronounced ah-Mee-cus). Amicus, which comes from the Latin word for "friend," was designed as a quality exchange program where international students could experience "the greatest *year* of their lives."

To do this, Amicus focused on building relationships with the foreign students by placing them in homes of adults with Young Life backgrounds, inviting them to clubs and then to camps at the end of their school year.

The program was also designed to have a more comprehensive system for the mission to help students grow in their faith, or exploration of the faith, when they returned to their home country. Many went back home ready to live as followers of Christ, as the next generation of leaders reaching out to their communities. "We felt the missing ingredient in most student exchange programs was follow-up," Ann Reeverts said. The program, therefore, focused primarily on students who could stay involved in Young Life upon their return.

Amicus completed its first year on October 1, 1981, with five students from Germany, Austria, France, and Australia. The next year the number doubled, and by the end of the decade, 197 students from sixteen countries had completed a year of education in the United States, enjoying vital connections with the ministry of Young Life.

MILITARY COMMUNITY YOUTH MINISTRIES

In the twenty-one years since Jim Rayburn met Colonel Henry Amen near Frankfurt, Germany, Young Life continued to reach out to kids on military bases overseas. Separation from parents serving in the theater of war, combined with frequent moves and accompanying re-introductions into the new and unknown, often produced feelings of insecurity and hopelessness in military dependents.

By 1980, at the height of the Cold War when the number of overseas troops was swelling, many in Young Life and Youth for Christ felt more needed to be done to reach their kids. Staff in both ministries began dreaming of a cooperative effort to achieve a greater result.

In July 1980, Bob Broyles, who was on Young Life staff in Austria, invited the leaders of Young Life and Youth for Christ to a meeting at the Fellowship House in Washington, D.C., to discuss the idea of a joint ministry to military youth. Along with Broyles and Doug Coe, who hosted the time, those present at the meeting were the presidents of Young Life and Youth for Christ, Bob Mitchell and Jay Kesler respectively, along with their directors of International Ministry, Bob Reeverts and Earl Schultz.

Not long into the gathering, the group unanimously agreed that the time was right to start a new military outreach ministry and the two ministries should "join forces."

"It was a history-making event," Broyles said, "for it was the first instance in which these two global ministries agreed to work together, in partnership, on a national and international scale. They [also] agreed that the organization needed to be separate from each of the partners, and that, to be attractive to the military, it needed a recognizable name."

The new venture was entitled Military Community Youth Ministries (MCYM), and the parties agreed that Broyles should serve as MCYM's first executive director. That fall it was decided that MCYM's club meetings would be known as "Club Beyond," distinguishing them from Young Life and Youth for Christ clubs back in the States.

"All present felt the movement of the Holy Spirit as we stood at the conclusion of the meeting, hand in hand in the living room of the Fellowship House, praying for God's blessing upon this new, dramatic undertaking," Broyles said. "We left knowing there were many obstacles immediately ahead, not the least of which was a huge recruiting task to find staff for the many new contracts being offered for youth ministers on American bases in Europe where over a half million American soldiers, airmen, and their families served."

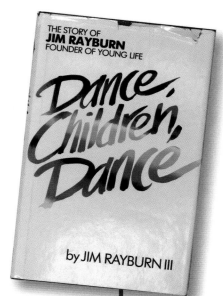

In 1984, Jim Rayburn III told the story of Jim and Maxine Rayburn from a son's perspective. The book was an intimate look at their hopes, dreams, struggles, and triumphs as Jim pioneered the work of Young Life. The book was later updated and reprinted in 2000 under the name *From Bondage to Liberty: Dance, Children, Dance*.

Kids on a Club Beyond outing in Germany, 1985.

Oakbridge

In 1974, former NBA All-Star John Block and his wife, Margie, along with tennis great Stan Smith, who won both the 1971 U.S. Open Championship and the 1972 Wimbledon Championship, started Oakbridge Christian Family and Sports Camp in Ramona, California, located fifty miles northeast of San Diego.

The dream for the property was to reach kids and adults through sporting programs such as basketball and tennis camps as well as through retreats for individuals and churches. Throughout the seventies and early eighties, Young Life increasingly rented the property for middle school camps and staff retreats. In 1982, the Oakbridge board felt led to give the camp to Young Life.

Four years later, a new central lodge and dining room were completed, and the Chatelain family donated an additional forty acres along with a home, which were adjacent to the property. In 1987, Oakbridge became Young Life's first camp exclusively for middle school kids, who for years to follow would enjoy the greatest week of their lives in a place just for them.

The vision of MCYM was to minister primarily to military dependents overseas, and the ministry was launched in Germany in 1980. Within ten years, MCYM had a presence in eighteen communities in four European countries as well as the United States.

INTERNATIONAL SCHOOLS

Thousands of American teenagers attend high school overseas for various reasons. Some have parents who are serving in the military, employed with U.S. businesses around the world, or possibly working as diplomats. While their parents are employed in a foreign land, the students are able to attend English-speaking high schools.

In 1982 Young Life began a concerted effort to recruit teachers, who had experience as Young Life leaders, to teach in overseas high schools and establish outreach ministries with the students there. Jim Meredith, MCYM's board chairman from 1982 to 1993 who was stationed in Greece in the early eighties, had experience in beginning the work from earlier military assignments in the country.

"We started a very large and successful outreach to two international schools in Greece while we were there," Meredith said. "We had done the same thing in 1970 in Thessaloniki, Greece. We were getting about fifty kids a week, and that was half of the school, because it was a small school in Thessaloniki. We just wanted to repeat in Athens what we had done in 1970."

Within five years, alongside the ministry in Athens, Young Life was also reaching kids in international schools in Vienna and Salzburg, Austria. In 1991, the mission appointed Meredith, the man who had helped start it all, to be the director of International Schools.

HELPERS

Young Life HELPERS was a short-term missions program that offered leaders and their Campaigners kids opportunities to work in a developing country or to assist nationals with their youth ministry overseas. The ministry was established in 1981 to 1) help national leadership reach more young people for Jesus Christ, 2) introduce young men and women to different cultures and how relational youth ministry is done within a particular cultural context, and 3) meet the physical needs of youth and their families in developing countries.

One of the first excursions was a trip led by longtime area director Charlie Scott for ten staff and leaders to serve in a Haitian orphanage. Within the first seven years, HELPERS enlisted the services of seventy-nine work teams, roughly comprised of nine hundred Campaigners kids and their leaders. The ministry was the forerunner to Young Life's Expeditions ministry, as well as short-term discipleship and service trips, which provided kids even more opportunities to grow in their faith.

ENCOURAGING SIGNS

Entering the eighties, Young Life's urban ministry continued to make strides. In 1980, the ministry received a $90,000 grant from Lilly Endowment, a foundation that had generously supported the work throughout the previous two decades. The following year the Board of Trustees approved a blueprint for a five-year urban growth plan, titled "Outreach '80s," which involved the designation of $5.3 million toward training and expansion. Part of the plan included development of two-year residential training programs in Boston, Chicago, Jacksonville, and San Francisco, not to mention spurring on new work in other major cities.

Also encouraging to the staff were the 1984 appointments of two African-Americans, Fred Davis and Lee Green, the first minorities to serve on the Board of Trustees. Davis, an owner of an insurance company in Memphis, and Green,

the founder and president of an investment group from Washington, D.C., were significant supporters of the urban work in their cities, and important voices on the board.

In 1986, twenty years after Young Life began work in Chicago, it was announced the city would play host to the mission's first black regional director. Harold Spooner, who had successfully served as an area director there for La Salle Street Young Life, was recognized and acknowledged by his peers as a man gifted and qualified for this important position.

On another front, there had not been a clear strategy for reaching the Hispanic community. By the end of 1981, there were no Hispanic full-time staff, even though the ministry had had a presence in Hispanic neighborhoods since the early sixties. An intentional effort to enlist Hispanic staff yielded positive results; by 1987 the mission had ten Hispanic staff reaching kids in seven cities. These inroads not only served kids in the eighties, but also laid a foundation for Latino initiatives in future decades.

The decade would end on a promising note for Young Life urban staff when Verley Sangster was named vice president of U.S. Field Ministries in 1989. In this role Sangster oversaw

Verley Sangster

Every Kid

Jesus' focus is every kid.
Rayburn's message was every kid.
Young Life's mission is every kid.

Not just rich kids . . . every kid
Not just white kids,
   nor just black kids . . . every kid
Not just my kids,
   not just your kids . . . but every kid

Not a lot of kids,
   nor even most kids . . . every kid
Not more kids than
   other organizations . . . every kid
Not giving just a few kids the opportunity
   to receive Jesus . . . but every kid

Not just the "in crowd," not just the beautiful,
   the charming, but every kid
Not just those with high potential, but every kid
Not just the loved and loveable, but every kid
Not just American kids, but every kid

Every kid!

A dream worthy of my time
A dream worthy of my energy
A dream worthy of my money
A dream worthy of my life

A dream of bringing "every kid" to Jesus
A dream of bringing great honor to God the Father
A dream requiring great dependence
   upon the Holy Spirit
A dream making a difference
   in heaven or hell for eternity!

*The above poem, "Every Kid," first appeared
in a 1984 book of the same name, which
told stories about inner-city kids and
Young Life's ministry to them. The poem
was written by consultant Bobb Biehl, who
after spending a day with the Urban Primus
Council, was moved by Young Life's heart
and vision to reach every kid for Christ.
Over the years, the poem was often quoted
throughout the mission.*

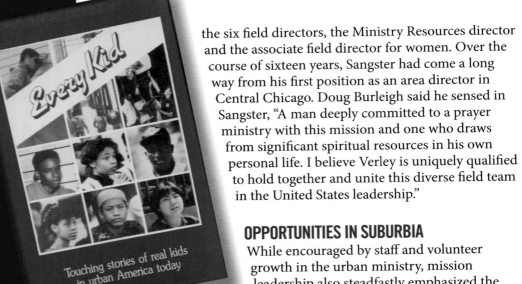

Touching stories of real kids
in urban America today

the six field directors, the Ministry Resources director
and the associate field director for women. Over the
course of sixteen years, Sangster had come a long
way from his first position as an area director in
Central Chicago. Doug Burleigh said he sensed in
Sangster, "A man deeply committed to a prayer
ministry with this mission and one who draws
from significant spiritual resources in his own
personal life. I believe Verley is uniquely qualified
to hold together and unite this diverse field team
in the United States leadership."

OPPORTUNITIES IN SUBURBIA

While encouraged by staff and volunteer
growth in the urban ministry, mission
leadership also steadfastly emphasized the
importance of not neglecting the traditional
suburban work. "The Lord has blessed Young Life with
remarkable results in our approach to suburban-oriented young
people," Mitchell explained in a 1982 Board of Trustees report. "This
work must continue and expand. The future is bright for reaching
more of those kids who will take community leadership roles in years
to come.

"When we speak of a commitment to the city and to minorities," he
continued, "we do not mean a shift of emphasis from our suburban
ministry to something else more important. Some have read it this
way—that Young Life is not excited and challenged anymore by its
opportunities in suburbia. On the contrary, we seek by every means
possible to reach typical high school kids."

Leadership also affirmed the effectiveness of the mission's traditional
methods, especially contact work and club, which had served so
well since the beginning. While acknowledging there will be times
where non-traditional models of ministry might work better, they
continued to uphold the challenging, but rewarding, work of building
relationships with kids who didn't know the Savior and explaining His
love for them in the safe, kid-friendly confines of club and camp.

CONTINUED CONSULTATION

Throughout the eighties Young Life held church consultations on
youth to continue building rapport with the church. *Christianity Today*
reported of the meetings: "Young Life is taking giant steps toward a
reconciliation with local church leaders . . . the pastors also noted with
approval of the increasing attention being given by Young Life to the
inner-city youth ministries and to educating seminarians for careers
as full-time youth ministers, as opposed to regarding such positions as
mere stepping-stones to top pulpit posts among adults."

In the fall of 1985, mission leadership, having recognized the need for
Young Life to better understand and articulate its relationship with
the church, established a Church Relations Advisory Committee.

Thereafter, the team, comprised of Protestant and Catholic leadership from across the United States, gathered together regularly with Mitchell, Bill Starr, and other mission leaders at Trail West to dialogue about theology and Young Life's place in the church.

LEARNING IN NEW PLACES

Theology was also the emphasis in training the staff. As the training continued to grow, so did the accompanying attendance at summer and winter classes. In January 1983, Eastern College in St. David's, Pennsylvania, just outside Philadelphia, hosted the first Institute of Youth Ministries (IYM) winter session. The experiment was a success and especially advantageous for East Coast staff.

The next year the summer session was moved to the joint campus of Hope College and Western Theological Seminary in Holland, Michigan. The IYM was no longer just for Young Life; that year the mission advertised the IYM to other ministries and the response was tremendous.

In June 1989, the program sponsored a staff trip to Stuttgart and Berlin, just five months before the Berlin Wall would fall. Eight staff had the opportunity to visit East Berlin and learn more about the kids who lived there.

Mike Ashburn, area director in Newburgh, Indiana, recalled his emotions from the momentous trip. "I was nervous about being 'behind the Iron Curtain.' I was really afraid we would not get back by the midnight curfew, afraid we would miss our bus. Would they hold us at gunpoint? Detain us in jail?

"I snapped out of my dream and looked into the faces of these kids. They were fourteen to seventeen years of age, dressed mostly in plain clothes, yet each had something to make him separate—a hat, an earring, or trench coat. Soon I realized they were just that . . . kids searching for identity, worth, and security. All the walls in the world can't keep a kid from being a kid. The thought gave me hope. I began to daydream, 'If I were an area director in Berlin, why I'd . . . I'd do just what I do in Newburgh, Indiana.' "

WHAT'S THE PURPOSE?

Throughout its history, Young Life's mission had been described in a variety of ways by a variety of voices. Determined to present a universal expression of Young Life's function, the leadership issued the organization's first official Statement of Mission Purpose in 1985. The statement replaced all former "statements of purpose," and helped provide consistency in the mission's direction.

1985 Young Life Mission Purpose Statement

Young Life is a mission community of Christ-centered people committed to reaching adolescent youth with the Gospel of Jesus Christ. We believe that we, as a community of adult Christians who belong to a broad diversity of church traditions, have been called and gifted by God to carry out this ministry.

*Our Purpose
Reaching adolescent youth with the Gospel of Jesus Christ.*

We do this by building personal relationships with young people, by sharing our lives and participating with them in a variety of experiences through which the Gospel can be heard and experienced.

We carry out our mission under the authority of Scripture and in accordance with our understanding of incarnational witness, seeking to enflesh the Gospel in our lives and relationships.

SAYING GOODBYE TO AN OLD FRIEND . . .

In 1983, the mission's second camp met a similar fate as its first. Like Star Ranch eleven years earlier, Silver Cliff was no longer able to provide the mission with an isolated setting where kids could be free to be kids. Over time, more homes were built close to the property and the new neighbors were not thrilled with the noise and activity that often accompany teenagers at camp. After thirty-four years playing host to campers from around the U.S., Silver Cliff was sold and the monies used to help the mission invest in its newest property.

AND HELLO TO A NEW ONE

By the early eighties, the two camps most accessible to the large population of the Northeast, Upper New York's Saranac Village and North Carolina's Windy Gap, were over capacity. In order to service more areas, both camps went from the traditional seven-day week to a six-day week, enabling them to host two to three more weeks' worth of campers. This was helpful in the short term, but the message was clear: Young Life needed a new camp to accommodate the populous East Coast. The answer would be found in a place that God had previously provided to two other ministries working with kids.

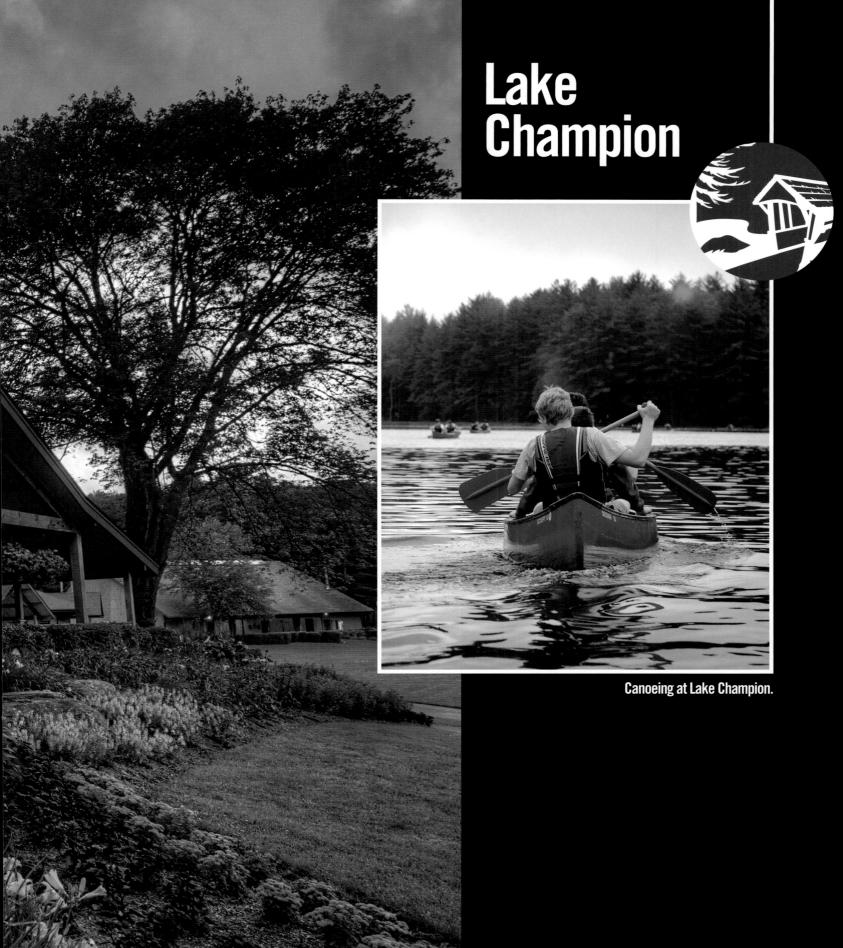

Lake Champion

Canoeing at Lake Champion.

Singing songs at club in the eighties.

In 1949, Jim Vaus, a wiretapper for noted gangster Mickey Cohen, met Christ at Billy Graham's Los Angeles crusades. In the 1950s, he set up a ministry for troubled teens called Youth Development International, aimed at helping the kids in New York City's Spanish Harlem. Vaus wanted a camp where he could take these kids, and in 1961, along with the financial assistance of George Champion, chairman of the board of Chase Manhattan Bank, they bought a 365-acre property in the Catskill Mountains located just ninety minutes outside of the city. The property, located near Glen Spey, New York, also boasted a fifty-acre manmade lake—perfect for all kinds of water activities.

In 1972, Vaus sold this property to another ministry designed for kids, Teen Challenge. After thirteen years of using the camp to reach out to kids struggling with drug abuse, Teen Challenge decided to sell the property.

Longtime New York staff member Bo Nixon learned of this opportunity and, knowing the property well from using it for Campaigners weekends and leadership overnights, excitedly told other staff about this treasure. At a divisional meeting at Princeton Seminary, Nixon shared about the golden opportunity with the other leaders there. At first the news was glossed over as the group broke for lunch.

A confused Nixon approached his friend Jack Carpenter. Nixon confided to Carpenter, "Jack, it doesn't sound like these people heard what I said. We need to go back into that meeting and bring camping back up again before we move onto the next subject. We need to go back in there and tell them that this is a camp that already has buildings and everything is ready to go."

After lunch, Carpenter made sure the topic of Lake Champion was back on the agenda. He told the group, "Bo was talking about this camp, and he feels no one really heard him. I've been at that camp, and I think we should look at it."

The testimony of two witnesses seemed to inspire the group to investigate the matter further. An exploration team checked out the property and was amazed. Doug Burleigh said, "I couldn't believe that here was a place that with only a few months of work, we could bring two hundred fifty young people in, tell them about Jesus, and they'd have the best week of their lives. God had in mind for us to have that place and to use it to tell kids about Jesus. One thing that's particularly special about Lake Champion is that it's so close to New York City, to Newark, to Philadelphia, to all the urban centers in the East, and we so desperately needed a place to take kids to tell them about Him."

Young Life purchased Lake Champion in March of 1986, with camp scheduled to open a mere three months later, on June 21. The staff were excited about the new camp's possibilities. Dave Carlson, director of Properties, remembered a pledge he made to Joe Paolella, then area director in Northern Virginia. "Joe was the first man to put a deposit down on camp spots for the first week and he said, 'Dave, you've got to promise me that our bus will be the first bus through the gates.' So on opening day I was out there and a van pulled in right in front of his bus. I had to tell that van driver, 'You've got to turn around and get behind this bus. We've got a line-up going here.' So Joe lays claim to being the first camp bus in!"

That month Burleigh served as the camp's first summer speaker, standing before one hundred fifty campers and their leaders and telling them all about the love of Jesus. "I'll never forget the feeling," Burleigh said, "when that first group of [fifty] kids stood up at the Say-So, and I was just trying to keep it together. The tears were flowing, amid the realization that God had given us a magnificent place."

A VILLAGE OF COMFORT

Certain moments hold a special place in the history of Young Life. Many of the dates for these moments (the first prayer in Gainesville, Texas, the initial contact work experience, etc.) are not recorded; fortunately, March 10, 1986, was. This was the day of the very first Capernaum club, an event that would help bring about a paradigm shift in the mission's thinking and, more importantly, hope for thousands of overlooked kids.

Six years earlier, Nick Palermo had entered the halls of Blackford High School in San Jose, California, where his own life changed in a matter of minutes. After nearly being mowed down by a contingent of twenty-five teenagers in wheelchairs on their way to lunch, Palermo asked, "Who are those kids?"

Nick Palermo, kneeling, second from right, with his friends at Capernaum club in the fall of 1986.

Unbeknownst to him, Palermo would be God's chosen instrument to begin the process of reaching out to this community. After that encounter in the hallway and his interactions with the teens moments later, Palermo couldn't get these precious kids out of his mind. As he describes in his book, *Missing Stars, Fallen Sparrows*, Palermo was on a lifelong journey to learn how to walk alongside kids with disabilities, to learn how "to be comfortable with being uncomfortable."

Six days before the first club, Palermo decided upon the name "Capernaum Project" for the ministry. The name came from the story in Mark 2:1–12, where four men lower their disabled friend through a roof to bring him to the feet of Jesus. The town where this occurs is Capernaum (*kuh*-PUR-nee-*uhm*), which means "village of comfort"—a perfect description for the environment they wanted to foster.

When the day of club finally arrived, Palermo picked up the kids in a lift-equipped van. As they drove to club, he said, "It was with five kids in wheelchairs, four able-bodied high school kids and four leaders. What an incredible hour! I had never seen such excitement in a club."

While the initial club was small by Young Life standards, Palermo and the team were excited about the endless possibilities in connecting with kids with disabilities. It seemed the sky was the limit! That's not to say, however, that the movement was without resistance. Often Young Life staff misunderstood the importance of the new work. "This ministry was new, different and, for many, threatening," Palermo explained. "Some Young Life staff concluded that since Capernaum was not really Young Life (as they perceived it, anyway), we should not even think about beginning this type of ministry."

The road to acceptance would be a long one, and like those before him who had started new work within the mission, Palermo's learning curve was steep. Among many other principles, Palermo learned that these were "kids who happened to have disabilities, instead of disabilities who happened to be kids."

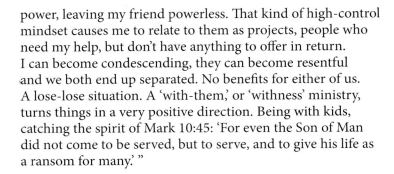

Palermo also discovered that this was not a ministry *to* kids with disabilities, but a ministry *with* kids with disabilities. "When I conduct ministry as a 'to-them' enterprise, I hold all the power, leaving my friend powerless. That kind of high-control mindset causes me to relate to them as projects, people who need my help, but don't have anything to offer in return. I can become condescending, they can become resentful and we both end up separated. No benefits for either of us. A lose-lose situation. A 'with-them,' or 'withness' ministry, turns things in a very positive direction. Being with kids, catching the spirit of Mark 10:45: 'For even the Son of Man did not come to be served, but to serve, and to give his life as a ransom for many.' "

Yet another lesson was the diagnosis that the ones with disabilities offered to those without. "The crazy, unexpected, and sad thing," said Palermo, "is that we—the able-bodied and fully functioning ones who are supposedly disability-free—are the ones who are so uncomfortable. Not only around kids with disabilities, but tragically, with ourselves."

Over the years, Palermo and his fellow leaders faithfully and patiently soldiered on, spreading the news about their friends with disabilities to other Young Life staff. "As we involved our friends in clubs, camps, and other activities, it slowly but powerfully began affecting the Young Life family and culture. When I spoke about our ministry, people were often shocked and shed tears. 'I had no idea,' they told me. 'I never thought about these kids.' God had made us a prophetic voice within our own organization."

A NEW ROLE FOR "MITCH"

The year 1986 was a transitional one for Bob Mitchell. During his nine-year tenure as Young Life president, he led the mission through some critical times, and his thoughtful navigation played a key role in the advancement of women and the work in urban areas.

Under his leadership, relations between Young Life and the church flourished, the mission gained a stronger international presence, and the staff grew in their theological training, most notably through the Institute of Youth Ministries.

Perhaps his proudest accomplishment, however, was encouraging the staff in their own spiritual development. "In the last few years that I was at the helm of Young Life, my major focus was in the area of spirituality and encouraging people in their own walk with Jesus, so that all that activity would flow then out of a secret center and an intimacy with God in prayer."

One unique way he sought to encourage the mission spiritually was through a publication named *Ventures*. From 1981 to '86, this "monthly aid to personal Bible study" arrived in the mailboxes of donors, staff, and kids. Each issue featured daily Scripture readings and accompanying insights written by Pamela Heim, the editor of *Relationships* magazine. "By following the *Ventures* outline," Mitchell explained in an early issue, "you can read through the entire Bible in three years."

His love for the Scriptures and the Savior they spoke of endeared "Mitch" to the mission. "If there was ever a person who epitomized the heart of Young Life, I think it was Mitch," said Doug Burleigh, who would soon become Young Life's fourth president. "We all loved to hear him speak. We have all laughed at his humor. We have all wept as he articulated the heartbeat of Young Life, Christ, and kids."

Mitchell's next assignment would be another presidency. As president of the Young Life Foundation, he would oversee the "effort to provide ministries to young people who had not previously been particularly well served by the mission's traditional program." Mitchell rallied a board of men and women to pray and financially support an expanding ministry to kids in "inaccessible, socially threatening, or far-away places."

Mitchell served in this role until 1990, when he followed the Lord's leading to join the ministry of World Vision. From his first involvement in 1940 as Jim Rayburn's club kid, through his four decades of service to Young Life, Mitchell grew up alongside the ministry, and his half-century presence left an indelible mark on the hearts of so many kids and adults.

Ventures, September 1986.

STANDING IN THE GAP

During the transition period between Mitchell and his eventual successor, someone was needed to ensure the daily work of the mission continued without interruptions or distractions. For this important task, the Board of Trustees called upon Hal Merwald.

Hal Merwald

Merwald had served on staff since 1963 in such diverse locations as Little Rock, Arkansas, Brazil, and New York City. His most recent role was Young Life's Operations manager, where he reported directly to Mitchell. Like his previous assignments, Merwald devotedly carried out the duties, and left his mark on those around him.

"Hal has faithfully done everything he's been asked to do in Young Life," Burleigh said. "Whether it was as the interim president, going to Brazil and learning Portuguese, moving to New York or Little Rock. Everywhere I go, I run into people whom Hal has loved and encouraged. And I just appreciate the quiet way he and Judy have faithfully done Young Life work."

His year as interim president served Merwald well; in the spring of 1987 the Canadian Board of Trustees unanimously appointed him to serve as the new director of Young Life Canada.

Doug Burleigh

FROM RELUCTANT CLUB KID TO PRESIDENT

For the mission's fourth president, the Board of Trustees turned to Doug Burleigh, a man with a strong history in the mission. Twenty-six years earlier, however, Burleigh could not have had a more humbling introduction to this ministry called Young Life.

As a sophomore at Seattle's Roosevelt High School in the fall of 1960, Burleigh had no involvement with Young Life until his mother intervened. She and Burleigh's father had attended an adult week at Malibu a few years earlier and wanted their son to experience what Young Life had to offer, so she contacted the area director, Tom Raley.

"Well, his mother called up," remembered Raley, "and said, 'I want my son to go to Young Life. Will you pick him up?'— which is not exactly the way you want to get a kid to club the first time!"

When the day of club arrived, Burleigh's mother notified her son that Raley would be coming over to take him to club. When the teen rebuffed the idea, his father informed him that he was outvoted and would, in fact, be going.

The reluctant attendee arrived and, to his surprise, found two hundred other high school kids there. "I started coming every week after that!"

The following summer, Burleigh went to Malibu, where he began a relationship with Christ. For the next two and a half decades, Burleigh was along for the ride. After enjoying experiences on work crew, summer staff, and as a volunteer leader in college, he served on staff in the Seattle, Tacoma, and Renton-Kent areas of Washington. From there he became a director for the Pacific Northwest Region and the Western and Eastern divisions. By 1986, Burleigh had demonstrated his leadership capabilities from Washington State to Washington, D.C., and so many places in-between. Because of his experience, the board felt Burleigh was the right man to lead the mission into the 1990s. With wife Debbie by his side, he began his tenure in January 1987.

POSITIVE STEPS

With Mae Page's appointment as associate director of Field Ministries in 1978, there was a strong push to continue integrating women into the mission at all levels of ministry. In the early eighties, Page formed the Women's Ministry Council, which helped encourage the development of women as ministers in Young Life.

The year 1986 was perhaps the most significant to date in the mission's advancement of women. In February, Trail West hosted the First Women's Conference, a rousing success attended by two hundred twenty-six adults, which focused on the giftedness of women while helping to equip and affirm female staff and volunteers.

On September 1, 1986, Young Life appointed Nancy Warden as the first female regional director. The former club kid and college volunteer leader who came on staff in 1977 to serve in Rockford, Illinois, and later as a regional administrator, would oversee the work in Northern Illinois and Wisconsin.

In 1987 Page was succeeded by Donna McClellan, who had served on staff since 1974. One of Doug Burleigh's first appointments, McClellan was someone he knew would partner with him to spur more women on to leadership.

McClellan didn't view herself as "an issues person," but rather a unifier looking to promote partnership. "Obviously Young Life in the beginning was white

Mae Page and Donna McClellan

male, as was typical of the culture, and that was hard to change. I wanted to see men and women work together; I didn't care who was in charge or what the title was, you bring the gifts to the table. I think we're healthier when we're more diverse."

While issues tended to divide, McClellan conceded the heartbeat of Young Life was what the Lord used to unite the genders. "My favorite memories are at an area, regional, and national level when I saw men and women in tears talk about relationships with kids. That's what brought us all together."

MY FIRST THIRTY QUIET TIMES

In 1984, Ty Saltzgiver, the area director in Winston-Salem, North Carolina, returned home with two busloads of kids from the area's camp trip to Frontier. Of the sixty-six campers who went, fifty-five began relationships with Christ that week. An excited (and exhausted) Saltzgiver quickly realized he needed to prepare something for these hungry, wide-eyed new believers. That afternoon he wrote out a five-day plan of devotions for the kids to read in their time alone with the Lord. In the following weeks, Saltzgiver repeated the process until he had thirty days' worth of material.

> " MY FAVORITE MEMORIES ARE AT AN AREA, REGIONAL, AND NATIONAL LEVEL WHEN I SAW MEN AND WOMEN IN TEARS TALK ABOUT RELATIONSHIPS WITH KIDS. THAT'S WHAT BROUGHT US ALL TOGETHER."
>
> —DONNA MCCLELLAN

As other Young Life staff heard of the resource, they requested copies. Saltzgiver had five thousand copies of *My First Thirty Quiet Times* published in 1985 and sold the booklet at one dollar so it would be affordable to every kid who requested one. The first printing sold out in six months. In its first thirty years, over five hundred thousand copies had sold, and Saltzgiver marveled at the response.

"I've never marketed it or taken an ad out anywhere," he said. "It was always just word of mouth. It's amazing how often people mention *My First Thirty Quiet Times*. They'll come up to me and say, 'Your book was the first thing I read after becoming a Christian.' Thanks be to God!"

TO (AND FROM) RUSSIA WITH LOVE

One of the lasting legacies from Doug Burleigh's presidency was the strong bonds formed through the U.S.-Soviet student exchanges. The Cold War was still very real in the late eighties, but diplomacy was slowly opening up between the two superpowers, providing ministries with opportunities to make in-roads into the Soviet Union. Burleigh's unique experience and training in Russian studies revealed him to be a man raised up "for such a time as this."

In college Burleigh received two undergraduate degrees in political science and Russian language and literature, and a graduate degree in political science. During this time he also studied for two summers in Russia. The education prepared him for a grand undertaking: organizing an exchange program with youth leaders in Russia.

The exchange actually happened, Burleigh explained, "because of a friendship with a high-ranking official within the Soviet Academy of Sciences (a very unlikely partnership during Soviet times.) When I would come and tell him about many kids who met Jesus, he would quietly admonish me, 'That is wonderful, Doug, but please don't tell me about it.' It's truly miraculous that under a communist system that says 'there is no God,' a key leader took a gigantic risk to help make it happen. It reminds us in Young Life once again, it's all about relationships."

In the summer of 1989, forty-four "highly qualified Young Life kids" gathered from twenty states to enjoy the trip of a lifetime. The group, made up of twenty-two boys and twenty-two girls, spent twenty-two days in the Soviet Union, comprised of a two-week stint with fifty Soviet teens at a sports camp, and two homestays with families from Moscow and Leningrad. One of the staff couples to accompany the American kids was Nobie and Carol Hill, who recalled their time at the sports camp:

THE IMPORTANCE OF *RELATIONSHIPS*

A few months after announcing its fourth president, Young Life also unveiled its fourth magazine, the aptly named *Relationships*. Unlike the fifties' and seventies' versions of *Young Life* magazine, which were aimed at kids, and the serious tones of *Focus on Youth* in the 1960s, *Relationships* served as a celebratory showcase of the work to donors, committee members, volunteer leaders, board members, and friends of the mission. Since first arriving in mailboxes in April 1987, the magazine has evolved through different iterations of size and frequency, but always remained true to the vision of telling the great story of what God is doing around the world through Young Life.

Relationships covers from 1989.

"Toward the end of the first week, we wondered if we could have a club. We'd been singing and doing mixers and we told the kids that Nobie was going to give a talk about Jesus Christ. We told the kids they could leave if they wanted to. Nobody left.

"There was an openness, a hunger in the kids that you don't often find here in the States . . . they asked questions about everything imaginable. We'd just have to mention we were an organization based on Christ and the questions would start . . . People would constantly tell us, 'Your group is different; there is something in your eyes.' "

On the same day the Americans left for the Soviet Union, forty-four Soviet teens arrived in Washington, D.C., for what would also prove to be a life-changing three weeks on the East Coast. After sightseeing, the group divided into three groups and enjoyed homestays in three areas: Rochester, New York; Annapolis and Baltimore, Maryland; and Greensboro, North Carolina. After this, each group attended a week at one of the three nearest camps: Saranac Village, Lake Champion, or Windy Gap.

The time there left a mark on many Soviet kids like Luba, who later wrote, "The talks about Christ touched my heart. I know that I'll think about Him all the time, that I'll read the Bible, the greatest gift from Young Life . . . I will never forget camp in Saranac Village, never forget the people who were around me; I'll never forget America!"

"It was a great reminder," Burleigh said, "that this God of ours loves all the nations. And that these kids—who for the last seventy-five years their country has said 'God doesn't exist'—met Jesus just as enthusiastically as kids from Keokuk, Iowa, or Peoria, Illinois. And that somebody from Leningrad or Moscow or Kiev had the same need for Jesus."

As a result of the special friendship formed between Young Life and the Russian people, the work began in Russia. Gary and Jeanne Parsons, who had accompanied the American kids on the summer trip, moved to Moscow in 1992 to recruit and train the country's first Young Life leaders.

"It was a thrill to see that barrier broken," Burleigh said, "as somebody who had a chance to start studying Russian in 1961, and go over there in '65, and twenty-some-odd years later, as the president of Young Life, to see Young Life work start there."

Reflecting on the great progress made, longtime staff member John Miller smiled and asked the president, "When you were in college, did you wonder why you studied so much Russian language? Now, do you see why?"

CRUMBLING WALLS

The move into Russia was symbolic of a rapidly changing world and the increasing need for ministries like Young Life to respond quickly and appropriately. As these walls around the world began to crumble, so did the barriers that had hindered Young Life from reaching every kid. From this point forward, Young Life now saw kids with disabilities as among those the mission hoped to reach with the Gospel. So were military kids, exchange students, and an ever-increasing number of previously unreached populations. This, then, was an era of liberation, both for the mission and thousands of kids who could now be reached with the Gospel.

The walls that came down for kids in the eighties foreshadowed a time with even more advances. Like this decade, the nineties would see more specialized ministries inaugurated, and other changes like the introduction of the mission's fifth president, new countries reached and more camps purchased. The 1980s not only made their own unique mark on the mission, but prepared Young Life for an era of unprecedented growth.

A Salute to Our Volunteers

A Reflection by Denny Rydberg, president

We love our staff in Young Life. Men and women who have said, "Yes," to God's call and joined the mission as full- and part-time employees. They are talented, motivated, fun-loving, serious when needed, kid-pursuing, Jesus-following men and women of all ages. They, in short, are amazing.

But our staff members are just a small portion of the army God has given this mission to reach kids.

Did you know that as I write this (and it changes almost monthly), we have over four thousand staff worldwide? But in our army, we are blessed with more than sixty thousand volunteers, and we hope to be near eighty thousand when we finish our seven-year goal of Reaching a World of Kids. Currently, our ratio of volunteers to staff members is fifteen to one. And guess what? Our volunteers are talented, motivated, fun-loving, serious when needed, kid-pursuing, Jesus-following men and women of all ages. Just like staff.

And what do these amazing (yes, amazing) people do?

They lead, serve, help, coordinate, pray, and give of their time, energy, money, and skills—just like our staff members do. There's really no difference between these members of our team. All are called! All have said, "Yes."

Our volunteers work in a club. They do contact work. They go to camp. They lead Campaigners. They are at the heart of our direct ministry. You see them at football games, band concerts, school plays, hanging out at McDonald's or Starbucks with kids, helping coach, chaperoning school and community events, etc. You'll see them welcoming kids to club. Knowing them by name. And, when it's time for winter or summer camp, there they are giving up a week's vacation, sleeping in the same cabin with kids who are having the best week of their lives but not the best week for keeping their clothes or cabin fresh and orderly! And for the vast majority of our leaders, they're having the best week of their lives once again, because they've done it before and will the next time as well. Our volunteers are all ages. Some are high school Campaigners

who help with WyldLife ministry. Many are college-age young adults. There are men and women from all walks of life in their twenties, thirties, forties, fifties, sixties, and seventies (and maybe some in their eighties who are flying under the radar because they're having too much fun making a difference in the lives of kids and don't want to be asked, "Should you really be doing this at your age?")

We also have thousands of committee members. These are the adults in the community who keep the local ministry going. They rally around the area director and mentor him or her and the volunteer leaders. They care about making sure the finances are in good shape. They want the family members of our staff and leaders to be secure and supported. They serve as the public relations directors for the mission when people wonder about Young Life. And they pray, pray, pray that kids might be reached in the community.

And when I describe sixty thousand of these great volunteers, I'm not counting those who also pray regularly for schools, communities, and kids by name. These unnamed warriors may not hang out with kids or serve on the committee and some may no longer be able to get out as much as they'd like, but they know what a difference their prayers make.

In the eighties, I was not on Young Life staff, but as Marilyn and I led a college ministry, many of our students were Young Life volunteer leaders living with one foot on their campus and one foot on the campus of their high school or middle school friends. I knew the challenges they faced. And at the church where we served, we knew men and women who were on the local area committees, those who each summer went to Malibu as "yacht hosts and hostesses," and those who volunteered on work weeks at camp, etc.

For seven decades, Young Life has been made up of called and committed staff members, volunteer leaders, local committee members and thousands and thousands of prayer warriors, helpers, investors—all friends of the mission.

It's one of the major reasons we can reach more and more kids each year!

MAKE 'EM LAUGH

Humor is serious business in Young Life. From the beginning, it's been a tool for engaging disinterested kids and a key to unlock their guarded hearts.

Classic camp characters like Dirty Bert and Squinty Newton have captivated even the most reluctant campers. Duct Tape Man, Leonard Jenkins, and Bobby the hapless matador have invited kids to laugh. With them and even at them. It's okay to laugh. Loud. Because the characters have a secret they can't wait to share—the story has a happy ending.

The humor in Young Life celebrates Gospel truth: Loners find love. Losers become heroes. Gaffs resolve into grace. And disasters end in happily ever after. That's the joy at the heart of our humor.

"YOU WERE LUCKY!"

"I HAVE ♫ COME TO SEE THE KING . . ."

"THEM HOGS HAS GOT TO BE FED."
—SUNG BY SARAH RHODES (BELOW)

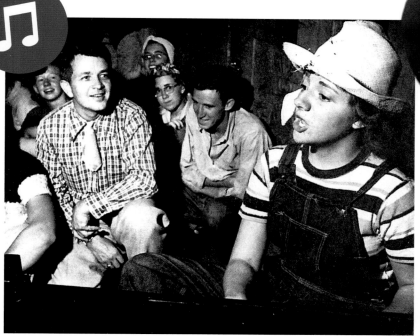

"THAR'S A BAR!"

"IF I WERE NOT IN YOUNG LIFE . . ."

the 1990s

Whatever . . . it Takes

"**W**hatever." Often uttered in a spirit of apathy, this catchphrase came to epitomize much of the nineties. From the grunge sensitivities and lyrics of bands like Nirvana and Pearl Jam, to *Seinfeld*, a self-proclaimed "show about nothing," a sense of indifference existed throughout the popular culture.

Young Life also subscribed to an attitude of "whatever," but with a twist. The decade marked a renewed spirit to do *whatever* it would take to reach even more kinds of kids.

After years of working with teen moms as well as kids in rural areas, the mission officially established new ministries with these populations. There was also a renewed emphasis on how to bring on staff, train them well, and place them where they could help the work flourish. Added to this was the introduction of several new camps, which the mission desperately needed, each one strategically located to serve the most kids.

With unprecedented expansion to new kids in new places, the 1990s represented an era of unparalleled growth throughout the mission.

CELEBRATING FIVE DECADES OF THE LORD'S WORK

By 1990, it seemed right to bring the mission together again. The last time the entire staff gathered together was eleven years prior at the Broadmoor in 1979. (The 1980s consisted of divisional conferences with specialty conferences in alternate years.)

The 1990 staff conference was billed as "The Young Life 50th Celebration," a time where the mission could reflect on what the Lord had done since the work was *established* in 1940 (Young Life was incorporated in 1941).

Held in San Diego from January 3-7, the conference welcomed twenty-five hundred staff and friends of the mission for five days of worship, prayer, reminiscing, and vision casting. Many of the "patriarchs and matriarchs" of Young Life came and shared with the staff, most of whom were younger than the mission itself.

"I felt it was important that all the eras of Young Life would be represented," Doug Burleigh said in a 1999 interview. "Jimmy Rayburn [the founder's son], Bob Mitchell, and Bill Starr shared. It was important to review what God had done over the fifty years.

Opposite: Kids and leaders from Chicago ham it up at camp.

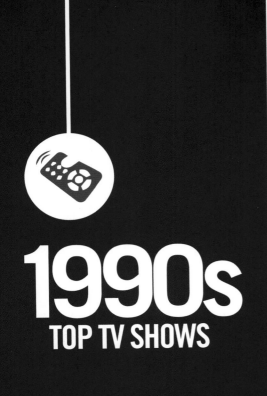

1990s
TOP TV SHOWS

Comedies
Seinfeld
Friends
Roseanne

Dramas
ER
Murder, She Wrote
Touched By An Angel

News Programs
60 Minutes
20/20
Primetime Live

Reality/Game Shows
Who Wants to Be a Millionaire?
Unsolved Mysteries
Rescue 911

The Young Life 50th Celebration logo.

"We were able to thank God individually and corporately for this mission. I think of the concert of prayer, just a chance to get on our knees together and ask God to make the next years the greatest in the history of Young Life. And I believe He's answered that prayer."

ORGANIZED ORGANIZATIONS

One of the highlights of the celebration was the attendance of the presidents of five other ministry organizations who also worked with young people. The five other leaders Burleigh introduced to the audience were: General Dick Abel of Fellowship of Christian Athletes; Dr. Bill Bright of Campus Crusade for Christ; Dr. Steve Hayner of InterVarsity; Dr. Jerry White of The Navigators; and Dr. Dick Wynn of Youth for Christ. Dr. Bright said the invitation gave the men "an unprecedented way for us to demonstrate unity."

Three years earlier—around the time Burleigh became president—the leaders of these organizations and their spouses began meeting twice a year for times of fellowship. The six men were tremendously encouraged by their time together and the bonds they developed.

"As I look at the decade of the 1990s," Burleigh explained in 1990, "I'm convinced that the challenge of reaching a generation of future leaders for Christ is larger than any one organization alone can meet. And as I study Scripture, I see our Lord repeatedly calling us to labor together in love so that we may reach more with the Good News. The incredible needs of today's adolescents for meaning and direction in their lives force us to think in terms of the Body of Christ—church and parachurch—working hand in hand to mobilize an army of leaders to befriend young people and share the life-changing Gospel with them."

The cooperation was not only visible in presidential level meetings, but in joint ministry opportunities, such as when Young Life and The Navigators collaborated on

Ministry presidents at the Young Life Celebration (left to right): Dr. Steve Hayner of InterVarsity; Dr. Bill Bright of Campus Crusade for Christ; Dr. Dick Wynn of Youth for Christ; General Dick Abel of Fellowship of Christian Athletes; Dr. Jerry White of The Navigators; and Doug Burleigh.

a college outreach to the Soviet Union during the summer of 1989, and the ongoing work between Young Life and Youth for Christ through Military Community Youth Ministry. These early efforts helped to build great bonds among the organizations, which would last for decades. Verley Sangster, vice president of Field Ministries, reflected, "I think meeting with other parachurch ministries was one of the great legacies of Doug Burleigh's presidency."

A MINISTRY TO TEEN MOMS

Diapers. Bottles. Two a.m. feedings. Not what most kids in the nineties spent time thinking about as they navigated the already tumultuous tides of adolescence. But for hundreds of thousands of kids in the U.S. alone, they were part of their everyday lives.

By 1991, the teenage pregnancy rate was at an all-time high, and the U.S. led all other countries in the industrialized world in teen pregnancy, birth, and abortion. Facing fear, confusion, guilt, and extreme loneliness, these young moms only had a one in three chance of finishing high school, and within five years of the birth of their babies the majority would be on welfare. As far back as the seventies, there had been teen pregnancy ministries, like those of Angela Reeves on the West Side of Chicago, but never a missionwide approach to helping these girls. Teenage moms, because of their many needs, were a population traditional Young Life clubs were not reaching.

Betsy Stretar, who would eventually lead the mission's outreach to these girls and was once a teenage mom herself, articulated what so many others experienced. "I felt like my life was over at seventeen," the Cleveland, Ohio, staff woman said. "I was overcome with guilt and shame." Stretar simply verbalized what teenage moms knew all too well: they were in need of love and support at this vulnerable time.

Young Life was eager to respond, and areas such as Visalia, California; Vancouver, Washington; and Lee County, Florida, spearheaded initial efforts. In Visalia, where nearly one thousand babies were born to teen moms each year, the local Young Life committee recognized the need to reach out to these girls. After much prayer, discussion, and a realization that there was no budget to meet this need, they stepped out in faith by acting on what they sensed God was calling them to do: hire a staff person who could lead this ministry.

A pastor's wife with previous Young Life staff experience, Mary Somerville, was the ideal candidate. Armed with a master's degree in pastoral counseling and great experience in relational mentoring of other women, Somerville was already at work with teen moms in the area.

She quickly enlisted the help of many women in local churches to come alongside the girls and serve as volunteer mentors. In the fall of 1991, there were thirteen pairings of mentors and teen moms. The program at that time was aptly named "Mentor Moms."

Somerville eventually came on Young Life staff, and within two years the first national Mentor Moms camp was held at Woodleaf.

Betsy Stretar and Mary Somerville

In 2002 the ministry was renamed "YoungLives," an acknowledgment that the program not only touches the life of a teen mom, but her children—and quite often the child's father too.

TAKING DONORS SERIOUSLY

Throughout its history, Young Life had excelled in caring for kids; unfortunately, this was not always the case when it came to donors. Traditionally, staff and leaders were comfortable in the world of kids, but many felt less confident when speaking to adults about the subject of financial support. Consequently, while the kid work was friendship-based, relationships with donors could sometimes have more of an impersonal feel to them.

Donors were invited to fundraisers like banquets and golf tournaments—events upon which the area's budget often depended. When these proved less than successful financially, the area would look for another "experience" to which they could invite potential contributors.

Director of the Young Life Foundation Greg Kinberg said at the time, "Young Life has been fundraising with principles we would never settle for in ministry. If there are just a few kids coming to club, we don't add a second club meeting during the week; we start spending more time at the junior or senior high school."

In short, the organization that had always prided itself on its ability to reach out to others with no strings attached, had neglected this very strength when it came to its financial supporters.

Young Life responded by formalizing its fundraising training. Bill Hautt, of FOCUS Consultants, introduced the mission to a concept called "Taking Donors Seriously," commonly referred to as "TDS." The idea was, as the name implied, to better care for those who might never work directly on the "front lines" with kids, but who were just as vital in their role to the ministry's success. By building genuine relationships with donors and ministering to them and their needs, staff could help ensure that donors would never again feel like a means to an end.

"In the end," Kinberg explained, "taking *fundraising* seriously is self-serving; we are doing it to meet our needs. When we operate this way, we use adults to love kids. Taking *donors* seriously means believing and acting like the way we treat kids is the way to treat people."

YOUNG LIFE FOR FAMILIES

By 1990, Trail West, which had begun as a window for adults to witness Young Life camping, was no longer the only destination that offered this service. Many of the camps now had adult guest programs—and much closer to home. Moreover, for sixteen years Trail West had sub-leased camp weeks to churches and ministries, who ran their own programs, while being served by the work crew and summer staff. This inevitably led to an identity crisis for the resort. "The camp," Stacy Windahl wrote in *Build It Here: Celebrating 50 Years at Trail West Lodge*, "was disconnected from the greater mission of Young Life."

"That changed in 1990," Windahl continued, "with a three-week experiment in something called 'family camp.' Doug Burleigh charged Neil Atkinson of Kansas City, Missouri, to assemble a team of mission staff to create a true Young Life camp experience for families from anywhere in the nation. That experiment yielded results. Guests called the week, 'the best family vacation we ever had!' By the end of the decade, Trail West's family camp grew so popular that Young Life once again ran every camp week of the summer.

In 2004 Trail West played host to the first of many Military Weeks, a critical respite for those in the armed services and their families. Most of the soldiers were fresh out of Iraq and in desperate need of a vacation. The precious time here provided them with the opportunity to relax, reconnect, and laugh with their families, while hearing about the Savior—a first for many.

While still giving adults a window into Young Life, Trail West now also provided the mission with a new way for new audiences to hear "the old, old story of Jesus and His love."

THE DECADE OF CAMPS

Within just three years of its opening, Lake Champion was almost filled to capacity with campers. Likewise, the overcapacity in other camps and the encouraging growth in field ministry around the country made it clear the mission was in dire need of new places to bring kids.

One of the most important relationships in Young Life exists between the field and camping staffs. Camp staff see their role as serving the field, providing the area staff with the best experience possible. This service primarily plays out when staff are at the camps with kids, but also extends to determining the geographical need and availability of campsites.

"We sit down with the field staff and decide together where and when the ministry vision is in need of another camp," said Dave Carlson, director of Properties. "At that moment we all start praying for what the Lord is going to have in store for us."

The Properties department [later known as the Camping department] recognized the need for flexibility, Carlson said. "We need to be very responsive to cultural trends, different geographies, and specific field staff needs as they perceive

Rockbridge Alum Springs

"Boarding is 10 dollars per week. This place is more crowded than any other in the mountains, and I have not heard of a single person who is dissatisfied." —Stonewall Jackson, July 12, 1852

The comments above are part of one of the earliest "camper letters" ever sent from Rockbridge Alum Springs. In the 1850s, the natural springs provided Southern clientele like Jackson and General Robert E. Lee with a resort where they could enjoy the restorative alum water.

More than one hundred twenty-five years later, there would be a different kind of healing taking place, and this time it would certainly be due to the Living Water that Jesus promises.

"Dave Carlson, Billy Branch (a Young Life board member) and I were always in the car together looking for that next camp," remembered Lee Corder, senior vice president of the International North Division. "And because of our region's commitment to that vision, we had a "Buy an Acre" campaign for our first location, Jump Mountain. When that pursuit encountered huge pushback from the local community, friends sent us to another property, landlocked within the George Washington National Forest. We found a very overgrown and rundown property, with huge potential. The 'God story' in this was that with our earlier campaign, we had raised virtually the full purchase price of the available Rockbridge property before we had even encountered it."

The 273-acre property located twelve miles northwest of Lexington, Virginia, was purchased in 1992. After four years spent on development and integrating new buildings alongside many of the existing structures, Rockbridge was ready for its first summer campers in 1996. Eventually, the fully developed resort provided the East Coast with a capacity of more than eighteen thousand campers and staff annually.

BACK TO THE BASICS

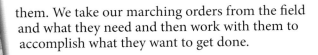

John Miller was one of the beloved caretakers, not only of Young Life's history, but its methodology as well. The man who proclaimed that he "came on staff shortly after Noah parked his boat," was often approached to write about what he had learned in his thirty-six years with the mission. Miller did eventually put pen to paper and what emerged would encourage and educate new generations of staff and volunteers for years to come.

Published in 1991, *Back to the Basics of Young Life* detailed not only the "hows" of incarnational evangelism, but the "whys"; among the many highlights from the book are the passages where Miller expounds on the four guiding principles of Young Life work he learned early on from Rayburn. Miller summed these up as:

'Number one: *'It's a sin to bore a kid with the Gospel.'* That is fundamental. What do kids think about God? They don't like Him. They have their reasons. So you've got to overcome a world of attitude to actually not bore a kid. And that's the key to Young Life: not to bore a kid.

'Number two: *'Walk in wisdom toward them that are without'* (Colossians 4:5, KJV). Jim said, 'When they're without Jesus Christ, they're without everything that matters. They're without hope, future, direction, purpose and fulfillment. So walk in wisdom toward them that are without.'

'Number three: *'Win the right to be heard.'* If you walk like Christ would among kids, you are winning the right to be heard. I think the reason Christianity works so beautifully is because Jesus Christ was so beautifully attractive.

'Number four: *'When you're speaking to kids about God, assume your audience doesn't know anything. Therefore, you're always in the posture of a teacher.'* Teaching and preaching are two different ball games. Teach them attractively about an attractive person."

them. We take our marching orders from the field and what they need and then work with them to accomplish what they want to get done.

When Young Life began camping, Carlson explained, there was no Properties department. "Field staff would come in the spring and they'd take the mattresses and the blankets out of storage and the first week or two, work crew or summer staff would be setting up the camp.

"Well then as things got bigger and more complex, you can see how the evolution happened. The field staff said, 'You know, we could start camp a couple of weeks earlier if we could get some full-time camp leaders to help us with this throughout the year. This began the full-time camp properties staff that is now a highly professional group in the mission."

This philosophy was most evident when the mission began to dream about acquiring more camps. In 1991 countless hours of research and listening to the field helped the Properties department identify three areas where camps were needed immediately—the East Coast, Colorado, and the Northwest.

Ultimately, the three targeted areas each received a camp; in the East, Rockbridge Alum Springs; in Colorado, Crooked Creek Ranch; and in the Northwest, Washington Family Ranch. In fact, the Lord led the mission to purchase seven properties over the course of the decade, six in the States as well as Pico Escondido, Young Life's camp in the Dominican Republic—each one a testament to the growth in the U.S. and beyond.

GROWING PAINS

By the time Young Life reached its fiftieth birthday, it was organized into six divisions. (The mission had been organized into divisions for about two decades.) Unfortunately, "division" turned out to be an apt description of the mission at that point. Not only was Young Life divided geographically, but in many ways, ideologically, as mission leadership often differed on the direction of the ministry. One senior staff said, "I believe we have become very 'divisional' in our mission, bordering on several separate 'Young Lifes' making up one whole."

Added to the danger of divisions becoming autonomous, was a confluence of issues, personalities, and other factors that made leading the mission especially challenging. "I think we were at a point in time where there were a lot of different visions about where Young Life would go," Burleigh said, "and I think we had a challenge during those years of asking the question, 'How do we still keep our focus on Christ and kids?' Sometimes trying to figure out how that worked itself out in the course of trying to give leadership to the mission was a real challenge. Those were pretty turbulent years for Young Life."

While a lot of great Young Life work was happening in the midst of this turbulence at the top, ultimately it became clear to senior leadership that a change was in order. At the Board of Trustees meeting on April 24, 1992, Doug Burleigh submitted his resignation.

Burleigh's tenure had been a challenging one, but like the three presidents who preceded him, he left his own unique mark on the mission.

"Doug came in with a great deal of energy," Bob Reeverts, vice president of International, said, "and worked as hard as any leader of the mission I've ever seen." That work helped create an important legacy with many accomplishments—two of which included his help in increasing the mutual support and encouragement between Christian organizations and, of course, the pioneering work in Russia.

"When Doug left Young Life, he still went back over there," longtime staff member John Miller remembered. "One day he said to me, 'My club is Russia.' That's a territory all right!"

In fact, Burleigh continued his work with his "territory" through the end of 1992 as the Young Life representative to the Republic of Russia. This work included leading the Youth Track of the Billy Graham Crusade, where they trained five thousand teenagers in discipleship in preparation for the October Moscow crusade.

"This experience," Burleigh observed, "provided the seed bed for the growth of Young Life's significant ministry in ten former Soviet republics and allowed me to continue discipleship work in a dozen locations around the former Soviet Union. Partnering with Gary Parsons in 1992 caused youth ministry in these former Soviet republics to explode in subsequent years."

TIME FOR TED!

As the mission began its search for the fifth president, the Board of Trustees asked Ted Johnson to take the reins in the interim. Since the fifties, Johnson, with the support of his wife, Nancy, had faithfully served in a variety of capacities throughout the mission, including as a volunteer leader, a member of several different Young Life committees, and as the last National Committee chairman for the mission. Before becoming interim president, he served as president of the Young Life Foundation.

Not content to see the mission coast during his tenure, Johnson focused on prayer and staff care. A great encourager, Johnson used that gift to lovingly challenge leaders to join

him in spending time in the Word and prayer.

Johnson told the staff, "Look, I'm going to do this. I'm going to get up at five o'clock [in the morning], and anybody else who will do the same, let's pray for each other, and let's pray for the mission together." Johnson experienced the power of those prayers firsthand. "I know that prayer made the difference, for me," he said. "So the focus was on Christ and prayer, and we turned the heat up. So if anything good happened during those eighteen months, the glory goes to God, period."

Johnson's service to the mission was not overlooked by others in leadership, noted Bob Reeverts. "I think these people like Hal Merwald and Ted, who came in for these brief interim periods were really wonderful gifts to the mission. Ted came in, not with a staff background, but said 'yes' to the Board of Trustees; 'yes' I'll sit in this difficult place—not an easy thing at all. So here were these interim people keeping this mission moving forward, and it was wonderful for us to see the continuum of the work of God's Holy Spirit through times like this."

When his time as interim was completed, Johnson reassumed his position as president of the Young Life Foundation. The mission, served so well by Johnson's faithful care, eagerly anticipated meeting the new leader . . .

"OUTSIDE" THE NORM

Over the course of fifty-plus years, Young Life had grown from five staff to 1,388 by 1992. By the end of that same

Ted Johnson

year, the mission also had 8,574 volunteer leaders and 7,170 committee members in its ranks. Many within these three groups, in fact, came to faith through their involvement in the ministry as kids. With five decades of history under its belt, Young Life had become a very unique subculture all its own.

Like any organization that has been around for that long, Young Life had developed its own language, style, mindset, personality, and quirks! Right or wrong, the belief among many within the mission was "You either 'get' Young Life or you don't."

Imagine the reaction throughout the mission, then, when someone "outside" the organization was named as Young Life's next president!

On April 23, 1993, 364 days after Doug Burleigh stepped down, the Board of Trustees unanimously approved the appointment of the mission's fifth president: Dennis I. Rydberg.

Although Denny Rydberg was an unknown to the majority of staff and volunteers within the mission, the forty-eight-year-old from Washington state had quite the résumé: youth director at First Presbyterian in Tacoma, the director of Christian Education at First Presbyterian in San Diego, one of the founders and vice presidents of Youth Specialties, director of Operations for Inspirational Films, the editor of the Christian humor magazine, *The Wittenburg Door*, speaker, consultant, author of ten books, and then finally, director of University Ministries, a position he shared with his wife, Marilyn, at University Presbyterian Church in Seattle.

Prior to this position, Marilyn had also served as the national women's coordinator for Campus Crusade, spoken on more than one hundred college campuses and put Campus Crusade's training together. The Rydbergs knew ministry, but could Denny Rydberg be expected to lead a mission of men and women, so unfamiliar with him, and he with them? Could this man, or any outsider for that matter, grasp the Young Life culture?

Initially, many assumed the answer was "no." Bill Garrison, like others on the Board of Trustees, had his doubts during the hiring process. "I thought the Young Life culture was so distinctive that no one could imbibe it from the outside," confessed Garrison. "No one could express it; no one could become a part of it from the outside. I just didn't believe that."

Garrison, while not alone in this concern, felt differently after meeting Rydberg. "I was converted in twenty minutes! I thought he handled himself so beautifully. He answered the questions so thoroughly and concisely. My impression of him was, 'This man can run this mission.' Hiring Denny was the greatest thing we ever did."

While the board members were convinced, the rest of the mission would also need to be persuaded—a much more challenging task, given the lack of face time with the new president.

It didn't take long, however, for Rydberg to convince the skeptics that he was more than up to the task. "Denny had to face an awful lot of people who didn't believe an outsider could come in and run Young Life, and if he did, for sure he would ruin it and it would become just a big church youth group," Greg Kinberg, Young Life's chief operating officer, explained. "He quickly startled them. He really did have a fix on contact work, relating to kids who don't know Christ, winning the right to be heard, building bridges of friendship. In that sense he was a real gift."

Rydberg was indeed a breath of fresh air for a fractured mission. "The people out in the field knew what they were doing and just went on doing it," Kinberg said, "but as an organization, we were not very focused. We had been through a decade of focusing on issues and a tough term for a president who was never fully supported."

For his part, Kinberg concluded, "Denny had a better focus of what Young Life should be doing than any of us did. He had a much clearer, simpler focus on kids hearing about and meeting Christ. It was very refreshing."

Denny Rydberg

Crooked Creek Ranch

For the second camp purchased in the nineties, the mission targeted a location in the Rocky Mountains of Colorado. At this point, Frontier Ranch was consistently over capacity and field staff were requesting a camp within striking distance of a major ski area.

The search process involved looking at more than sixty properties over two years. In 1994, Bruce Kramer, Western Divisional properties coordinator, learned of a family looking to sell part of their four thousand-acre ranch. The Murphy family owned a one hundred-year-old cattle ranch near Winter Park, Colorado, about seventy-five miles northwest of Denver.

"We felt it met all the criteria," Kramer said. It was free from encroachment, thirty-five miles from a major interstate, four miles from a train station, and ten miles from a major ski area. It really exemplified God's grandeur and His creation in a marvelous way."

With the board's approval, Kramer and the search team selected nine hundred sixty acres, and Young Life purchased the land in August 1994. Crooked Creek, the mission's second camp to be built from the ground up, hosted its first campers in 1999. "We build these camps," Dave Carlson explained at the time, "not for an eight- or ten- or fifteen-year turnaround to re-sell and make money, like the business world does. We build them with a one hundred-year time frame in mind. When we find something that's right, we stay with it."

Rydberg's predecessor, Doug Burleigh, agreed. "I believe the board acted correctly after I left in bringing in somebody from the outside. It was the right time to bring in somebody who perhaps looked at it a little bit more objectively than some of us who were involved all of our lives, basically, with Young Life. Denny had a lot of background in youth ministry, and therefore, brought a pretty rich understanding of ministry with adolescents. He's an idea person and somebody who has built a great team."

Chuck Reinhold, vice president of Young Life's Northern Division, among many other leaders in the mission, shared this belief. "I was confident that God would bring the right person to lead us," Reinhold said. "This conviction was confirmed when I met Denny and Marilyn. I was impressed that they were responding to God's call on their lives and not to personal desires or ambitions."

SURVEYING THE WALL

Rydberg diligently became a student of all things Young Life. "I think what he did," Garrison said, "was he immersed himself in what I call 'Rayburn-isms'—the fundamental, underlying, philosophic mission of Young Life. I think he caught it immediately."

For his part, Rydberg was eager to respond to God's call through study, yes, but also through action. "The first year, I used the concept of walking around the wall, the Nehemiah passage," he said. "I wanted to really survey the situation, and so I did a lot of listening. I used a yellow pad and just took copious notes."

Rydberg was pleased with so much of what he found in surveying the Young Life "wall." He smiled as he listed off many of his discoveries: "The staff and volunteers who were absolutely exceptional. The type of kids we were reaching who were just the type of kids you want. The rich history of Young Life. The brilliance of Jim Rayburn with the idea of going where kids are, winning the right to be heard. 'It's a sin to bore a kid with the Gospel.' The 'C's of Young Life [contact work, club, camp, Campaigners, committee]. The wonderful grace and favor that so many people have toward Young Life, whether they're still involved with Young Life or not."

That first year he also found areas in need of repair. "There was a feeling like 'everybody does what is right in their own eyes,' and they were doing some great things, but we weren't all pulling together. I think the divisional lines were no longer lines. I think to a certain extent they were barriers. That's sometimes good, because you really develop an esprit de corps in your division, but it isn't too good in trying to cross lines and getting people all working together. One of the things I discovered is when you have a vision and people are all moving in a certain direction, it cuts down on a lot of the ancillary stuff. You're so busy moving ahead and trying to reach more kids and do so with excellence, you don't have time to complain and so forth. It was a great organization, but it just needed a little bit of a vision, a little bit of tweaking."

Rydberg also proved to be a man of action. While he was happy to learn the culture, he explained, "I also made some moves right away in that first year. I made sure that I had direct contact with the field. Previous to that time, there was somebody between the president and the field directors, and I took care of that on July 26, and that was only two weeks in."

In addition, Rydberg continued to advance diversity within the higher levels of leadership as he assembled his team. In the nineties he placed three women in vice presidential positions: Margie Atkinson to vice president of Human Resources, Gail Merrick to senior vice president of the Midwestern Division, and Donna Murphy to vice president of the International department.

RECRUITING, TRAINING, AND DEPLOYING

In the first year of his presidency Rydberg developed a tri-fold vision for the mission: healthy people on healthy teams, harmony between the different ministries within the mission, and looking to God for growth in the outreach to kids.

The staff were eager to reach more kids and Rydberg was unapologetic about raising the bar. "This is an organization that's absolutely exceptional," Rydberg said. "I consider it the premier youth mission in the world. But we needed to get to more kids, because kids were dying out there. Kids were lost."

The question in Rydberg's mind was how to mobilize the great mission and get more people involved so these dear kids could be reached.

Mobilization came in the form of a strategic growth initiative called Recruiting, Training, and Deploying (RTD). "RTD started," Rydberg said, "with the idea that we were only in 6 percent of the junior highs and high schools in America, and we were barely touching some of the countries we were in."

Combining Rydberg's tri-fold vision and RTD led to the creation of five task forces of mission leaders who fleshed out the plan. The task forces addressed recruiting, training, deploying, area care (care for area ministry and staff), and the regional director job. Through much prayer and consultation, the leadership fleshed out the three components.

● Recruiting
In the first five years after Rydberg's arrival, the staff doubled in size, due largely in part to new recruiting strategies. Along with traditional roles (student staff for college students and intern positions for college graduates), new entry points into the mission were created. "Second Wind" positions were for men and women who had other careers prior to coming on staff, while "Fast Track" positions consisted of people who had some previous kind of ministry experience or seminary education.

● Training
For years, the Institute of Youth Ministries (IYM) had served the mission well by providing staff with a strong theological education in an atmosphere of fellowship. Building on this foundation, Rydberg sought to introduce a new iteration of training that would reduce the cost and shorten the time it took staff to finish their degrees.

"I think there was an emphasis on education over training," Rydberg added, "and we didn't really have a training wing for Young Life, so we decided to revamp that a little bit. We wanted to focus on training but also get seminary education in there."

The mission subsequently set up new training programs for its staff. The first training new hires would receive, appropriately named "New Staff Training," prepared college graduates with the foundations of strong Young Life ministry. The mission had been oriented to train people as if they were going to spend their whole work life on staff, one senior leader explained. "Denny made a fundamental change in that he wanted to create a program where we would train people for two years and if 50 percent of them left after two years we would still consider it a rip-roaring success. Because those 50 percent would go be great volunteer leaders, committee chairs, get involved in other ministries, etc. But the 50 percent

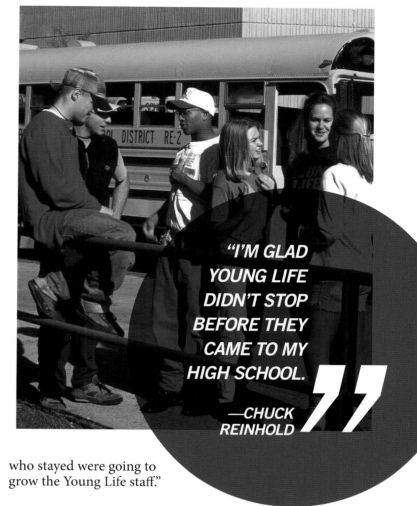

"I'M GLAD YOUNG LIFE DIDN'T STOP BEFORE THEY CAME TO MY HIGH SCHOOL.
—CHUCK REINHOLD

who stayed were going to grow the Young Life staff."

For those who did stay on staff after their two-year internship, Young Life provided a second program, "Area Director School," a mentoring program to train men and women in how to lead an area.

As for a staff person's theological education, the mission set up seminary partnerships to replace the IYM, relieving Young Life of some of the expenses it was paying to the seminaries, like overhead and administration. The access to more seminaries also helped staff find programs that were closer to them, and more flexible to their schedules.

The results helped staff in a two-fold manner, Rydberg said. "Now we have more people working on their Master of Theology or their Master of Divinity than we've had before and we're doing, I think, greater training than we have before."

● Deploying
Almost like faith without works, recruiting and training without deploying meant nothing. Mission leadership, therefore, identified twelve frontiers in the U.S. and abroad where the foundations could be strengthened. These frontiers included metropolitan areas such as Boston, Detroit, and Miami, while also targeting small town rural areas in the

Mississippi Delta and the Pacific Northwest. Outside the U.S., the plan also included establishing missions throughout Europe, and an expansion in the ministry at international schools. The tri-fold approach helped spearhead growth in the mid-nineties—not for the sake of growth, but for the sake of never giving up on lost kids. As Chuck Reinhold famously said, "I'm glad Young Life didn't stop before they came to my high school."

THE 1996 ALL STAFF CONFERENCE

The 1996 All Staff Conference was the first under Rydberg's tenure and also the first of many to be held in Orlando, Florida. While staying at Walt Disney World's Contemporary Resort, more than seventeen hundred staff, spouses, and friends of Young Life listened as Rydberg shared about what he had learned in his first two and a half years as president, as well as his vision for the mission's future.

It was here Rydberg laid out a ten-year plan for reaching more lost kids. "We want to move from 6 percent of the adolescent communities in the United States to 25 percent," he said. "That's a growth from 1,500 to 6,400 clubs; a growth of more than 400 percent. It is absolutely overwhelming; it is absolutely impossible; and that's why we're going to do it." Here, the staff broke into applause. He was quick to remind the staff, however, that the growth would not be up to them. "We're going to have to pray like never before. We're never going to be able to do this without the Holy Spirit's power."

From that point forward, All Staff Conferences represented special times where Rydberg would "bring the family together" every four years for a time of worship, vision casting, and mutual encouragement. The gatherings proved to be invaluable times for the spirit and health of an ever-expanding mission.

NEW LOCATION, SAME GREAT SERVICE!

When Rydberg arrived in Colorado Springs, he set up a schedule of brown bag lunches with each department at the Service Center to get a pulse on how things were going. One recurring theme from each session became the need for more work space—an impossibility in the current building.

"I realized they were right. We had moved into the building in the early sixties with fewer than twenty people and, although we had renovated some over the last thirty years, we were extremely cramped with more than eighty people in the building."

The Young Life Service Center in 1996.

Because of the spacing limitations, staff were also working in two other buildings across the city. "I felt that someday it would be great to have all of us under one roof to create a greater spirit of camaraderie, teamwork, and synergy—all designed to serve the field more effectively."

"Someday" was the key, because Rydberg wanted to employ a "first things first" strategy. "I wasn't going to make a new building one of my first priorities, because I didn't want all those hard-working people in the field to perceive that the new president was into a 'Service Center first, field last, let's build an empire in Colorado Springs' mode."

The answer came in the form of a downtown building "at an unbelievably good price that would meet all our needs and even allow for such growth over the years . . . to meet the needs of an expanding mission."

Rydberg and the board were committed that not one penny toward the project would come from the field. Funding came from current and former trustees, various foundations, and local downtown businesses wanting to keep Young Life near the center of the city.

In April 1996, Young Life moved into the new Service Center building located at 420 North Cascade Avenue. Once settled in, Rydberg reflected on how the move had improved the staff's morale. "It's a great place to work. I think it's been a wonderful gift for our staff. I think it's also raised how our field staff feel about the ministry when they come here and realize that this is a decent building, classy but not overdone, with people who work hard and really care. I think it's created morale, not just here but around the country."

THE BIG DREAM MEETS THE BIG MUDDY

The 64,000-acre, 100-square-mile Big Muddy Ranch has a backstory as big as the West itself. The ranch, located in the high desert country of Central Oregon, has existed since the late 1800s. It has been a stop on the Pony Express, home to several famous gun battles, and an area rich in ranching and mining ventures.

In 1978, a cult leader from India, Bhagwan Shree Rajneesh, bought the ranch and created a commune for his thousands of followers, who flocked to the area in 1981. For four long years the "Rajneeshees" inhabited the land and made their presence felt to the thirty-five residents of nearby Antelope, Oregon. In 1985 the cult disbanded after Rajneesh was deported for immigration fraud.

Much to the relief of the Antelope citizens, the land lay fallow for the next six years. In 1991 Dennis Washington, a Montana businessman, and his wife, Phyllis, purchased the land. Within six years the fate of the Big Muddy would change drastically.

Having learned of the couple's heart for the next generation, Rydberg invited Dennis Washington to spend time together at Malibu. Here Washington witnessed firsthand what Young Life could do with kids in a beautiful setting prepared just for them. Realizing a true kindred spirit with the fifty-five-year-old mission, the Washingtons graciously donated the entire property to Young Life in 1997.

Over the next two years, crews (many of whom were volunteers) remodeled and moved buildings, installed a pool, excavated a pond, and remodeled an 88,000-square-foot structure as a sports center. This particular feature was a teenager's dream, complete with basketball and volleyball courts, a skateboard

Washington Family Ranch.

SharpTop Cove

Even though Rockbridge had just enjoyed its inaugural summer camping season in 1996, it would not be long before it too began to fill to capacity. Meanwhile, its neighbor to the south, Windy Gap, was already overcrowded. The decision was made to continue down the eastern seaboard and look for another site close to a metropolitan center where strong, healthy ministry was taking place.

The exploratory team learned of a camp located an hour north of Atlanta, in the Appalachian foothills, surrounded by forests, streams, and waterfalls. Cecil Day, the founder of the Day's Inn hotel chain, originally purchased the land in the 1960s for the purpose of youth ministry. Here he built his own youth camp called Burnt Mountain Assembly.

As the mission researched the possibilities of this land, a longtime friend of Young Life, Lavelle Bean, heard about the search and was eager to make contact.

Bean's original interactions with Young Life occurred about fifty years earlier while he was at Wheaton College. "Lavelle was the person who would wait up for Jim Rayburn when he would come in at twelve, or one, or two o'clock in the morning," Dave Carlson said. Rayburn, who was scheduled to speak the next morning, would arrive by train, come to Wheaton, "and when Lavelle would open the door, Jim would say, 'What do you have to eat?' And they'd go and rustle up some eggs and bacon down in the kitchen, and Lavelle and Jim would talk until it was time to go to the student meeting the next morning."

Five decades later, Lavelle Bean just "happened" to be the chairman of the board for the Burnt Mountain Assembly! The doorkeeper for Rayburn would also prove to be the doorkeeper for the next Young Life camp.

The mission came to terms with Bean on the purchase of the camp in May 1997, and Young Life renamed the camp SharpTop Cove after the prominent mountain peak on the property.

park, a climbing wall, pool and Ping-Pong tables, weight training equipment, a juice bar, and more.

The camp would be named Washington Family Ranch, and with a vision that there might one day be more than one camp located within its expanse, a name was chosen for this first camp: Wildhorse Canyon, and eventually, simply "Canyon." The first buses rolled into camp in 1999. The camp was easily Young Life's largest, with the capacity to host seven thousand campers coming each summer to hear about Jesus.

THE FLAG THAT FLIES OVERHEAD

It had been thirteen years since Young Life's last Mission Purpose Statement had been crafted, and in 1998 Rydberg felt the statement needed some slight revisions. This in no way implied a change in the direction Young Life was heading; rather, Rydberg wanted to work toward a "common statement of our mission that will be virtually unforgettable."

To accomplish this, Rydberg sought counsel from his cabinet, the Board of Trustees, the National Field Leadership Team, senior staff in the mission, and well-respected pastors around the country. He reiterated to these groups the differences between an organization's mission statement and its constitution. He wrote, "A mission statement is not meant to be the constitution of an organization. It is not the critical document that defines an organization in specific and exhaustive terms. In other words, it is not the rudder that guides the ship as much as it is the flag that flies overhead . . . In Young Life, the Articles of Incorporation serve as the rudder for guiding this massive ship."

The board affirmed the proposal, opening the way for a new mission statement:

Introducing adolescents to Jesus Christ
and helping them grow in their faith.

The mission appreciated this clear, concise description that would be easy to memorize and share with others. This was a helpful tool, and one that in future years could still be "tweaked."

FOR THE LONG TERM

Meanwhile, things didn't remain status quo on the international front. Young Life had ministry in forty countries by the end of the decade, a period that saw new ministries begun in countries such as Japan, Cambodia, India, and Mongolia, while established work in places like Russia and

A WyldLife leader and kid spending one-on-one time at camp.

Nicaragua continued to strengthen. The growth inspired the mission to create four international divisions in 1996, which were eventually consolidated into one International division in 1999, with Donna Murphy appointed as the senior vice president of International ministry.

Over the previous four decades, many lessons had been learned in building the Young Life ministry outside the U.S. The model that worked most effectively in cross-cultural ministry was establishing Young Life staff in the country for the long term. Just as Young Life's model with kids was to "move into the neighborhood," so the international work would require men and women who would practice the power of presence in each country. Sometimes this involved nationals who already lived there coming on staff; other times a staff person from the U.S. or another country would go. With a commitment to stay and live among the people, discipleship of other leaders would more naturally occur— and last.

● **Russia**
An excellent example of this incarnational strategy occurred in 1992, as Gary and Jeanne Parsons responded to the Lord's call and moved their family of five to Moscow. Since 1987, the Parsons had been ministering to Russian kids and felt the time was right to live among them to not only share the Gospel with them, but also equip older Russian believers in relational ministry. While Moscow was a city in turmoil, its citizens were very hospitable to the Parsons. "The people were leery of Westerners," Gary said, "but welcomed us with open arms. They were so gracious."

Lost Canyon

The mission's growth in Southern California, Arizona, and New Mexico practically demanded that a new camp be located in the Southwest. Spearheading the movement was a group consisting of twelve families, each one contributing at least one million dollars toward the cause, not to mention prayer, sweat, and tears. Eventually known as the "Lost Canyon Founders Team," the group helped Young Life staff narrow their search around the Flagstaff area.

This area, however, came with certain challenges. Most of the land was owned by the Federal or State government. To make matters more difficult, land that had water was especially hard to find. These two hurdles highlighted the Lord's hand in the process when they came to Williams, Arizona, in 1997.

In Williams, the team found a forty-acre property surrounded by national forest, with a water source that could produce over two hundred eighty gallons a minute—an amount unheard of in that area. The choice was obvious.

When Young Life presented the proposal to the Williams City Council, they granted immediate, unanimous approval . . . with a caveat. The mayor said, "We'd like to have the kids of Williams be able to go to this camp."

Young Life staff member Stu Graff said, "In Young Life we don't send kids to camp, we take them to camp. So in order for that to be true, we'd have to start a Young Life club in Williams, Arizona."

The mayor said, "Then that's what you have to do in order for us to approve!"

"Through tears of joy," said Marty Caldwell, senior regional director in Arizona, "we said that's exactly what we'll do." Within a month, volunteer leaders started a Young Life club and that year took eighteen kids from the high school to Woodleaf.

"A bunch of these kids met Christ and became the best PR people for what we were going to be building in this city's backyard," Caldwell said.

The construction of Lost Canyon began in 2000 with Elkhorn dining hall, the largest free-span log structure in North America; furthermore, Lost Canyon itself was the first and only camp site of its size and quality in the state. Summer camp began in 2001, hosting the first of thousands of campers who'd experience the message of Jesus' love . . . so that they may never be lost again.

While spending two years faithfully building ministry there, Gary also established work in other countries. In 1994, adults in Chernovtsy, Ukraine, organized a ten-day summer camp attended by one hundred kids. One kid, named Sasha, had spent years on the streets and wasn't particularly receptive to the messages Gary delivered during club. "He would sit in the front row at club and taunt me as I spoke. But I knew that Sasha was more important than the club I was trying to lead. He just needed to be loved."

Gary continued to pursue Sasha that week. He looked past the tough, blustery exterior to the heart of this hurting kid. Sasha's resistance to the message was overcome by the messenger's love. On the eighth day of camp, Sasha's walls came down and he began a relationship with the Savior.

After he left camp, Sasha went from mocking those who spoke of Jesus, to actively pursuing his peers with the Good News. He became a Young Life volunteer and began organizing "forest camps," where even more kids like him would hear about the One who loved them.

Throughout the decade, similar "Sasha stories" were occurring throughout the Commonwealth of Independent States and the Baltics. Through the faithfulness of the Parsons and other caring adults, the Lord was beginning a new "Russian Revolution" that would last for generations.

● Nicaragua

Like the Parsons in Russia, Jim and Sarah Hornsby wanted to make inroads in a hurting country. Having come to Nicaragua in 1984 with Habitat for Humanity, the couple decided (after their assignment was over) to bring Young Life to the country. Because of civil war, the adult population had decreased to the point that 50 percent of Nicaraguans were under the age of sixteen.

The Hornsbys, Young Life veterans who had founded Pioneer Plunge in North Carolina in 1973 and also helped start the urban work in Jacksonville, Florida, began work in Matagalpa in 1988. As basketball had been a successful introduction to kids in other parts of the world, baseball would be Jim's way of meeting kids. He walked down the streets of Matagalpa, bat and ball in hand, and in his broken Spanish, began to build relationships.

By 1991, the ministry offered kids their first Young Life weekend. More than sixty kids attended and heard the message of God's love, but they were still trying to discern what a personal relationship with Jesus meant.

"We found it a slow go trying to get beyond recreation to the new life that Christ offers," Sarah said. "Then a Young Life team from Costa Rica came and held another camp. It was when they served the Nicaraguans a banquet—beautifully decorating the tables and room, serenading them, serving

Russians and Americans together in front of St. Basil's Cathedral in Moscow's Red Square during the summer of 1990.

La Finca.

with such love and thoughtfulness—that the Nicaraguans realized the love of Jesus was real. There is a traditional gulf of hatred between Costa Ricans and Nicaraguans, the former having a prejudice toward Nicaraguans that can be compared to racial struggles in the States. But at that camp, the Costa Ricans visibly transformed those feelings into a love that penetrated the hearts of our kids."

An hour north of Matagalpa lay land the Lord would eventually use to also penetrate the hearts of Nicaraguan kids. In 1992, Young Life Nicaragua purchased La Finca ("The Farm") and began the work of creating a national camp there in the lush rainforest. The camp would eventually host more than two thousand campers each year.

SMALL TOWNS

"Touch a kid in a small town, and you touch his family, his barber, and his football coach."

Young Life enjoyed a long history of reaching out to kids in rural areas; in fact, the honor of "the first small town to have Young Life" goes to Tonkawa, Oklahoma, with a population of fewer than five thousand. Ernest Wetmore, who lived in Tonkawa and served on Young Life's national board, asked Rayburn to send a staff person to his town, and the small town ministry was unofficially born there in the 1940s.

Tonkawa would become the exception to the rule, however, as most small town work was really the result of volunteers rolling up their sleeves and reaching out to kids. In fact,

the areas with the most long-term success were those that were volunteer led. Don Stuber, the mission's first director of Small Towns/Rural, said, "History supports what we strongly believe: small town ministry is best led by insiders—professional people who have a long-term stake in the town."

For half a century, Young Life had work going on in rural communities, but it wasn't until the 1990s that the approach became an organized initiative. In February 1999, Oakbridge hosted the first Rural Conference, with forty-one staff in attendance. There the leadership defined a small town as "a one-high school town of fewer than twenty-five thousand that is NOT a suburb."

In December of that year, staff drew up the Small Town and Rural Constitution. A few of the beliefs they affirmed in this document were:

- Rural teens are important to God and should have equal priority to suburban and urban ministry. They need to hear the Gospel the way Young Life proclaims it. Every kid. Everywhere. For Eternity!

- Rural ministry has the capacity to involve 100 percent of the adolescents in a community and impact the whole town.

- Where He wants ministry, God has placed enough people around the school to do effective ministry there.

- The trust of rural communities may take longer to win, but it will be very difficult to lose.

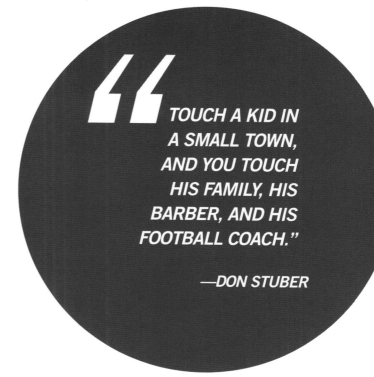

" TOUCH A KID IN A SMALL TOWN, AND YOU TOUCH HIS FAMILY, HIS BARBER, AND HIS FOOTBALL COACH."

—DON STUBER

CHRIST IN THE CAFETERIA AT COLUMBINE

In Young Life, the high school cafeteria comes close to sacred ground. For more than sixty years, it has been a key place of contact between Christ and kids through the flesh and bone of Young Life leaders who drop in for a visit.

On April 20, 1999, however, that sacred ground became a battleground when hundreds of kids hit the cafeteria floor at Columbine High School in Littleton, Colorado. Among the faces pressed against the cold concrete that morning was Young Life Area Director Kevin Parker.

Kevin was on campus to grab a friend for lunch when a janitor ran through the room screaming, "Down! Down! Down!" According to Kevin, the next three minutes were "the most intense and fearful" moments of his life. There were gunshots and pipe bombs, and then a mass exit of students and adults from the building. Kevin escaped unharmed. Sadly, fifteen others didn't. Fourteen students and one teacher lost their lives that day at school.

That night, Kevin and Kerry Parker's home was flooded with hurting kids. Several Young Life staff members from around the state were already on hand to help steady kids as the first waves of grief began to crash against the community. In some respects, it seemed God had been bracing Littleton for this tsunami for years. Young Life was twenty-five years deep in the community and more leaders were connected with kids than ever before. As a result, the ministry served as a sturdy breaker against the storm.

Kids continued to fill the Parkers' home for many nights following the shootings. A common question among the crowd: Where was God that day at Columbine High School?

Not an easy question to answer at such a tragic time. But for kids who came to the Parkers for comfort and consolation, one answer became increasingly clear. Jesus was lying on the cafeteria floor that day as the bullets and bombs exploded. And now Jesus was extending a healing hand through these two faithful friends.

Shortly after the shootings, Kevin wrote these words in a letter, "Young Life leaders will never step into the schools again with the same confidence we once did, but we will continue to be there because our faith compels us to go."

—Donna Hatasaki,
Collecting Lost Coins

WALKING WITH TEENS THROUGH TRAGEDY

As the decade neared its end, there was an alarming increase in the number of school shootings in the U.S. Within eleven months of each other, the shootings at Thurston High School in Springfield, Oregon, and Columbine High School in Littleton, Colorado, were the deadliest in the nation's history. At Thurston on May 21, 1998, four people were killed and twenty-three wounded; nearly one year later, on April 20, 1999, fifteen died and twenty-one were injured in Columbine's massacre. Both days would forever be etched into the hearts and minds of high school kids, their families, their teachers and administrators, their communities, and a watching nation.

The area director in Springfield, Ron Sauer, had a daughter who attended Thurston. The morning of May 21, after finding her okay, Sauer rushed to the high school to offer any help he could. Sauer's part in helping to address the heartache was needed in both the short term of that day and the long term of the days, months, and years that followed.

Part of the healing occurred in the form of a gift from the Young Life community in Springfield. Sauer and his team came up with the idea to offer free camp trips to any of the injured victims. Fourteen kids responded to the gift and on July 11, 1998, arrived at Woodleaf. Many heard the Good News of God's love for the first time while at camp, and four stood up at the Say-So to affirm their decisions to follow Jesus. In April 1999, God also used the Young Life team's presence in Littleton to care for the many kids and adults affected by that tragedy. This presence literally began as shots were fired, since Area Director Kevin Parker was spending time with kids in the cafeteria that fateful morning. (See sidebar.)

Timber Wolf Lake

"Rick, more kids could come if we had a camp closer to home."

The harsh reality of that statement by a Young Life area director left a mark on Rick Poll. In 1994, Poll and his wife, who hailed from Hamilton, Michigan, were visiting Castaway Club as adult guests. The geographical problem was one shared by many areas in the mission. Because of where the camps were located, some Young Life areas were just financially handcuffed when it came to bringing kids.

The upper Midwest faced a critical need for a camp, because of the many rural areas in Michigan and neighboring states, not to mention the many city kids living in places like Chicago, Indianapolis, Detroit, and Cleveland—"a void with a seven hundred-mile diameter."

Poll took the area director's statement as a personal challenge and began to investigate what would be needed to bring a camp to the region. Poll's vision ignited a five-year search process, covering three states and more than seventy site visits.

In 1998 God introduced a generous benefactor into the equation. The benefactor not only surprised Poll by putting him on his payroll so he would be freed up to continue the search, he also found an ad in *The Wall Street Journal* advertising land outside of Lake City, Michigan.

After the search team gave the thumbs up on the site, the benefactor astonished them again—he purchased the 876-acre property for $1.6 million and gave it to Young Life. In 1999 Greg Carlton moved from his position as camp superintendent at Frontier Ranch to oversee construction.

Within two years of the purchase, in the summer of 2001, campers arrived at Timber Wolf Lake—the newest Young Life camp that wasn't too far from home.

Pico Escondido

Teenagers in the Dominican Republic first encountered Young Life in 1986 through José Postigo, a local volunteer who started the ministry there. Marv Asfahl, the Latin America regional director, came alongside Postigo, and in just a few years the need for a camp was apparent. The acquisition, however, proved to be anything but conventional.

After a period of roadblocks and discouragements for Asfahl and his team, Chad Wallace, who would become the first camp manager, scouted the country looking for just the right place for a camp. In 1998 he found in the mountains above the town of Jarabacoa the ideal location—a large parcel of land owned by a group of brothers. They were eager to sell with one stipulation: they must be paid in cash.

Scott Steele, national director of the Dominican Republic, did not let this minor detail stand in the way of such a beautiful acquisition. What followed would prove to be a one-of-its-kind transaction in Young Life's history. Steele met up with his lawyer, "a really big guy" who no doubt doubled as Steele's security detail, and the pair quietly went to secure the deal. "I literally converted $35,000 cash into pesos (what an ordeal!), put it in this huge hockey bag and went with our lawyer up to the brothers and gave it to them," Steele laughed. "And then we owned Pico! It was crazy!"

The hilly pastureland contained no infrastructure, buildings, or roads, but it was the answer to countless prayers. For years, work teams from the United States came at their own expense to help with the construction, as did local men from the nearby Vida Joven (Young Life) ministry. The camp filled a void in the Dominican Republic for facilities that could host Latin American kids at an affordable price in high-quality accommodations.

Pico Escondido, which means "hidden peak," gave visible evidence to thousands of kids of a loving Creator, who desires to be hidden from them no longer.

While the school shootings were sadly neither the first nor the last to occur that decade, they seemed to mark a critical turning point in the escalation of violence at schools. Like many organizations that worked with teenagers, Young Life would need to be prepared for whatever might come.

GROWING INTO THE TWENTY-FIRST CENTURY

Throughout the highs and lows of the mission's sixth decade, Young Life continued to live out the spirit of "whatever it takes" in order to introduce kids to Jesus and help them grow in their faith. This spirit enabled the organization to reach more middle school and high school kids than ever before.

The results were difficult to miss: Over the course of the decade, the numbers of kids involved in club and Campaigners alone grew by more than 50 and 80 percent, respectively. Not surprisingly, so did the numbers of adults working hard to bring their young friends to Jesus. Full- and part-time staff nearly doubled, while volunteer leaders grew by 50 percent and committee more than 40 percent.

Asked about the importance of numbers, Rydberg responded, "Numbers represent people. I'm not a big 'numbers guy,' but I look at numbers. I love to see how many kids are accepting Christ at camps, and how many kids we're reaching. We know that when we gave out ten thousand Bibles at camps this summer (1996) that ten thousand kids had made a commitment to Christ or were interested enough that they wanted their own Bible.

"And numbers represent accountability. I've got to send the bill for the Bibles to the donor who wants to pay for them, and he wants to know how we're doing. Numbers let us know how we're doing. It doesn't always measure quality, but sometimes it does."

Striving for quality growth would continue to be a point of emphasis as the mission, along with the whole world, anticipated what lay ahead in the new millennium. The nineties prepared Young Life for a world that would be changing far more than anyone could have dared realize.

When God Wants to Teach You Something

A Reflection by Denny Rydberg, president

Bruce Larson was a hero in my life—senior pastor for six years, mentor, and friend. He was filled with one-liners, and one that meant so much to Marilyn and me was, "When God wants to teach you something, He takes you on a trip."

Bruce was right. Our journey with Young Life has been a trip of a lifetime and here's how it unfolded.

I was the first president to come from outside the mission. The board had decided in advance that Young Life needed the perspective of an outsider, and through a rather rigorous and definitely prayerful yearlong process, Marilyn and I were selected. (I say "Marilyn and I" very deliberately and enthusiastically. She and I came to this post as partners and have continued to serve side by side for more than two decades.)

We were surprised by the choice and, I'm sure, so were many staff members and others involved in the mission. Marilyn and I knew we weren't worthy enough to hold this important position, and we weren't talented enough to lead it. But we also felt totally called to do it and knew God's strength would be made perfect in our weakness, so we said, "Yes."

But it was a process—one step at a time. One evening in December 1992, Marilyn and I were talking about how settled we felt. We had lived in our home for twelve years, we had been on the staff of University Presbyterian Church for nine, and we had developed some wonderful lifelong friendships. Our parents all lived in the Pacific Northwest and we enjoyed that extended family feeling. Then less than a month later, we received a phone call from the head of the search firm Young Life had hired, saying I had been mentioned as a potential candidate and would I be interested.

Frankly, Marilyn and I were reluctant. We had what we considered the best job (ministering to and with collegians) in the best church in the nation. We loved students and could see ourselves involved with them the rest of our lives. We loved the church and one of our great friends and mentors, Earl Palmer, had followed Bruce Larson as our senior pastor. Why move?

But I also had learned a lesson by that time: You don't ignore anything that might have God's fingerprints on it. We concluded, after a bit of wrestling with the opportunity, that we needed to go through the process as an act of obedience and as part of the constant adventure of walking with Christ. Three months later, after many phone calls, numerous meetings, and a final interview process before the whole board in April 1993, we were told we were their unanimous choice to lead this great mission. Then, for the first time, we met the senior leadership staff who all had been invited to come to the board meeting on the last day and meet us. We told them the best analogy we could use in describing the process was walking down a hallway with some windows, but no doors, to an arranged marriage.

I think we—the staff and us—all felt like this when we first met. The staff had not chosen us (nor had any of the volunteer leaders, committee people, and friends of the mission). We had not chosen them. And we were now on the road together. United by our call.

I wrote in my first article as president that, "I have a strong sense that God has called me to be a leader and not a caretaker. My leadership style revolves around a team concept, and I'm looking forward to being teammates with you."

I had no idea how long my call would be. But we enthusiastically plunged into the battle for the hearts, minds, and souls of kids. For over twenty-two years, we have worked with an amazing team and seen literally millions of kids around the world begin a relationship with Jesus and grow in their faith. In the process, Marilyn I have felt our Young Life tagline has come to fit us: We Were Made for This. And we're thankful for the opportunity.

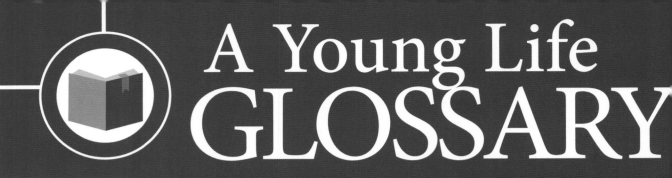

A Young Life GLOSSARY

adult guest

Adults invited to see Young Life camp in action. Hosted by couples or an individual at a beautifully appointed adult guest lodge, guests can experience their own "best week." (see Best Week of Your Life)

Amicus

Young Life's student exchange program through which students come to the United States and live with Christian families. During their stay, students are exposed to the Gospel through host family relationships, host family churches, local Young Life, and camp.

Best Week of Your Life

The common experience of kids from every decade who have spent one week at a Young Life camp.

assignment team

Staff members and their families who spend a summer session at one of Young Life's camps to serve in various capacities, from speaking to program to leading volunteer work crew and summer staff.

donors

Essential partners in ministry with local areas around the world. Regional and area staff are responsible for raising 100 percent of their budgets, and donors allow staff the freedom to focus on kids and not on finances.

Celebration

Also known as All Staff Conference, the quadrennial gathering of staff in one location for the purpose of thanksgiving, equipping, rejoicing and renewal.

Campaigners

A weekly gathering for those who want to go deeper in their faith, capitalized because the word derives from the Young Life Campaign, our original mission name.

blob

An oversized, inflated pillow in Young Life camp lakes used to catapult campers into the lake, after a brief period of suspended animation (and terror?).

every kid

Athletes, band kids, nerds, cheerleaders, goth, popular, lonely, average kids of all kinds whom Young Life seeks because every kid has the right to know the truth about Jesus Christ. Young Life is for every kid in every life stage and unique life circumstances:

- Young Life for high school kids; WyldLife for middle school kids; Young Life College for college and university students.

- YoungLives—for teen moms.

- Capernaum [kuh-PUR-nee-uhm]—for kids and young adults with disabilities.

- Young Life Military–Club Beyond —for kids on military installations around the world, offered in partnership with MCYM (Military Community Youth Ministries).

- Multicultural and Urban—for kids of color and kids in under-resourced communities.

- Small Towns/Rural—for kids in areas with fewer than twenty-five thousand people.

"earn the right to be heard"

The demonstration of sincere affection, authentic faith, and trustworthiness that, over time, inclines the hearts of kids to listen to and receive the Good News of Jesus Christ. [Also expressed as "Win the right to be heard" and "earn a hearing."]

fun

A defining attribute of Young Life and by-product of Young Life activities.

furthest-out kid

The least receptive, most disinterested kid in the room, school, camp, or community whom we seek to love anyway.

C's (Five) – The Five C's

The time-tested methods by which Young Life introduces kids to Jesus Christ; **contact work**—building authentic friendships with kids by going into their worlds. [see incarnational]; club—a party with a purpose to gather kids for fun and a simple message on what we celebrate every day; **camp**—resort-quality properties where kids experience the Gospel [See Best Week of Your Life]; Campaigners— see definition above, and committee—adults who love Christ and kids, advocating for and supporting Young Life.

global leaders

College students around the world who are supported through our sponsor-based, tuition-funding and mentoring program to raise indigenous leaders who are making an eternal impact in their communities.

Good News

The greatest story ever told; the birth, death, and resurrection of Jesus Christ.

program

The umbrella term for the combination of mixers, skits, gross games, and clean humor at club, weekend and summer camps that, together, captivate the most disinterested and "furthest-out" kids, and everyone in-between.

property staff

Those men and women who serve year round at a Young Life camp to create a unique and inviting environment where everyone can encounter Christ.

volunteer

The lifeblood of Young Life; adults who serve in direct ministry with kids or on a local area committee.

work crew

A volunteer experience at a Young Life camp for students who are in high school that deepens faith through service and community.

incarnational (ministry)

The essence of Young Life's approach to ministry, modeled by Jesus Christ, who "became flesh and blood and moved into the neighborhood" (John 1:14, *The Message*).

(the) night that never ends

At camp, the midweek dress-up-for-dinner night (usually with a theme, like fifties night or western), which typically includes elements like the "tableau," an opera, a carnival, and a square dance. Usually follows the "sin talk" in the proclamation progression. It allows a release from the weight of reckoning with sin, a time to bond with leaders, more clean fun than kids have ever had, and in this way, it is a foretelling of the Good News of the cross that will be shared the next day.

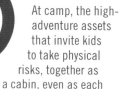

rides

At camp, the high-adventure assets that invite kids to take physical risks, together as a cabin, even as each one takes the personal risk of exploring the condition of their hearts. These could include water sports like skiing, parasailing and tubing, and land activities like completing a ropes course, trail riding on horseback, rappelling, go-cart racing, and mountain biking.

twenty minutes

At camp, following the message about the cross, a time of silence for campers to consider in solitude what the message means to them.

eXpeditions

One-week to three-month short-term volunteer opportunities for groups and individuals to serve in countries where Young Life exists or is developing.

Jesus

"Not just what Young Life's all about; that's ALL that Young Life's all about."—Jim Rayburn

opera

Complex musical drama featuring characters appearing throughout the week and a dilemma, like camp solvency, that is resolved in this great operatic act.

run-on

A skit that is played out in scenes over many clubs, or nights at camp.

tableau

From the French, "Tableau vivant," meaning "living picture"; in a setting from the past (e.g., a soda shop or old west town), a scene enacted silently by motionless work crew and summer staff attired in costumes and with props who strike story-telling poses. Together, the effect is to have entered another world. On cue, the actors spring to life and act in character, as campers watch and then enter the scene, attired in their dress-up costumes.

Say-So

The opportunity for kids to declare to friends, leaders, and fellow campers that they have made a decision to follow Jesus Christ. See Psalm 107:2 (KJV), "Let the redeemed of the Lord say so."

summer staff

A volunteer experience at a Young Life camp for those who have completed one year of college or who are college- or post-college age, in positions requiring maturity and a strong non-verbal witness.

the
2000s
Ready!

The arrival of a new year traditionally brings with it an air of speculation, but 2000, of course, also marked the beginning of a new century and millennium. As January 1 approached, many were concerned with the day's earliest hours. Specifically, when the calendar hit "00," would the feared "Y2K bug" ultimately wreak havoc on the world's computers and their networks?

After successfully navigating the Y2K "crisis," another strange question hung in the air. For a twenty-eight-day span in November and December the world watched and wondered who would be declared the next president of the United States. Over those four weeks, conversations swirled around electoral votes and "hanging chads," before George W. Bush emerged the winner.

Issues like these made for great headlines and late night talk show fodder in the early days of the decade. All that abruptly changed, however, a mere 615 days into the new millennium.

A "hinge point" in American—if not world—history, the morning of 9/11 left a reeling nation wrestling with life's ultimate questions, while searching for meaning and hope.

As it had experienced with the school shootings in Oregon and Colorado in the late nineties, Young Life was again reminded of the importance of being ready. In this climate of unease another question emerged: How could Young Life continue to proactively introduce adolescents to Jesus and help them grow in their faith, and yet be responsive to the unforeseen?

The 2000s were a decade where the mission did more than just survive. Along with shining a light in the darkest of moments, Young Life grew by continuing to go after kids in the darkest of places. By the end of the decade, Young Life had ministry in more than seventy countries around the world and was uniquely positioned to build on this presence through the principles it had learned over nearly seven decades.

JUST BEING THERE

Every American remembers where they were on the morning of September 11, 2001. The terrorist atrocities brought unspeakable horror and pain to a speechless nation and changed the course of history.

Opposite: A Cambodian leader engaged in contact work, 2008.

2000s
TECHNOLOGICAL INNOVATIONS

eBay	1995
Google	1997
USB Flash Drives	1999
Play Station 2	2000
eHarmony	2000
iTunes	2001
iPod	2001
Wikipedia	2001
Xbox	2001
MySpace	2003
Skype	2003
Facebook	2004
Gmail	2004
YouTube	2005
Twitter	2006
Wii	2006
Amazon Kindle	2007
iPhone	2007
Mobile Apps	2008
Spotify	2009
Instagram	2010
iPad	2010
Pinterest	2010

Like any traumatic event, the tragedy caused a stunned world to ask, "Why?" As hard as it was for adults to try and make sense of the senseless, it was even more challenging for kids. They asked the age-old questions so many were wondering: "Why would God allow this? Where is He? Why did these innocent people have to die?"

Those living near the attacks, especially those who had lost loved ones, were particularly in need of attention. Like the leaders who had responded to tragedies throughout the previous decades, Young Life staff and volunteers quickly mobilized to care for any and all the Lord would bring their way.

In the Times Square/Hell's Kitchen area of New York City, leaders began meeting with kids the day of the attacks in a space at a local church. Originally designated to be the area's club room, the space quickly became a disaster relief area for Ground Zero workers. The next few days were filled with staff and volunteers continuing to do what they do best—being present in the lives of kids.

Meanwhile, in Washington, D.C., leaders also reached out to kids in the aftermath of the attack on the Pentagon. Sam Branham, area director for Central Fairfax, Virginia, wrote in a newsletter that fall:

"On Wednesday, September 12, fifty or so high school students piled into my family room, sat with solemn stares, and just wanted to talk about what had happened the day before. I was so impressed with the maturity of these teenagers. When they boiled everything down and reached a final conclusion, it was that people need to know God. They saw Jesus as really the only solution to any of the world's problems."

In an effort to help kids in New York City and the children of those who died in the attacks, the mission established two funds. The September 11th Camp Scholarship Fund provided camperships to those who lost parents in the attacks, while the Young Life Manhattan Project helped fund new ministry sites in New York City: Times Square/Hell's Kitchen, Harlem, Union Square, Gramercy Park, and the Upper West Side.

Less than a month after the attacks, on October 7, 2001, the war in Afghanistan began. The mission rolled up its sleeves to once again care for those affected by war. Young Life staff and volunteers continued investing in relationships with former high school kids entering the conflict, while Club Beyond leaders reached out to kids who were military dependents. This worldwide ministry, which had come to mean so much to so many in the military community, continued to faithfully serve kids both stateside and abroad, as their parents served the nation.

MORE THAN JUST RELIEF

In many ways, Young Life's response to 9/11 helped prepare the mission for other times of crisis. When Hurricane Katrina hit the Gulf Coast the morning of August 29, 2005, causing massive destruction from Texas to central Florida, Young Life was there.

The Young Life community throughout the Gulf region (and beyond) looked for ways to help, in both the short and long term. Through the crisis, Young Life Expeditions, the mission's international initiative begun in 1997 to serve areas through short-term service, mobilized its forces and beautifully came alongside those who were hurting. For months and years afterward, the Expeditions leadership provided teams of volunteers from all over the States to come and serve however needed.

Meanwhile, other teams of leaders, kids, and friends of Young Life from all over the Southern Division volunteered in the cleanup efforts. Furthermore, Young Life staff and leaders throughout the south welcomed the displaced kids and their families, helped them relocate to places where they'd be cared for, and connected them with the Young Life ministry in their new communities. Basic needs were met, jobs were found, and kids were enrolled in new schools.

Tarneisha Smith, Young Life Urban staff in Baton Rouge, Louisiana, put the mission's response in perspective. "One thing I love about Young Life," she said, "is the relationships. We have relationships with kids so we're able to help in all aspects. Someone said the other day, 'What's so great about Young Life is, when the Red Cross leaves and FEMA stops helping people, Young Life is still going to be there. We're going to be with kids and walk with them through this. We're more than just relief. We're there to aid kids throughout time. This is not just an event for us. We can show them something that lasts.' "

The mission established a Hurricane Recovery Fund to assist members of the Young Life family who lived in areas affected by Katrina. In only two months, the fund raised close to $250,000, with nearly $50,000 of that donated by other Young Life areas and regions.

Another resource, Young Life's Benevolence Fund, would also come into play three years later when the mission sought to help those affected by Hurricane Ike. One staff person, Cristina Azios was able to repair her badly damaged home through a generous gift from the fund. The fund, established back in 1998, was created solely by the gifts and donations of Young Life staff and friends of the mission to help fellow staff withstand the storms of

> " WE'RE GOING TO BE WITH KIDS AND WALK WITH THEM THROUGH THIS. WE'RE MORE THAN JUST RELIEF. WE'RE THERE TO AID KIDS THROUGHOUT TIME. THIS IS NOT JUST AN EVENT FOR US. WE CAN SHOW THEM SOMETHING THAT LASTS."
>
> —TARNEISHA SMITH

Young Life supporters come from all walks of life, and in 2001 the mission was proud to partner with Mike Edwards, a National Hot Rod Association (NHRA) driver. Over the course of the decade, Edwards not only sported the logo on his Chevrolet Cavalier racecar, but at each national event, the Mike Edwards Motorsports Team shared with kids about drag racing as well as the Gospel. The team also partnered with Young Life in a project called "A Team on a Mission," which gave drivers, sponsors, racing teams, and fans a chance to send disadvantaged kids to camps across the country. In 2009, Edwards captured his first NHRA Full Throttle Pro Stock World Championship.

Young Life reinforced its commitment to middle school kids in the 2000s.

financial distress resulting from extraordinary emergency or hardship.

For the mission and the world, the decade included a time of unprecedented tragedy and heartache. While many would experience the physical, psychological, and spiritual effects throughout their lifetimes, they could also see how the Lord had used Young Life to be there for them in their darkest hours.

GROWING WYLD-ER

Young Life began working with middle school kids in the late 1960s. While the middle school work was strong in certain places, by the late nineties the mission was looking to take WyldLife to the next level. Young Life formed a WyldLife task force to give thought and attention to growing the work, which had often taken a back seat to the high school ministry.

For some, the idea of working with middle school kids was treated as "pre-evangelism." Randy Giusta, who had been working with middle school kids in Encinitas, California, since the 1970s, had a different perspective. "From my experience," the veteran staff member said, "middle school kids are totally ready to hear the Gospel and to respond to it."

At the 2000 All Staff Conference, Denny Rydberg announced, "From now on, Young Life will be as committed to reaching junior high kids as it is senior high kids." Rydberg was affirming the work that had been done, while spurring on more staff to begin WyldLife in their areas. Veteran staff member Rick Beckwith, who was asked to lead the new WyldLife rollout, viewed this as an opportunity "to change the mission's thinking with regard to pre- and early adolescents." The WyldLife task force helped reaffirm principles such as these:

- Middle school kids need Jesus, and reaching them is a fulfillment of Young Life's mission statement.

- Middle school kids are different from high school kids and, therefore, a different program should be developed for them.

- The camping program should also be different for middle school kids.

- High school Campaigners can grow tremendously in their faith and leadership skills by serving as leaders in a WyldLife club.

- Leadership training must also be modified, so the mission can best recruit, train, and deploy WyldLife leaders.

The added attention to the middle school ministry paid off. Throughout the 2000s, WyldLife became one of the fastest growing segments in the mission.

ASIAN YOUNG LIFE

In 2006, nine of the top ten U.S. communities (minimum population: 100,000) with the highest percentage of Asian residents were located on the West Coast. One of those cities was San Francisco, where Young Life already had a thriving ministry, thanks to the efforts of people such as Steve Chung.

Chung came on Young Life staff in San Francisco in 1979 and focused his work specifically on kids living in Chinatown. These kids hailed from countries such as Vietnam, China/Hong Kong, Cambodia, Laos, and Thailand.

Like every good Young Life leader, Chung knew it was important to tailor the ministry specifically to the cultural needs of the kids. "The Asian culture is very different from American culture," Chung said. "They have a very strong family structure. It is rare for a student to rebel against his family."

To properly respect family values, which includes a high emphasis on education and studying, Chung was sensitive to the logistics of the Young Life clubs. "We hold six different clubs so kids can fit it into their schedules," he said. These six

Kids enjoying their time at Woodleaf.

Steve Chung (second from right) and Capernaum friends dressed up for Halloween.

clubs also reflected the rich diversity of the area—as leaders ministered to kids from various cultural backgrounds.

The Asian culture also differed from typical American culture in regard to volume! Unlike traditional American clubs, which tend toward the loud and wild, Asian clubs more closely resembled a Campaigners meeting. In an Asian club, Chung explained, "there are no high-profile skits, no loud songs. We sing maybe twenty minutes of mellow songs and have forty-five minutes of club talk and discussion."

Chung's efforts to reach the Asian population on the West Coast were mirrored in the East through the work of Brian Hall, a high school teacher in New Jersey. In 2003, Hall and his friend, Tony Lin, began a ministry to Asian kids living in Bergen, Middlesex, and Morris counties. The two volunteer leaders took eight Asian kids for a week at Saranac and that fall began doing contact work. By the spring of 2005 they were ready to hold the first "Asian Young Life" club, which hosted sixty-five kids. A few months later they brought eighty-five kids to camp.

The ministry was hitting its stride and the "Asian" designation was an important part of the success. "It's not to be exclusive but having Asian in the name indicates this is for them," Hall said. "We welcome kids from all races, but there is a desire to be with people of the same ethnicity when you're the minority, especially the kids who are recent immigrants. We are providing a sense of community they are looking for but often don't find in high school."

"There's a lot we are still learning along the way. We're trying to think outside the box and, so far, I think what we're doing is working. Paul said, 'I become all things to all people to save some.' I think we've just begun to scratch the surface of what we can do. There are so many kids out there still to be met."

MORE KIDS IN MORE PLACES

Midway through the decade, Rydberg reiterated the mission's commitment to kids around the world. "I have heard some reputable leaders from other missions give this stat: 95 percent of kids live outside the United States and 95 percent of youth workers work within the United States. Something is wrong with that picture.

"Now we're in fifty-one countries from A to T (Armenia to Tanzania)," Rydberg continued. "That's progress and a good start, but it's barely scratching the surface of what we want to accomplish. We want to renew our focus on international. We want to build sustainable movements more than we do individual ministries. We are praying, talking, thinking, and strategizing about how to have a greater impact on the 95 percent of the world's youth population who live outside the borders of the United States."

Pyneath Sor with kids in the computer room in Phnom Penh, Cambodia.

In 2005, both Donna Murphy and Bob Reeverts sensed the Lord calling them to step down from their international posts. With their departures, Rydberg turned to two staff veterans familiar with the demands of leadership. Marty Caldwell, who had most recently served as the regional director of the Sunbelt Region in Arizona, was a staff veteran of twenty-seven years. He would oversee the work in Latin America, Africa, and Asia. His counterpart would be Lee Corder, formerly the senior vice president of the Eastern Division, who came on staff in 1974. Corder would oversee ministry in Scandinavia, the United Kingdom/Ireland, Europe, the Former Soviet Union, and the Eastern Caribbean.

This intentionality paid off. Over the course of the decade, the mission would grow from forty countries in 2000 to more than seventy in 2009. Around the world, staff found creative ways of beginning the ministry in their own cultures; a prime example of this ingenuity could be found in many Asian countries, such as Cambodia.

CAMBODIA

By the late nineties, young people made up about 65 percent of Cambodia's primarily Buddhist population, a fact not lost on Pyneath Sor. Sor lived in Phnom Penh, and after a meeting with Bob Reeverts, the Young Life Asia regional director, he realized God was calling him on staff with Young Life. For the next six months Sor focused his energies on building relationships with kids in the city.

Sor asked friends to pray with him for wisdom on how to start Young Life in the local high school. The group offered to organize sporting events for the kids, but the principal declined their offer. Undeterred, Sor and his friends continued to brainstorm, and decided upon another idea: What if they taught a computer class at the school?

This time the principal agreed. With the help of Reeverts, enough funds were raised to provide the class with five computers (in a room that could only contain five desks).

The class was a natural way for leaders to serve kids and get to know them. In 2001, Young Life moved into a center near the school. The location afforded the leaders the opportunity to teach kids English and guitar (as well as computer). Several hundred students took advantage of these opportunities each week. While the student numbers rapidly multiplied, so did those of the Phnom Penh Young Life leadership team. By the middle of the decade, the team had grown to thirty-six, six staff assisted by thirty volunteers, and the class had grown to twenty computers and an enrollment of one hundred twenty kids—all because Sor continued to ask the Lord what would serve students best.

In 2008, staff gathered at the first Africa All Staff Conference in Tanzania. They represented more than fifty African tribes speaking (and singing) in a wide variety of languages.

MADE FOR AFRICA!

While countries across the globe experienced tremendous growth throughout the decade, nowhere was the explosiveness more evident than on the continent of Africa. Young Life had a presence in Africa since the 1970s, and in the late nineties began a reinvigorated work there, beginning in Ethiopia.

● Jesus with Skin On

In 1999, longtime staff member Chuck Reinhold and his wife, Linda, began ministry in Addis Ababa, Ethiopia. Living among the Ethiopian people, who struggled daily with hunger, disease, and death, the Reinholds, alongside the Ethiopian staff, modeled what it was like to be "Jesus with skin on."

"The Bible says that 'The Word became flesh and dwelt among us,'" Reinhold said. "Young Life is a natural ministry. It's a ministry of friendship that transcends all cultures. People just need us to be with them and love them."

Joining the Reinholds in 2002 were Steve and Dyan Larmey, who had served for eight years in southern Indiana. The couple would become a fixture in Ethiopia, and later, the continent.

● For the Many and the One

By 2006 Young Life Africa was looking to establish a pilot camp, where kids could experience the best week of their lives. The first part of camp consisted of leader training, equipping staff and volunteers to run the camp. The second part was camp itself, where kids would come and enjoy the Young Life camp experience—Africa style.

That summer, seventy-eight staff and leaders from Congo, Ethiopia, Kenya, Liberia, Malawi, Rwanda, South Africa, Tanzania, Uganda, Zambia, and Zimbabwe took part in the pilot camp in Tanzania.

After the training, the staff and leaders welcomed the buses of incoming campers, one hundred seventy-four kids from Dar es Salaam. The joyous week began immediately upon the campers' arrival, as they were royally greeted by a traditional African brass marching band.

Due to many roadblocks, the last bus to arrive had only one rider, a kid named Michael. "We always ask the question to leaders in training: 'Would you do everything the same if it was for just one kid?'" Larmey said. The response was a resounding "yes," and Michael stepped off the bus with one hundred work crew cheering him on, the brass band trumpeting his arrival, and leaders putting him on their shoulders and bringing him into camp to join the others.

That week, Michael began a relationship with Jesus. "And he was carried into the kingdom of God," Larmey said. "Was it worth it for just one kid? I think I know what Michael would say."

● Africa Blesses the Mission

The growth in the work led to new "firsts" which served the whole mission. In 2008, Young Life assembled a U.S. camp assignment team (a group of staff working at a camp property for a month in the summer) that represented the true reach of its ministry. Staff from Kenya, Congo, Tanzania, South Africa, and Sudan joined staff from Argentina, Costa Rica, England, Paraguay, Portugal, and the U.S. to be a part of the up-front and behind-the-scenes workings at Lost Canyon. That summer hundreds of kids began a relationship with Jesus, and witnessed a beautiful picture of what the kingdom looks like.

That same year the Board of Trustees welcomed its first member outside of North America, when Moyo Kamgaing, a native of West Cameroon and citizen of the United Kingdom, began serving in November. This was a powerful reminder that Young Life sought to have a board that represented the mission around the world as well as in the U.S.

● One Kid at a Time

Over the course of the 2000s, Young Life Africa grew rapidly, reaching over 230,000 kids. The leadership was quick to point out, though, that this was accomplished "by reaching one kid at a time." Steve Larmey, who would become the vice president of Young Life Africa in 2011, said, "An African proverb teaches the 'slow way is the fast way' and that proverb has guided our vision for reaching every kid in every country in Africa."

Perhaps it shouldn't have been a surprise that Young Life proved successful in Africa, which has the youngest population among all the continents; in fact 50 percent of the inhabitants are nineteen years old or younger.

Young Life's new tagline reminded everyone who saw it that they "were made for this." Young Life Africa staff insisted, however, that *Young Life* was made for *Africa*! The mission's emphasis on going to where kids are, building relationships of trust, and sharing the Gospel through leaders' lives fit beautifully and seamlessly into African culture.

PROCLAIMING THE GOSPEL

Over time it often becomes necessary to articulate the foundational truths an organization holds. For Young Life in the 2000s, this meant upholding, in both style and content, the mission's historic proclamation of the Gospel. In 2008, senior leadership created a document to help provide direction and clarity to a mission growing increasingly diverse, in both background and cultural sensitivities.

On the opening page of Young Life's Proclamation Paper, leadership explained the reasoning behind the document's creation:

In recent years, challenges have arisen both inside and outside the mission regarding how we proclaim the Gospel of Jesus Christ. Our goal is to clearly define what we believe are the non-negotiables of the Gospel message proclaimed by Young Life staff and volunteers in camp, club and one-on-one settings. The intent of the paper is not to squelch the creativity of our staff, but to provide a foundation on which their creativity can be expressed. However, these are not suggestions. They are the key elements of what we will present and what our audiences can expect when they are involved with Young Life. With a prayerful posture, we affirm these essentials of our proclamation:

1) *We proclaim the Person of Jesus Christ in every message.*
2) *We proclaim the reality of sin and its consequences—that apart from divine grace, we are estranged from God by our disobedience and incapable of a right relationship with God.*
3) *We proclaim the crucifixion of Jesus Christ as the ultimate proof of God's love and the only solution to our problem of sin.*
4) *We proclaim the resurrection of Jesus Christ.*
5) *We proclaim the risen Christ's offer of salvation by inviting our middle school, high school and college friends to confess Jesus as Lord and Savior.*
6) *We proclaim God's call to discipleship by encouraging all who respond to grow in their faith.*

The paper went on to more fully develop the above points, and the scriptural interpretation of each. The leaders concluded, "As a mission we seek to be faithful to the Scriptures. We base our proclamation on our understanding of God's Truth contained therein, and we stand on the shoulders of faithful men and women who have effectively proclaimed the Gospel of Jesus Christ throughout Young Life's history, to the glory of God."

The Proclamation Paper drew out healthy discussions within the mission. While some found it stated the obvious, others disagreed with leadership's stance on certain theological points. This led to difficult conversations, and ultimately, some staff and volunteers having to break ties with Young Life. A vast majority, however, were in overwhelming agreement with Young Life's restatement of the message the mission seeks to proclaim.

REACHING A WORLD OF KIDS

By 2008 the mission had hit a significant milestone—this was the year Young Life reached more than a million kids around the world. While celebrating the milestone, Rydberg sensed God calling the mission to more. What if, he wondered, the million kid milestone became a launching-off point to go after even more kids?

This Spirit-led inspiration encouraged Rydberg and mission leaders to pray about a larger-than-humanly-possible goal. The result was an initiative called "Reaching a World of Kids" or RWOK for short. Quite simply, RWOK was the dream to move from one million to two million kids annually . . . in the span of seven years!

"It took us about sixty-seven years to get to our first million annually; we want to get to our second million in much less time than that!" Rydberg proclaimed. In order to pursue the two-million-kid mark, the mission would also seek to mobilize more than eighty thousand volunteers and establish eight thousand ministry locations around the world. Of course, to undertake such a great endeavor would require an extensive plan and extensive resources. The estimated cost for RWOK would be $260 million, another large vision within the vision. Because of the size and the scope of what it would take to reach the next million kids, the mission would need to enlist the help of generous financial partners.

Rydberg enlisted the wisdom of the mission's senior leadership as well as regional directors from around the world to help support and design the initiative. "We brought fifty-five people together in Colorado Springs for twenty-four hours to flesh out ideas to turn RWOK from a dream to a reality," Rydberg said. "These fifty-five were divided into six working groups that focused on prayer, kids, leaders, staff, hard-to-fund areas, and communication."

Out of this time, Rydberg and the senior leaders decided this immense initiative would hinge on three growth strategies: leadership development, sustaining and starting ministries, and camp impact.

LEADERSHIP DEVELOPMENT

Experience had proven that the mission would never reach a critical mass of kids through staff alone. Reaching a world of kids would depend on leveraging the power of volunteers, and there were many avenues where more volunteers could be found. Among these initiatives were Young Life College, the Latino Student Staff Initiative, the Teachers in Mission project, Alumni and Friends, and the Developing Global Leaders program.

Young Life College

One important way to invite leaders into the work would be through the mission's newest ministry, Young Life College. Working with students entering their college years, Young Life was well aware that adolescence doesn't end with graduation from high school and sensed a critical need to continue reaching out to them. Young Life College could minister to students during this next critical phase of their lives.

Young Life College officially began in 2005, when Rydberg assembled a college task force of regional directors, area directors, mission staff, leaders, and trainers. While working extensively with college students who were leaders, mission leadership recognized the need to expand ministry especially to former Young Life kids who were not yet ready to be leaders, but with whom the mission had already earned the right to be heard. (For years, many areas were already unofficially serving college students not involved in leadership.)

In 2007, Rydberg hired Mike Gaffney, a twenty-year veteran of college ministry, to become the director of Young Life College. Gaffney likened the beginnings of the ministry to childbirth. "There is anticipation and great expectation, but there is also uncertainty and fear. In the numerous conversations I had with Young Life staff at the 2008 All Staff Conference, there were a few common reactions to Young Life College. Some were saying, 'It's about time, we've been waiting for this!' Others were apprehensive, wondering how this 'new addition' would impact the Young Life family."

The idea took hold and within five years there were eighty-five Young Life College ministries (seventy-three inside the U.S. and twelve outside). As the ministry connected with students who had previous Young Life experience in high school, it also made an

> "IT TOOK US ABOUT SIXTY-SEVEN YEARS TO GET TO OUR FIRST MILLION ANNUALLY; WE WANT TO GET TO OUR SECOND MILLION IN MUCH LESS TIME THAN THAT!
>
> —DENNY RYDBERG

Young Life College students from Arizona State University serving in Mexico.

impression on those who did not. Sixty percent of students involved with Young Life College had no prior experience with the mission. The obvious conclusion: Young Life College was introducing thousands of students to Jesus Christ for the first time.

As Young Life College served both believers and non-believers on college campuses, the effort was also translating into more Christ-followers, and in turn, more potential leaders for the mission. "I believe Young Life College is one of the most strategic initiatives in Young Life," Rydberg said. "As Young Life College grows, we believe that we will see a corresponding expansion in the number of leaders raised up on these campuses to help us care for kids all around the globe."

● **Latino Student Staff Initiative**
According to the 2010 U.S. census data, Latinos were the largest and fastest-growing people group in the nation, growing 43 percent during the decade. To ensure Young Life indeed met the specific needs of this booming population, the Latino Student Staff Initiative was born. In 2006 the mission designed this two-year leadership development initiative for emerging Latino leaders beginning in their sophomore year of college

and focused on four key pillars: character, theology, professional management, and leadership development.

One graduate of the Latino Student Staff Initiative was Jay Miranda, who went on to become area director of Chiapas, Mexico. "It gave me the training and support needed to become a strong voice in my community," he said. "I am excited to be the first Latino Student Staff member to lead international ministry."

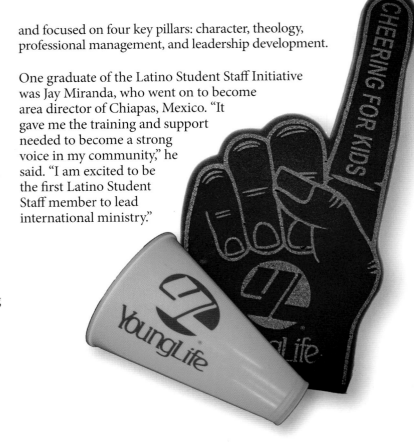

Teachers in Mission

Educators have always been powerful allies in the attempt to positively influence kids; after all, who spends more time interacting with kids in the course of a day than their teachers? Moreover, those teachers who have a relationship with Christ know the extra burden of not only wanting to see their kids excel academically, but in matters of faith.

Historically, many of Young Life's strongest volunteer leaders had been teachers. On top of their time in the classroom, these men and women continued to build relationships with kids outside of school hours.

Young Life recognized the great need to link arms with teachers and began a new initiative, "Teachers in Mission," to aid in these connections. Pete Fritsch, area developer for the Gateway Region, explained that the initiative helps Young Life staff and committees "find, thank, encourage and learn from every Jesus-loving educator in a school, and invite some of them to join the existing Young Life team at their school or assist them in starting one."

Some of these educators emerged as "Teacher Staff" candidates, a program the mission started in 2000, where teachers would be compensated for their after-school hours, which included leading club, continuing contact work with kids outside the classroom, introducing administrators and parents to Young Life, and recruiting more teachers into the program.

To set teachers up for success, Young Life held training conferences at various camps each summer to help "educate the educators." At one such conference, Fritsch humbly proclaimed, "There is a group of people who already know the next million kids who will hear about Christ. God is way ahead of us. This group of people is called educators."

Alumni and Friends

Technically there have been Young Life "alumni" ever since the first kids involved in Jim Rayburn's club graduated from Gainesville High School. Over the years, one of the primary ways staff cared for graduating high school seniors, the "youngest" alumni, was by connecting the students with Young Life staff in their new college towns.

Staff also looked for ways to connect older alumni with the local area by inviting them to become leaders, join the committee, attend camp as adult guests, contribute financially, or commit to pray.

After six decades, Young Life alumni numbered in the millions, and the mission was eager to assist local areas in their attempts at connecting with these important allies. In the 1990s the mission established the Alumni department which, in 2000, launched a strategic effort to find "any adult who's ever been involved with Young Life in any way" and reconnect with them.

By 2009 the ministry was called "Alumni and Friends," an acknowledgment that many people first become connected with Young Life in their adult years. Under the direction of Jonathan Schultz, the initiative exploded with a database of thousands of names and contact information, enabling more adults than ever before to reconnect with the mission and their friends. And of course, Alumni and Friends continued to assist in the efforts of connecting high school graduates with Young Life staff and friends in their new college towns, military placements, or workplaces.

Developing Global Leaders

Born in Ostrava, Czech Republic, Tyna Kvasnickova was raised an atheist. Through friends, the sixteen-year-old began a relationship with Christ, and not long after, met Al and Stacy Anderson, Young Life staff in the Czech Republic. The couple encouraged Tyna to become a volunteer leader, a role in which she excelled. The demands of volunteering, studying at university, and working a job, however, proved to be overwhelming. Tyna thought her leading days were over.

"I loved my ministry with Young Life," she said, "but I came to a point that I couldn't do it anymore. I told Al and he told me about this new opportunity with Developing Global Leaders."

In 2009 the mission created Developing Global Leaders (DGL), a college scholarship and leadership development program, to identify, support, and equip young adults to make

Developing Global Leaders student, Tyna Kvasnickova, left, with Stacy Anderson.

THE DIARIES OF JIM RAYBURN

Throughout most of his adult years, the founder of Young Life wrote daily accounts of the goings-on in his personal and professional life. In 2008, Kit Sublett, an author and publisher who served on Young Life staff for twenty years, sifted through decades of diary entries to compile, edit, and contextualize this unique look at the man. The book was a gift to those who wanted to hear more from Rayburn himself about what the Lord was teaching him, his passions and his struggles, his rich prayer life, and his vision for what the mission could be.

an eternal impact in their home country. DGL targeted high school graduates in developing countries who were already volunteering with Young Life and demonstrating high leadership and service potential. The hope was that a percentage of DGL graduates would continue ministering in Young Life or enter other fields of service such as education, health, and government.

Chad Edwards, director of DGL, said, "Our main aim is to help alleviate the poverty of leadership in the developing world through Christ-centered leaders. We work with many students who could go to college, develop intellectually, and make an impact for Christ, but because of their financial situations, they have limited opportunities."

"I was really excited because I love the ministry and loved the idea of being on staff—more a part of the organization," Tyna said. "DGL has helped me to continue the work with Young Life. Without the financial support, it would have been impossible. I can't imagine life without being a part of Young Life."

Tyna, upon graduating the program and to the delight of all involved in her training, went on Young Life staff in Poland.

SUSTAINING AND STARTING MINISTRIES

The success of RWOK would ultimately begin and end at the local level. In looking to grow both deep and wide, the mission's leadership committed to several initiatives to strengthen the existing work and expand into new countries, areas, communities, and schools. One such initiative was providing "resources and strategies for established ministries." The idea was to grow from a point of health. Ways to accomplish this financially included greater fundraising training for staff and developing an area sustainability fund to assist areas in financial difficulty. In regard to personnel, the mission increased efforts in retaining current staff, training new staff, and even equipping Campaigners kids to reach out to their peers.

Other critical initiatives focused on bolstering the work of Young Life's specialized ministries, like Capernaum, Young*Lives*, Multicultural/Urban, and Young Life Military—Club Beyond. Some of the greatest progress came from two particular programs: small town jumpstarts and the Texas Latino Initiative . . .

● Small Town Jumpstarts

"Did you ever drive by a school that does not have Young Life and wonder, 'How can we get it here?' " asked Don Stuber, field director of Young Life's Small Towns/Rural Initiative. The traditional model for starting ministry in new frontiers usually required spending a few years laying the groundwork.

What if the mission could do it faster, Stuber wondered, like say in a week?

This idea, which came to be known as a "jumpstart," would revolutionize how area work started not only in small towns, but larger areas as well. A jumpstart, as its name implied, involved bathing a new community in prayer, then engaging key people there with a vision of what Young Life could mean to the town . . . but doing so in a shorter amount of time.

"It's three hundred phone calls and thirty meetings in one week," Stuber explained. "You can sense the flow of Holy Spirit momentum. And the key is ownership. You need people stacking their hands together saying, 'Let's do this.'"

Patsy Goers, area director of Lakeland, Florida, shared about her jumpstart experience: "We were able to make more contacts with influential people in one week than what I could have done in a year."

The jumpstarts, however, did not focus solely on quantity. Quality also came through in the process. "A jumpstart builds the infrastructure in a town to allow for unprecedented

growth," Stuber said. By finding advocates early, the work was better set up, not only in terms of planning and leadership, but solid financial backing as well.

Texas Latino Initiative

The Latino population across the United States had been exploding for years, and one of the major centers of growth was in Texas, a fact not lost upon staff in the Lone Star State. Annie Mays, south San Antonio area director, voiced what many were thinking, "We can't afford to ignore the fact that in five years, 60 percent of the teenage population in Texas will be Hispanic. We have to be intentional about it now."

In 2009, the mission started the Texas Latino Initiative in four key Texas areas: Dallas/Fort Worth, Houston, San Antonio, and the Rio Grande Valley. More than one million Latino kids lived in these four areas.

Success in these communities would help the work expand even beyond state lines. "We hope in Texas we are creating a pipeline for future staff and volunteer leaders who will go north to the rest of the country and south to Mexico," said Gerald Garcia, the Texas Latino Initiative director.

Washington Family Ranch —Creekside

In 2008, ten years after Dennis and Phyllis Washington donated the Washington Family Ranch property to Young Life, their foundation gave the mission another gift. This one would completely finance the building of another camp on the sixty-four thousand-acre property.

Called Washington Family Ranch Creekside, the new water park-themed camp was designed especially for WyldLife campers, the first of its kind in Young Life. The park featured eight waterslides, a pool, an indoor ropes course, climbing area, and miniature golf.

Creekside would accommodate more than three hundred fifty guests, increasing Washington Family Ranch's capacity to more than one thousand guests per week. Within three years the new camp welcomed its first guests. "This is without doubt an unprecedented gift to the mission of Young Life and a cause for celebration," Rydberg said. "It will allow us tremendous flexibility as we look to the future growth of our ministry to kids in the Northwest."

CAMP IMPACT

About one-third of kids who attend Young Life camp begin a relationship with Jesus during their week at camp. To double the number of kids who would experience the greatest week of their lives, the mission expanded seven North American camps and continued construction on new camps in the U.S., Central America, Europe, and the Former Soviet Union. Moreover, leadership also looked to adapt camping strategies to new countries and cultures and committed to finding new ways to increase campership funds for financially challenged kids.

● Campership Legacy Fund

In 2009, the Young Life Foundation created the Campership Legacy Fund to provide camp scholarships for first-time, unreached kids who couldn't afford summer camp. The idea, inspired by Ted Johnson, quickly proved to be a win-win for everyone involved.

For the investor, it was designed for "today and tomorrow." The fund, based upon current and end-of-life giving, enabled investors' gifts to extend their "footprint" beyond their lifetime—as many as fifty years, or five generations of kids!

One of these kids was Caleb, whose application and follow-up report read as follows:

Before camp
I am seeking a scholarship for Caleb because he does not have a saving relationship with Jesus and cannot afford his camp trip. Spiritually, Caleb is seeking answers in his life before he leaves for college. He has started attending Young Life events, even though

Comedian Jeff Foxworthy and his wife, Gregg, share at the 2008 All Staff Conference. The couple served as WyldLife leaders in Atlanta.

his friends make fun of him for coming. Financially, Caleb's family could not even afford to pay his entire deposit to go to camp. Caleb has started fundraising by doing yard work and working at a local thrift shop. But this has gotten harder, because Caleb has developed some health issues. Caleb lives with his mom, stepdad, and four younger siblings. Caleb's biological father is not in his life and lives three states away. Please consider giving Caleb a scholarship to camp and pray for Caleb to invite God into his heart and start a saving relationship with Jesus.

After camp
Caleb loved camp and hearing about Jesus. My favorite memory was two days after camp when Caleb's mom called me and told me that he was a different person. He stopped hanging out with his old drug-using friends and was being respectful. It was cool to hear that Caleb's inward desire to follow Christ was also dramatically affecting his outward actions as well.

In the Campership Legacy Fund's first six years, 11,263 kids received a scholarship. Donors had contributed more than $4 million to the fund and committed to more than $65 million to continue helping kids like Caleb encounter Jesus at camp.

REAL CONNECTIONS

In the new millennium, it became obvious that an increasingly significant contributor to effective relational ministry would be . . . technology! Advances in technology helped staff and volunteers reach out to kids in the virtual world where they spent more and more of their time. Leaders went "online" in the "frontlines" with kids. The proliferation of blogs (web logs) and social media sites, like MySpace and Facebook, created an instant virtual community attractive to many kids. By the mid-2000s, it was estimated that more than half of all blogs and web journals were created by thirteen- to nineteen-year-olds.

Trained to "go where the kids are," Young Life leaders learned to navigate yet another frontier—increasing their "touch points" with kids through social media, cell phones, and texting. The immediacy was extremely helpful, but could only go so far. Kids, who were created for relationships, still needed interaction with real flesh-and-blood human beings.

In a 2004 edition of *Relationships* magazine, Tom Combes, a regional training coordinator, shared a story about a hurting kid, "Cory," whom he had met at Windy Gap. "We're Internet people," Cory said, "and my friends and I have online journals." Cory went on to share with Combes about his year (he entered a new high school), his interests (he was learning to play guitar), and his struggles at home (his parents were divorced and his father hit him).

"I was amazed at his openness," Combes wrote, "so I asked him if kids in his cabin knew all these things. 'No, they haven't asked me.' He paused, looked at me and said the most revealing thing, 'I told you because you asked.' "

"The growing popularity of online journals and web diaries," Combes concluded, "remind us that many kids today are still quietly longing for a place to be heard and someone to listen."

As the week continued, Combes watched "Cory's countenance gradually change from guarded and fearful to open and vibrant. On the last night of camp, I was in the back of the club room, and I watched him stand up and say, 'My name is Cory, from Texas, and this week I gave my life to Jesus.' "

Despite all the technological revelations in the modern era, it seemed there was still no match for the simple, time-tested approach of a life on a life.

CAPTURING THE GREATEST WEEK ON VIDEO

Since the 1950s, film and video had been an important part of telling the Young Life story. From early movies like *Judy Makes a Date* to *Time for Living* in the 1970s to the modern short promo videos for every Young Life camp, thousands of kids had come to camp, in part, because of the amazing "movie trailers" they saw back home.

Video wasn't just critical for drawing kids to camp, however. Once there, video continued to speak to kids in a host of ways. Each night at club kids might catch a glimpse of themselves in a short clip of the day's camp activities. By the end of the week, a longer video was available for kids to purchase as a way to take home a video reminder of their time at camp.

This "Video Scrapbook Program" was a labor of love put together by video interns, who worked long hours every week to turn around such a special keepsake. It would take interns at least sixty hours every week to construct the twenty-minute scrapbook, which came with many extra features (program clips, mp3s of club talks, club songs, etc.).

The program became a beautiful way to continue sharing the Gospel with kids long after their camp week was over. "The goal of the camp video program," said Dan Dyer, who became the mission's Video Services manager in 1998, "is to extend the ministry of camp past the borders of the property. Because the goal of camp is to introduce kids to Christ, the video scrapbook should be something kids can take home with them that will further that ministry. For some kids it's a commemoration of their spiritual birthday, and as such, it needs to be great."

With DVD in hand, kids now took home a visual time capsule of the week, a reminder of the moment where many came to know the Savior.

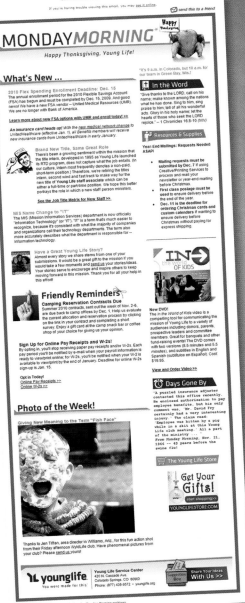

MONDAY MORNING

As the decade drew to a close, Young Life was fully committed to sending electronic communications to staff, volunteers, and committee whenever possible. Recognizing a trend towards digital communication, and seeing an opportunity to save the mission money, the Communications department replaced previous print communications with a weekly eNewsletter called *Monday Morning*.

The title was a tip of the cap to the original Young Life internal publication of the same name. Early on in the mission's history, Bob Mitchell, the first editor (and eventual president of Young Life), would sit down every Monday, type out the information staff would need to know, make copies, lick envelopes and stamps, and mail out the letter. Begun in 1950, when the staff numbered in the thirties, the publication lasted until 1977. When *Monday Morning* was revived on June 8, 2009, the audience numbered approximately thirty-two thousand recipients. The first edition stated the goal of the weekly newsletter:

"We echo the sentiments of Mitchell who explained the feel behind the original *Monday Morning*: 'We want to give an honest presentation of what is going on, and shall include items of encouragement as well as those needing our prayerful attention. As Young Life grows, every attempt will be made to keep the personal touch and the family spirit that has been so appreciated by us all.' "

ONE YOUNG LIFE

Young Life ministry logos, before and after the rebranding process.

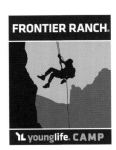

BRAND NEW!

By 2007, the mission had a unique challenge on its hands. Young Life had grown to such an extent that it was in danger of diluting its identity through the many names and logos of its different ministries, areas, and camps. Young Life was, in a sense, competing with itself for people's attention through its diffused messaging.

At that point Young Life managed one hundred forty-nine distinct logos (and these were just the official ones!). Terry Swenson, vice president of Communications, said, "Whether I presented our team findings to the board, or senior leadership, or to folks from the field, when I showed the slide revealing forty of our logos in one array, the understanding was instantaneous. The 'ah-has' and moans were audible. In this case forty logos spoke a thousand words."

A new logo was the first step in more clearly communicating Young Life's mission. Its shape formed the familiar "YL," but in a more abstract way than the previous logo, known affectionately as "the bug." The arrows forming the YL, symbolically pointed upward to God and outward to kids; they leaned back toward the mission's past and forward toward its future.

This new logo was the most visible aspect of a much larger "brand identity" system intended to give appropriate visibility to each ministry and location while reinforcing the overall Young Life brand.

The other significant branding change was the new tagline: You were made for this®. When the team working on the new branding process heard the tagline for the first time, the approval was unanimous. It was clearly Young Life.

"The tagline begins with 'you,' just like we do in Young Life as we go to kids, learn their names, and meet them where they are," said Stacy Windahl, a member of the team who helped with the new branding process. "And the phrase, like Young Life, invites people into something bigger, something that is just right for them. It says, 'We hope that your encounter with Young Life attracts you, and draws you closer to the person of Jesus, because we believe all of us were made for this purpose.' "

CONTINUED FAVOR

In 2001, after thirty-nine years of working with Young Life, Vice President of Recruiting, Training, and Deployment Cliff Anderson, observed, "Growth spurts have always been a vital part of our mission, but I can't recall a time when we have had such a clear, missionwide strategic growth initiative in place." To be sure, the late nineties were a tremendous period of growth. The number of outreach ministries almost doubled from 1,606 ministries in 1996 to 3,114 in 2001.

Staff and leaders from Young Life's North Central Texas Region.

Yet, within a mere eight years, the initiative known as Reaching a World of Kids took the best of those previous efforts and further multiplied them into a comprehensive worldwide movement. The goal to reach two million kids in seven years galvanized Young Life, rallying mission leadership and the local area around a Holy Spirit-inspired vision.

In a decade when the mission employed more resources than ever before to care for a hurting world, the love of God compelled mission leadership to continue taking the Gospel out to the farthest reaches. The RWOK initiative would go on well into the next decade, culminating the same year the mission would celebrate its seventy-fifth birthday (2016). The years leading up to this celebration continued to see the Lord rain down His favor upon Young Life.

Coming Together:
All Staff Conferences

A Reflection by Denny Rydberg, president

Staff conferences have existed from the beginning of Young Life. As soon as we had staff, we had staff conferences. The first ones took place in a car—like the regular weekly road trips Jim Rayburn and his fellow leaders took late at night from Houston to Dallas. Jim and his buddies led clubs in Houston and then drove through the night to get back to seminary the next day. The whole staff could fit in a car to pray, evaluate, and learn how to more effectively introduce kids to Jesus Christ.

As the staff grew, these meetings continued as times of prayer, leadership training, fellowship, encouragement, and exhortation. Sometimes well-known speakers from outside Young Life spoke, and always there was the Young Life distinctive of great humor and entertainment. Greg Kinberg, a staff member who served forty-four years before retiring in 2013, recalls the 1960s when Chuck Reinhold left his new area in Rochester, New York, and picked up staff in the next closest areas in Baltimore and Philadelphia on the way to Silver Cliff for a "staff conference." As Greg said, "The times traveling were as good as the conference, and sometimes more adventurous!" Participants in these early staff conferences were photographed together, and there are some memorable pictures on the walls of the Service Center of these staff gatherings in the forties, fifties, and sixties.

In the seventies, staff conferences took on a new look as we gathered the whole staff at Asilomar on the Monterey Peninsula in 1970 and at the Broadmoor in Colorado in 1979. And in 1990, we celebrated fifty years of Young Life with an all staff conference in San Diego.

When I joined Young Life in 1993, I had the firm conviction that we needed to get together on a regular basis to celebrate what God had been doing with us and through us, to enjoy fellow team members and be reminded that we were not alone in the mission, to pray together, and to catch a vision for the future like a coach exhorting his team at halftime. And so, in 1996, our leadership team inaugurated an "every-four-year event." I've been privileged to be a part of five of these, and my sixth will be in 2016 in Orlando, Florida, as we celebrate seventy-five years of Young Life.

The staff conferences have grown and broadened from a few guys in a car late at night in the forties, to a four-day event (with a few pre-conferences and two additional travel days thrown in) attended by five thousand people. From just staff to "staff plus"—with some folks representing our volunteers, committee people, and investors in the mission. From primarily just staff in the U.S. to now international leaders as well. We can't bring every staff and volunteer leader reaching kids outside the U.S. to the conference, but we can give thanks for what they're doing and honor them up close and from a distance. In all of this, we're still doing what Jim did: helping all of us be more effective in introducing kids to Jesus Christ and helping them grow in their faith.

So we come together, worship together (five thousand Young Life voices united in praise is a special experience), hear from great speakers, laugh, cry, pray, play, and celebrate. I'm sure Jim would enjoy this as much as we do.

The 2008 All Staff Conference at the Marriott World Center in Orlando, Florida.

COVER-ING YOUNG LIFE

A look at the mission's magazines throughout the years.

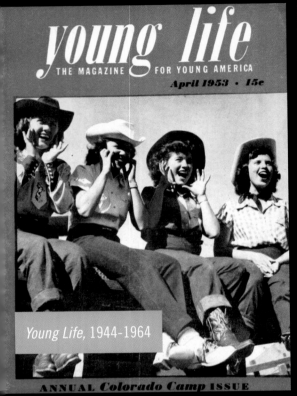

Young Life, 1944-1964

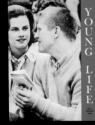

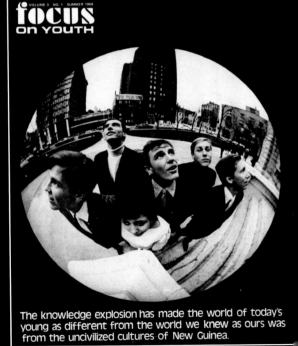

The knowledge explosion has made the world of today's young as different from the world we knew as ours was from the uncivilized cultures of New Guinea.

Focus on Youth, 1967-1975

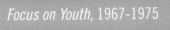

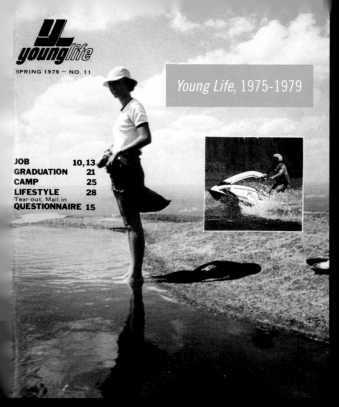

young life

SPRING 1979 — NO. 11

Young Life, 1975-1979

JOB   10, 13
GRADUATION   21
CAMP   25
LIFESTYLE   28
Tear-out, Mail-in
QUESTIONNAIRE   15

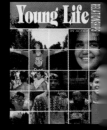

A PICTURE-PERFECT DAY FOR SENIORS NEEDING YEARBOOK PHOTOS

RELATIONSHIPS

Spring 2015 | Vol. 29 Issue 1

TENNESSEE'S
BILL HASLAM
GOVERNING WITH GRATITUDE

FINDING REFUGE AT THE

THIS YEAR'S
ALUMNI AND
FRIENDS
AWARDS

*Relationships,
1987-Present*

the 2010s

The Now and the Not Yet

The second decade of the new millennium picked up where the first left off. Around the world, conflict and terrorism continued making headlines. Technology advanced at breathtaking speed, providing more advances in fields as wide ranging as healthcare, engineering, and personal entertainment. Meanwhile, social media's popularity and influence grew to unprecedented heights—in 2014, Twitter had 255 million users who collectively sent 500 million tweets each day; there were more than 1.35 billion monthly active Facebook users and 50 million pages; and 20 billion photos were uploaded to Instagram.

In the midst of this dizzying array of cultural and technological news, a world of kids still needed to hear about Jesus. Young Life entered its eighth decade more positioned and prepared to respond than ever before.

The year 2010 found the mission—as well as the rest of the world—emerging from the worst economic decline since the Great Depression. The financial instability was unsettling to many staff and threatened to derail the progress the mission was making in the Reaching a World of Kids initiative. In the midst of "the Great Recession" and its aftermath, however, the opposite occurred. Donors continued to give faithfully and sacrificially to the work, which was stronger than ever and thriving in many new clubs, areas, cities, and countries. Young Life had never known such great expansion. The Lord had continued to give a grateful mission grace and favor in the eyes of many.

As Young Life neared its seventy-fifth birthday, the mission's growth became more "reciprocal." Local area growth influenced other parts of the mission, most notably, camping, which adapted to accommodate the growing numbers of campers. In turn, when kids returned home from camp having begun a relationship with the Savior, their excitement helped spur on even more local growth.

ALL KINDS OF CAMPING FOR ALL KINDS OF KIDS

The first half of the mission's eighth decade witnessed the need for more Young Life camps as the Reaching a World of Kids initiative continued to explode. The years 2010-2015 marked a time when the mission met this need in various ways. From developing traditional camps to providing specialty weeks to finding alternative sites, Young Life left "no stone unturned" in offering kids the opportunity to enjoy the greatest week of their lives.

Opposite: Poolesville, Maryland, kids "embody" the Young Life logo, 2013.

2010s
Notable greats from 1941 still going strong!

March 1   Captain America appears in comic books
May 1   Cheerios cereal is introduced as CheeriOats
May 1   *Citizen Kane*, hailed by many as the greatest movie of all time, premieres
May 12   World's first programmable, fully automatic computer introduced in Berlin
July 1   NBC television begins /The world's first TV commercial for Bulova watches airs
July 17   Joe DiMaggio's fifty-six-game hitting streak ends (and the record remains unbroken)
Aug. 1   First U.S. Army Jeep produced
OCT. 16 **YOUNG LIFE INCORPORATED**
Oct. 31 Mt. Rushmore completed

CAMP ON WHEELS

From the very start, bringing kids to camp had been a part of the mission's DNA. Years before there was a "Young Life" or even Young Life camps, Jim Rayburn took kids out into the wilderness to experience adventure and fun and introduce them to the Creator.

Over the many years the process continued until 2013, when Young Life flipped the idea on its head and brought *camp to kids!*

That was the year the mission introduced Camp On Wheels, Young Life's brand new mobile camping operation. All the fun supplies that could fit (tents, inflatables, games, and more) were loaded into a trailer that Young Life staff and volunteers could drive all over Central America.

In 2013, Camp On Wheels traveled to more than twenty-two locations in five Central American countries (Costa Rica, El Salvador, Honduras, Nicaragua, and Panama). The program proved to be the perfect "vehicle" for weeklong camps, day camps, and all-city clubs. More than seven hundred kids came out to the first Camp On Wheels club in San Jose, Costa Rica. One year later, a second Camp On Wheels was deployed on the African continent in the country of Zimbabwe.

Once again the mission was living out the incarnational principle to serve kids by meeting them where they were. By bringing the fun to them, some kids who faced substantial challenges in life could now experience a Young Life camping experience. Whether they were kids from poor neighborhoods, kids with disabilities, teen moms, or others with the odds stacked against them, the time spent here proved life-changing for many.

Costa Rican kids outside the Camp On Wheels tent.

CAROLINA POINT

During the nineties, it became increasingly clear the mission would need another camp in the southeastern part of the U.S. In fewer than twenty years—from 1990 through 2009—attendance at southeast camps had increased by more than 300 percent. The summer of 2009 witnessed 16,723 kids attending one of Young Life's three camps in the region, an 84 percent increase over the 9,100 kids who attended in 2000.

Relief came in Brevard, North Carolina, a small town on the border of North and South Carolina. Here, businessman Jim Anthony purchased land to begin building a camp where young people might consider life's biggest questions in the context of the Christian faith. In 2001, when Anthony learned of Young Life and its rich history of camping, he graciously donated the site to the mission.

Chuck Scott, campaign director for the new camp, helped lead the charge, and after several years of development and construction, Carolina Point was completely accessible to all campers, including kids with disabilities, by including features like wider sidewalks, built-in ramps, and automatic doors, as well as a zero-entry pool.

The newest Young Life camp offered every kid another place made especially for them, where they could encounter Jesus. John Vicary, executive vice president of U.S. Ministries, was there to witness the very first camper in Carolina Point's history:

"On June 30, 2013, she stepped off the bus with no idea what she represented. Of course, there was the usual line of work crew kids singing and cheering her on as she walked through the gauntlet giving high-fives with every step. I was there with my wife, Carol, and forty to fifty other field staff, camp staff, and donors who didn't want to miss this moment. If this girl would have looked closely, she would have seen a tear in every eye because of who she represented—kids we had been praying for . . . for years. At the end of that historic first week, she caused more tears as she stood with more than forty-five others to say, 'This week, I began a relationship with Jesus Christ.' Holy ground."

Clearwater Cove

At the turn of the century, six camps lined the eastern U.S.; nine more lay from the West Coast to Colorado, while Michigan and Minnesota boasted another two. This left a glaring void in the middle of the country, a geographically strategic location for serving kids from many states.

The mission began an extensive search for property in the Ozark Mountains, specifically in the region of southwestern Missouri. In 2000, Young Life purchased two hundred sixty-eight acres along Table Rock Lake within the Mark Twain National Forest. Named Clearwater Cove, the new site was situated within a six- to twelve-hour drive from a dozen major metropolitan areas including Chicago, Houston, Nashville, and Denver.

Table Rock Lake is considered one of the most beautiful man-made lakes in the mid-South. Clearwater Cove sits on more than a mile of the lake's scenic shoreline, which provides the perfect setting for activities such as water-skiing, parasailing, kayaking, swimming, and fishing. The surrounding hills are ideal for hiking, rock climbing, and rappelling.

During Clearwater Cove's development, areas in the Missouri Gateway Region used the camp for leadership retreats, work camps, and other small group activities. In the summer of 2014, Young Life broke ground for The Landing, a dining hall and multipurpose building, which sits in the heart of camp. Clearwater Cove opened in the fall of 2015, and Young Life areas from all over the central U.S. gave thanks for a camp sitting in the heart of the heartland.

A NEW CAMP IN ARMENIA

Like the story of Washington Family Ranch in the nineties, God again took a camp once enveloped in darkness and redeemed it into a place that would speak of His wondrous love.

In 1991 the Soviet Union collapsed and Armenia officially won its independence. Armenians longed to fill the spiritual void resulting from seventy years of Communist rule. The country had warmed to outside influences, and in 1998, Young Life officially entered Armenia.

The next decade witnessed great strides in the work there, so much so that kids and leaders willingly camped in crowded facilities and tents to experience a week of Young Life camp. By the summer of 2013, approximately twenty-one hundred campers and leaders attended camp somewhere in Armenia; the time was right for Young Life to move ahead with its first camp there.

One hour and fifteen minutes north of Yerevan, the capital and largest city of Armenia, lay a youth camp that had been abandoned for two decades. The description "youth camp," however, is where the similarities with Young Life ended. This was a Young Pioneer camp for kids between the ages of ten and seventeen. Akin to a "Communist Boy and Girl Scouts organization," Young Pioneers was designed to grow and replicate good communist party members. With communism extinguished in Armenia, the camp was no longer of use—at least for that purpose.

Located on almost nine and a half acres with existing buildings that could be repurposed, the Armenian Young Life camp would house more than double the number of campers from previous summers. This was good news for every kid,

because like the other countries from the Former Soviet Union, Armenia had a large population of orphans and kids with special needs. The camp would accommodate them, and in the process, proclaim to these dear kids their great worth in God's eyes.

The new camp would also be a catalyst for sustained growth in Armenia, and potentially open doors into the nearby countries of Georgia, Iran, and Turkey.

Looking forward, looking back: above, the design for the new camp in Armenia; right, kids in the former Communist "Young Pioneer" camp.

Gary Parsons, Young Life's senior vice president of the Russia/Former Soviet Union Division, was ecstatic about the potential. "The camp, located at the doorstep of the Middle East, is destined to be one of the most significant camping ministries in all of Young Life."

CREATIVE CAMPS

Young Life staff and volunteers are willing to go to any lengths to reach kids. In some places, traditional camping is not feasible nor accessible, and in these situations the adaptability, and often fearlessness, of the leaders shines through. Their ability to tailor a camp to the needs and interests of kids is second to none. A small sampling of this creativity could be found just about anywhere:

- **Kyrgyzstan**—Kids painted all day and heard stories about Jesus at night at Graffiti (!) camp, perhaps Young Life's first such endeavor.

- **Portugal**—Young Life staff created surf camp, on the shores of the Atlantic just north of Lisbon.

- **Germany, Northern Asia**—Staff held English camps where thousands attended day camps or virtual camps to learn the English language, as well as the language of God's love.

- **Jamaica**—Young Life Expeditions teams ran annual orphan camps for kids outside of Montego Bay.

- **Balkans, Greece, Turkey, etc.**—Eastern and Western European kids from Young Life and Club Beyond participated in weeklong service projects, helping those less fortunate, while experiencing a week of camp.

The mission also created camping experiences for those in the midst of overwhelming crisis. In Western Africa during the 2014 Ebola outbreak, staff held the first of several camps for Ebola survivors. The time was life-changing for the 117 survivors in attendance. Steve Larmey, senior vice president of the Africa Division, shared accounts from this historic time:

"Decontee Davis, one of our Developing Global Leaders who herself barely survived the virus, was one of the campers. 'This was unbelievable. For the first time in months we felt like we belonged. The Young Life team slept right next to us and ate with us and hugged us—nobody does that. Walls of stigma were broken down and we were able to let go of pain and hate, and forgive.'

"Many of the survivors said the same things: 'Now I have hope.' 'I can't believe people love us and touched us and served us.' 'I have not laughed in a long time.' 'My life is starting over.' But the most common response was, 'I have a new family. Young Life has given me a family.' One camper, Cecelia, lost over twenty family members to Ebola. 'Young Life is my family now,' she said through tears at the Say-So.

"Of the 117 survivors, seventy-six stood up and declared that they wanted to follow Jesus."

GREAT REPORTS!

As Young Life camping continued to expand internationally, the kids' responses were overwhelmingly positive. Summer after summer, reports flooded in about how kids were reveling in the greatest week of their lives. In a 2012 newsletter from camp, Tate Johnson, associate regional director in the U.K., who was serving at Lake Champion, told of two kids at the hot tub reliving the events of the previous night:

"I overheard them say, 'Last night was amazing. I thought it was over after the funny skits. Then there was the dance party, and I thought it couldn't get any better. Then there was the pool party. And I thought, yeah, and then there were these amazing fireworks.' Another camper told the leaders, 'That was the best three hours of my life!' What an awesome statement. All wholesome and guilt-free."

The fun went hand in hand with the message: There is a God who loves you and is calling you to be in relationship with Him. Worldwide, kids like "Selena" longed to hear this

A work camp in Macedonia; kids enjoy experiences designed just for them like Graffiti camp in Kyrgyzstan.

CAIRN BRAE AT LOCH MONZIEVAIRD

In 2008, longtime staff member Randy Nickel met Don Stephens, the founder and president of Mercy Ships, a ministry that converts retired cruise ships into floating hospitals. As the two spoke, Stephens declared that Young Life was his favorite organization in America and both his daughters had met Christ through Young Life.

Stephens asked Nickel what he was currently working on. "I told him I've been in Kenya and I'm transitioning to Scotland," Nickel said. "When I said that, his jaw dropped. He said, 'Well the chair of our board is a woman named Ann Gloag. She has an adopted child from Kenya, lives in Scotland, and you need to meet her.'"

While he established the ministry in Scotland, Nickel did in fact connect with Gloag, who in 2009 was given the Susan B. Anthony Humanitarian Award for her charitable work in Europe and Africa. As she learned more about Young Life, she longed for her grandkids and nephew to discover Young Life, too. The next summer they were part of eight kids from Perth who spent a week at Lake Champion, where many gave their lives to Christ.

Once he was back in Scotland, Gloag's nephew Calum Souter learned that thirty acres of lakefront property, which sat next to their estate, was up for sale. (With a history dating back to the second century, Loch Monzievaird had most recently served as a vacation destination offering holiday cottages.) Calum told his dad the property reminded him of Lake Champion and that their family "should help Randy." His idea? "We need to buy this so it can be a Young Life camp!"

Calum's parents, Sir Brian and Lady Souter, embraced their son's idea, told Nickel the story, and encouraged him to check out the property. "I couldn't believe this was happening," Nickel exclaimed. "I went over to look at the property. There were twenty-four stunningly beautiful three-bedroom cabins sitting on this incredible lake. I was overwhelmed."

The Souter Charitable Trust, which had financially supported Young Life Scotland in the past, purchased the property, with the plan to lease it long term to Young Life for one pound a year. Following this generous gift, Gloag told Nickel she wanted to help with the cost of renovating the property.

"This seven-year story," Nickel said, "goes back to Don Stephens, who didn't know me but trusted Young Life because of how it touched his daughters in Texas. He trusted me enough to introduce me to Ann Gloag. But the story goes back even further to the area director in Texas who reached out to Don's daughters, which has opened doors for me all over Scotland."

Young Life's camp in Scotland opened in 2015—an answer to one teenager's dream that would ultimately bless kids throughout Western Europe.

greatest of news. Marty McCarty, vice president of Young Life Military, wrote about her story:

"This summer, twenty Air Force kids from Spangdahlem, Germany, joined more than four hundred other military kids and adults from all over Europe in a service project trip to Romania. One of them, Selena (not her real name), informed her leader at the trip outset that she doesn't like to be told what to do and won't do anything during the week she doesn't want to do. She also said she doesn't like to be touched. On night three, the speaker was talking about secrets and the need to be real and honest. When Selena got back to her tent, she collapsed on the floor . . . sobbing. Her leaders realized she just needed someone to be near her so she wasn't alone while she cried. They just sat and cried together. In the weeks since, Selena has been a constant at Campaigners. She eventually explained why she doesn't like to be touched. 'It's not because I don't like the feeling of being held on to; it's because I don't like the feeling of being let go. I'm so tired of saying goodbye.' She desperately needed to find the one thing that will truly never let her go, the unchanging love of Jesus Christ. Young Life was made for military kids like Selena."

At the end of each camp week, it was common to witness great numbers of kids like Selena respond positively to the Gospel. Before these kids climbed back on their buses to return home, staff and leaders shared with them what a new life in Christ looks like. Often this was done on what was called the "New Believer's Walk." John Vicary, executive vice president of U.S. Ministries, shared what happened on one such camp week at SharpTop Cove:

"The New Believer's Walk on Day Seven is for those who have just begun a new relationship with Jesus Christ that week. Their guided walk ends at the bridge where they hear again about the bridge Jesus provided so we now have access to God. Once on the bridge, they all take a small rock and throw it into the pond to symbolize their old lives being dead and gone forever. On this particular week, however, they weren't able to let everyone throw their rocks, because there were so many kids, the bridge started to sink! Thank the Lord it didn't. It's not the lasting image and memory we want them to have about stepping on the bridge that Jesus has made for them, but what a great picture of what God did in the lives of kids this summer and this year!"

THE BEAUTIFUL SIMPLICITY OF THE GOSPEL

The 2012 All Staff Conference Celebration, the fifth under Denny Rydberg's tenure, offered the nearly four thousand staff and friends of Young Life a time filled with laughter, worship, rest, a renewed call, and poignant reminders of why they pursue lost kids.

One reminder came in the person of Michael Crofton, a Young Life Capernaum friend. Taking center stage with Mike "Ash" Ashburn, special assistant to the president, who on that day became temporary special assistant to Michael, the young man with Down syndrome captured hearts through his story and humor. As his time in the spotlight concluded, Michael gave perhaps the shortest club talk in the history of Young Life:

> *"Jesus suffered.*
> *He died for you.*
> *On the third day, He arose.*
> *He wants to be in your heart."*

Michael received a standing ovation.

Mike Ashburn and Michael Crofton at the 2012 All Staff Conference.

SHARING OWNERSHIP

Reaching a world of kids did not mean having to reinvent Young Life. Flashy new formulas and sleeker programs were not needed to carry out this Spirit-inspired vision. What was essential, however, was reliance upon the foundations, which had always served the mission well: an unwavering focus on Jesus, a dependence upon prayer, and an emphasis on relationships. These would continue to be the clarion call for a mission seeking to double its reach.

One way to accomplish this was by further giving away this vision to the kids already involved in club and Campaigners. Allowing kids to have more ownership renewed the vitality of the ministry.

Brian Summerall, Young Life director of ministry strategy, led this charge by training staff and volunteers throughout the U.S. on how to help kids take responsibility and leadership in their clubs. Summerall understood the challenges many leaders had faced through the years and the doubts that may have crept in about Young Life's effectiveness in the modern day. "Over my twenty-nine years of involvement," Summerall said, "I fear sometimes we all have given in to myths and simple untruths . . .

- Today's kids don't like to get together in large groups anymore.

- Young Life club no longer works, and we have to do something different.

- What works in one part of the country won't work in another.

- There's no way more than one hundred kids from our school can show up to Young Life club every week.

- Adults are too busy today to give up ten-plus hours a week so kids will hear about Jesus.

- In a bad economy, Young Life can't double the number of kids it reaches."

The Young Life Welcome Center
After several years of dreaming, concepting, and refining plans, the Young Life Welcome Center (located in the Service Center in Colorado Springs) opened in 2012. The project was a gift from friends of the mission whose company, Exhibit House, designed, built, shipped, and installed all of the display elements at no charge to the mission. The new space welcomes visitors and staff to the building and engagingly shares the vision and mission of Young Life.

But the mission, he continued, "is busting myths and charting a new course previously thought to be unattainable. I've seen clubs across the country more than double and triple in size. I've been from New York to Alaska and Hawaii and learned that regardless of geography, kids really were made for this. I am convinced the million kids we are reaching now already know the next million kids we will reach. Once our kids are given a vision and a challenge, I have no doubt they can reach them."

"What Brian does is both simple and profound," Rydberg said. "He travels across the country helping leaders understand how to build and sustain a robust club. Regions who have been involved with him have seen an increase of 29 percent in number of kids coming to club. Amazing!"

Young Life continued to serve as a comfort to those in the theater of war, just as it had in its previous seven decades. Here in 2012, Anthony Fernandez, deployed with the Oklahoma National Guard, proudly displays a Young Life banner in Afghanistan. About life in the war-torn country, Fernandez said, "I see a lot of teenagers and think, 'What a cool place [it would be] to start Young Life.'" The mission thanks Anthony Fernandez and the thousands of alumni who serve their country so sacrificially in the Armed Forces.

GROWING DEEP

In the United States, Reaching a World of Kids helped the mission connect with more kids through its longest-running ministry: traditional high school work. In 2009 there were 649,437 kids involved in Young Life club; by 2015 that number was 842,987. During that same period, the number of high school ministries also increased from 2,381 to 2,796.

Discipleship was flourishing too. Over the course of those six years, weekly Campaigners attendance expanded from an average of 42,331 to 66,804. Outside the U.S., the weekly attendance grew from 8,978 in 2009 to 33, 299, thereby doubling Campaigners numbers from 51,309 kids attending every week to 100,103. More kids than ever were learning the timeless truths of what a relationship with Jesus offers and how to put that into practice.

GROWING WIDE

While the traditional work was deepening, the mission was also reaching more kinds of kids than ever before through its various ministries. Three of the ministries experiencing explosive growth were Young*Lives*, Capernaum, and Young Life College.

● Young*Lives*

In 2011, Young*Lives* celebrated its twenty-year anniversary, and by this point the ministry was growing at a rate of 25 percent annually in both number of ministries and camping.

Lindsey Patchell, vice president, who led Young*Lives* in this explosive and healthy growth, was quick to acknowledge the strong team she was supervising. "In 2014 Young*Lives* impacted close to fourteen thousand teen moms plus their children," Patchell said. "More than sixteen hundred volunteers made this happen."

The year also marked the sixth consecutive year of camp growth as nearly twenty-six hundred kids attended one of the seven weeks of Young*Lives* camps.

"It gets even better," she continued. "More than one thousand teen moms are currently being discipled in Young*Lives*. These ladies are going on to do stunning work: starting new Young*Lives* ministries, serving on work crew, summer staff, and as childcare volunteers, graduating from high school and college, and raising their children to love God."

Capernaum

The year 2011 also marked the twenty-fifth anniversary of Capernaum. Nick Palermo, the founding executive director of Capernaum, reflected upon the surge of growth the ministry had recently seen. "With Capernaum, I feel like we're reading the book of Acts—it's a Holy Spirit wave. In 1986, there was one ministry, and for fourteen years we consisted of five. But from 2000 through 2010, we've gone from five ministries to 148 in fourteen countries."

In 2005 the Capernaum Board and Palermo invited Pam Harmon to join him in leading the ministry. The pair co-led for nearly a decade, during which time the Lord continued to raise up an amazing team of board members and divisional coordinators who prayed and advocated for kids with disabilities.

By 2015, the number of ministries had grown to two hundred fifty. Harmon, who was named the vice president of Capernaum that same year, emphasized the critical addition of leaders. "It's just amazing how we've grown from having one leader for every six to seven kids to one leader for every two. This means our Capernaum friends are receiving individual attention and really making friends."

"We've also doubled in the number of Campaigners we have meeting," she said, "which shows our staff and leaders believe young people with cognitive challenges can grow in their relationships with Jesus. We are committed to ministry 'with' people with disabilities."

Young*Lives* mentors, moms, and babies at Lost Canyon.

Young Life College

In 2015 Young Life College celebrated ten years of ministry, a surprising accomplishment to some in the mission. During the early days of the movement, Mike Gaffney, then mission director of the new initiative, heard people comment on several occasions, "I wonder how long before people are asking, whatever happened to 'that college thing'?"

The numbers bore out the important place Young Life College now had in the mission. By 2015, there were one hundred seventy teams of leaders on over two hundred campuses in twelve countries, impacting over seventy thousand college and university students' lives. These were not just high school alumni "re-enlisting" with Young Life on a college campus. Sixty percent of students involved in Young Life College had no prior Young Life experience.

Another delighted Capernaum camper arrives to raucous cheers at Young Life camp. Capernaum celebrated its twenty-fifth anniversary in 2011.

During the ministry's first decade, Gaffney made another important discovery—Young Life College provided a powerful platform for the mission's older staff. "Did you know that 41 percent of Young Life College directors are over the age of forty-one?" Gaffney asked. "In case you're wondering, 21 percent of all other area directors are over forty-one."

A decade later Gaffney, who had since become vice president of Young Life College, wrote in *Monday Morning*, "We are happy to report that the 'college thing' is still around and has clearly moved from an initiative to an essential part of the family of Young Life."

FINDING FAVOR AROUND THE WORLD
In order to fulfill the promise of "Reaching a World of Kids," the mission would have to grow internationally, and to the delight of all, Young Life continued to find favor with kids in countries around the globe.

Lee Corder, senior vice president of the International North Division, said, "The remarkable discovery so many of us are making on the international front is that those often-presumed mission values at the heart of our Young Life experience work virtually everywhere around the world. As we learn to walk alongside young people, 'move into their neighborhood,' engage them relationally, serve them compassionately, and lift up Jesus when the opportunity is 'right,' hearts and lives open up from Northern Asia to western Canada, from Moscow to Madagascar. And these themes of relational ministry come in as many frameworks as there are individual leaders, each expressing those gifts in unique expressions.

Friends of Young Life "climb for change" as they trek up Mt. Kilimanjaro.

"In a large Asian country, a young student who has been loved by a volunteer from the United States, asks, 'Why do your eyes and heart match?' and comes to discover the Jesus within who is the answer. In an unnamed country in Central Asia, heroic Young Life leaders were arrested and jailed just days ago because they had been so effective in loving kids that a Bible study (forbidden by local law) had broken out. Or in Spain, a thirty-year missionary veteran points at our phenomenal leaders gathered for training and says with tears in his eyes, 'You don't get it; you don't know what you are seeing; that just doesn't happen here.' "

The names and faces may have been different, but the same excitement abounded in countries far and wide . . .

● The United Kingdom and Ireland
As the decade began, Tim Keller, pastor of Redeemer Church in New York City and best-selling author, observed, "I can think of nowhere on the planet more spiritually needy than the post-modern, post-Christian United Kingdom and Ireland, and I can think of no better organization to reach the teenagers in those five countries than Young Life—because Young Life's strategy is the strategy of Jesus. Young Life goes to kids where they are, engages them in their world, loves them in His name, and earns the right to tell them about Jesus."

The need-and-response was observed firsthand by one Scottish pastor as he visited the Young Life summer camp in Scotland. The pastor commented, "From the moment I first heard of the weeklong outreach in the southeast of Edinburgh, being led by a group of American missionaries from an organization called 'Young Life,' I began to see and sense a feeling of excitement growing within my heart and soul. Our time together was the most fantastic week of mission and evangelism I have yet experienced among the youth in Scotland in my life. More than twenty-three years ago I became a Christian, and I have been a pastor for thirteen years. Over these years I have seen fewer and fewer teens coming to faith in Christ. However, in just five or six days I witnessed a team that was in total unity arrive, become friends with the Scottish volunteers, and then under the American leadership we took this mission to the kids and gave them an incredible week filled with laughter, excitement, sports, and adventure that I would have scarcely believed possible. From the word 'go' until the last prayer on Friday night, these kids were enthralled and caught up in the work of the Spirit and the Word of God through testimony, games, comedy, and preaching."

● Tanzania
Young Life Africa organized its first hike up Mt. Kilimanjaro in 2006. Modeled after previous prayer

Hunter Lambeth makes new friends at the Separation Wall in Bethlehem, laughs with kids at the first-ever Middle East Young Life camp, and joins hands in solidarity with Yousef Khalil, the first Palestinian Young Life staff director, at the 2012 All Staff Conference.

walks by other groups, hundreds of Young Life leaders and friends of the work in Africa would walk and pray as they ascended to the 19,341-foot summit. Over the course of the next decade, the annual trips earned the name "Climb for Change" and became a way to benefit African kids by helping them attend camp.

By 2014 there was ministry in twenty-one countries throughout Africa with thousands of kids participating. The Young Life Africa staff declared this the "Year of Freedom." That summer they embarked upon a "Freedom Walk" that traced the exact route across the entire country of Tanzania— the old East Africa slave caravan route—a trail of blood and tears walked by as many as fifteen million Africans in shackles on their way to a life in slavery.

The 1,400-kilometer (about 932 miles) trek allowed staff, leaders, and supporters to minister to those they met along the way. The aim was simple, Steve Larmey, senior vice president of Young Life Africa, explained. "We will walk that same trail releasing the presence and power of God, breaking chains and declaring freedom, and looking for men and women who will want to be Young Life leaders in every town and village along this route."

The results were more than Larmey and the other leaders could have dreamed. "We found leaders, we've begun clubs, and we'll follow up," he said. "We hope to have a new ministry

in every major town we walked through. That's the work that's yet to be done."

Denny Rydberg, who participated in part of the journey along with his wife, Marilyn, and many others from around the world, understood what the walk meant to not only the country of Tanzania, but to the entire mission. "The Freedom Walk is much bigger than just Africa. We have people all over the country and in the U.S. who are participating in the Freedom Walk. Africa is the fastest-growing part of Young Life. We've had tremendous growth everywhere, but in Africa it's been absolutely off the charts."

● Middle East
In 2011, Young Life's seventieth year, work officially began in the homeland of Jesus Himself, as the mission celebrated the first-ever Middle East Young Life camp, held on the shores of the Dead Sea.

On July 8, 2011, Hunter Lambeth led fifty-one Arabic-speaking Palestinian campers and fifteen leaders from Bethlehem and Zababdeh, as well as a seven-member assigned team/work crew from areas in Georgia, Arizona, Nevada, and Texas.

"Each kid was presented with an Arabic New Testament after the final club," Lambeth said. "There were many highlights, but one that stands above the others was the final night of

younglife.

TWEETS	FOLLOWING	FOLLOWERS	FAVORITES	LISTS
2,237	1,675	39.2K	10.6K	1

"Young Life leaders have always been in the world of kids, speaking their language, so we can share the truth with them," said Josh Griffin, Young Life's senior director of Strategic Services. "Our efforts on social media are one more extension of a seventy-five-year-old principle."

Young Life's "social media" in the early days consisted solely of kids' responses to the latest edition of *Young Life* magazine:

> *"I've been reading Young Life for some time now and I think it's very good. My shipmates enjoy reading it as much as I do."—Charles, A/S U.S.S. Helena*

> *"I think 'Say, Gang' is swell. I feel I can hear Jim as he is talking."—Sara, Tulsa, Oklahoma*

By 2015, Young Life's social media presence was flourishing. Between mentions on Facebook, Twitter, Pinterest, Instagram, and other social media, the mission engaged in the give-and-take available in the "Social Media Age."

> *"Beyond excited to drink coffee, laugh a lot, and talk about Jesus with my @YoungLife girls in the morning. Nothing compares to Wed mornings."—Kay*

> *"@YoungLife has shown me the true love of God and I'm so beyond thankful for that."—Trevin*

Another exciting development was the new delivery system for Camp Video Scrapbooks. By 2012, kids returning from Young Life camp could now see highlights from their time by simply going online to scrapbook. younglife.org. Every week from every camp was available for kids, who now had free access to reliving the memories from the greatest week of their lives.

camp when we held club in the city of ancient Jericho, on the side of the Mount of Temptation, the traditional backdrop. We talked about the fact that in that very spot some two thousand years ago, Jesus' love for us and His determination to reconcile us to the Father gave Him the strength to resist the devil, allowing us the opportunity on this night to respond with our very lives."

The Lambeth family sensed the Lord's call and after much prayer, moved to Nazareth in September of 2012. Within one year Lambeth and his wife, Lauri, along with the help of local volunteers, had established three clubs, one in Israel and two in Palestine. By 2015, they had ministry among Jewish kids, as well as Young Life College and Capernaum ministries among kids from Islamic backgrounds.

The ultimate hope for the ministry was that it would slowly break down the centuries-old walls between the people of Israel and Palestine. Nowhere was this hope more poignantly demonstrated than at the All Staff Conference in 2012, where a new member was welcomed to the team.

"We placed the flags of Israel and Palestine together on stage as we commissioned Yousef Khalil as our first Palestinian Young Life staff director," said Marty Caldwell, executive vice president of International Ministries. "Yousef said he has lived all of his life with those two flags but had never seen them together. The power of the moment moved all of us to tears, but none more so than Yousef."

● Canada

In 2012 Mike O'Leary and his wife, Carol, made their third move in thirty-three years of being on Young Life staff. O'Leary had most recently served as a senior leader in the mission and as a consultant with different entities in Young Life, including Young Life Military ministry. The latest move for the couple was to the "Great White North" where he became the national director of Young Life of Canada. The move was celebrated by Young Life leadership in the U.S. and Canada, both of whom were delighted at the continued synergy between the two organizations.

Two years later, Young Life of Canada celebrated sixty years of ministry, with more than eighty full-time staff working in four provinces across fifty communities.

● New York City

For more than half a century, caring adults had worked with teenagers in "the city that never sleeps." By 2012, Bo Nixon and his wife, Mary, were still working on the Lower East Side, faithfully loving kids in that community since the 1960s. Their faithfulness paved the way for others to come—leaders like Paul Coty and John Wagner, two staff veterans who yearned to reach the 3.1 million kids in and around the city.

During the spring of 2006, Coty and the Young Life team prayed from the roof of a local church. "The rooftop allowed us a full view of the entire city. As committee, staff, and

Paul Coty on a rooftop in New York City.

The Future of Young Life

A Reflection by Denny Rydberg, president

Futurists have a short shelf life. People listen to them pontificate and then often laugh at them later. I enjoyed what Jeff Chesemore, the author of this book, included from 1965 on what we thought we in Young Life might face after hearing futuristic predictions. "Population predictions are frightening. Can you visualize high schools in the form of skyscrapers in order to handle the crowds in the year 1990? Will Young Life still be conducting clubs in homes? Will our present beautiful camp sites be gobbled up for living space? We face these prospects confident that God will give wisdom to keep pace with the changes that occur."

I'm not a futurist. I'm not a prophet. I won't even attempt to define any specifics on what Young Life will face. I won't mention high school high rises, or clubs that are homeless, or camp sites gobbled up for living space. But let me give some general bullet points on what I think the future holds.

- **Hopeful.** I believe that until Jesus returns, He will give us grace and favor in reaching kids. But this statement comes with a caveat. There have been many great missions who have lost their way and either no longer exist or are a shell of their former selves. I am hopeful as long as Young Life stays true to who we are. We are centered on Jesus Christ. We proclaim Him passionately, fearlessly, and winsomely. We pursue lost kids. We go where kids are. We win the right to be heard. We know it's a sin to bore a kid with the Gospel. We know kids and because we spend so much time with them, we can make mid-course adjustments in how we reach them. As long as we stay true to whom God has called us to be, I am hopeful.

- **Wary.** I believe it will be tougher in our society to have the freedom to share the Gospel. I'm not a "doom and gloom" person. But as I see culture change, I am convinced that we may not have access to kids like we have now, and we may have interference from certain groups. But the good news is that God is in charge and for centuries, followers of Jesus have been faithful despite the outward circumstances or cultural climate.

- **Needy.** Soon, we will be impacting more kids internationally than we are in the U.S. That makes sense, of course; there are many more kids living outside the U.S. than inside, and God has called us to "go into all the world." We have been able to find the leaders we need around the globe. But many of these nations are poor or have not yet become a culture of givers. In the future, we will need additional financial resources in the millions and millions of dollars to reach more millions of kids. We will need more people and more money. And, it is my guess, that even though funds will come from many countries, the bulk of the resources will come from the U.S. We will be needy, but we will be confident. We will give investors opportunities, and they will respond generously and the work will continue to explode.

- **Thankful.** We will be overjoyed with grateful hearts for God's goodness in the future in providing staff, volunteer leaders, committee people (but we may not call them "committees" years from now), and donors/investors. We will be grateful that God has chosen to use us. We will be ecstatic as we see lost kids meet Jesus, grow in their faith, and share the Good News with others.

I am bullish about the future. I am excited about what will happen in and through Young Life in the years ahead. I am absolutely confident that the best Young Life is yet to be done.

volunteers prayed, the Lord gave me a vision of the city's kids coming to the feet of Jesus and then transforming the communities where they live. My prayer was, 'Lord give me the kids and don't move me until You allow me to see both the transformed and those transforming.'" Five years later Coty was thrilled to be joined by a kindred spirit, Wagner, who moved to the city in a brand-new role for the mission: senior vice president for the Greater New York Division.

Wagner understood the immensity of the challenge facing the work in New York. "It's been said Manhattan is 'the island where the world came to live.' I have also heard that within a twenty-five-mile radius of the Empire State building, there are twenty-one million people. Twenty-one million! That's a big club."

This "big club" required many leaders, and the Lord generously brought them to the work.

Over the Labor Day weekend of 2013, three hundred fifty staff and leaders gathered together for the city's Third-Annual Leadership Weekend. "It was unbelievable," Wagner said. "Someone remarked to me, 'You won't see a gathering like this anywhere else in the world.' Asian, African-American, African, Latino, Caucasian—it really was the gathering of 'all nations.'"

By the autumn of 2014—just one year later—the growth continued to flourish. The number of staff and volunteers in the Greater New York Division had nearly doubled, as seventy-two staff, five hundred fifty volunteer leaders, and three hundred fifty-seven adults involved on committees or in ministry support were part of the ministry.

"But maybe the most overwhelming part," Wagner remarked, "is not the number of people, but the quality. They are amazing. I would want any one of them to be my kids' Young Life leader. They are strong, courageous, called, and ready."

There was still so much to be done in the city, but there was no denying that the work begun more than five decades earlier continued on in the grandest of traditions. In a place lovingly referred to as "Gotham City" and "Metropolis," the real superheroes were those caring men and women faithfully going to kids and introducing them to the only One who always "saves the day."

WHAT A DIFFERENCE SEVENTY-FIVE YEARS MAKES!
The growth in New York was emblematic of Young Life's growth throughout the world. The number of adults involved in the mission had come a long way over seven decades. In 1940 it was not hard to "call roll" when the work consisted

Young Life staff take over Sea World for a night during the 2012 conference.

of five staff (Jim Rayburn, Gordon Whitelock, Add Sewell, Wally Howard, and George Cowan), and a three-man board of directors (John E. Mitchell, Dr. Lewis Chafer, and Ted Benson). These eight men unknowingly paved the way for the thousands who would follow in their humble footsteps.

Fast forward to 2015. If the mission were to assemble everyone involved in the work, they would fill to overflowing Soldier Field, the stadium that's home to the Chicago Bears. Young Life is made up of 4,609 staff; 42,591 volunteers; 12,584 committee and ministry support members, and a 27-person Board of Trustees. Every day, these men and women are involved in ministry to 1.9 million kids in ninety-five countries, from Argentina to Zimbabwe.

The current growth puts the mission in a promising position for the future. "As we near the close of the Reaching a World of Kids initiative, there's an incredible sense of momentum," declared Josh Griffin, Young Life's director of Marketing and Strategic Initiatives. "Not only are we poised to reach two million kids a year, the Lord is prompting us to push forward, to go into more countries and schools, to take kids deeper in Christ, and to do the best Young Life yet. So we're preparing a new plan to take us through 2020. It's the next, natural step of faith for the mission."

The more things change, the more they stay the same.

THE BEST YOUNG LIFE WORK

On its twenty-fifth anniversary, Young Life produced a booklet looking at the past, present, and future of the mission. As the authors of the 1965 piece speculated about the upcoming twenty-five years, these were some of their musings . . .

"Population predictions are frightening. Can you visualize high schools in the form of skyscrapers in order to handle the crowds in the year 1990? Will Young Life still be conducting clubs in homes? Will our present beautiful camp sites be gobbled up for living space? We face these prospects confident that God will give wisdom to keep pace with the changes that occur."

While these questions may seem humorous decades later, in the middle of the swirling sixties, these concerns were understandable. At present, the mission faces different concerns that future generations will need to address.

Denny Rydberg reflected on these challenges. "There's a great change going on in our culture and society. It's becoming more and more unfriendly toward the faith. It's not going to be as easy to stand up and proclaim Jesus or face some of the social issues coming our way.

"You compare this with the forties and fifties, and I think it's a whole new day. It took great courage in the early days to get this mission started and then tackle some of the issues of the sixties, but we're going to need courage and creativity for this new day. How do we contact kids, conduct clubs, and do all we do in an increasingly hostile environment?"

While specific answers to these questions may be unclear at the moment, the foundational, bedrock principles of Young Life must continue to play a part. "Young Life will never be into clever techniques designed to get big numbers fast," Rydberg said. "We will not be a ministry of cowboys putting evangelistic notches on our Gospel gun belts. We will always be a mission of committed people who develop meaningful relationships with kids because they are worthy of honor and significance. We will always continue to go where they are and win the right to be heard."

In 1953, Jim Rayburn penned the following sentiments in *Monday Morning*: "As I travel across the country, I feel continually humbled that the Lord would bless me so and bless the work so much. We are utterly unworthy of all of this. It has gone beyond our fondest expectations, and now this great growth is pointing us to things that we could not have dreamed of a few years ago."

The amazement continues today. The Lord has blessed the mission of Young Life in ways no one could have predicted, and only His hand will grant favor to the work. As long as the mission continues to faithfully follow the Lord's direction, the words of Jim Rayburn will still ring true:

"The best Young Life work has yet to be done."

The same needs, wants, joys, and hurts still remain in young people as they did seventy-plus years ago. While their dress, style, music, and culture may be decades apart, Young Life's mission to them remains clear: To introduce adolescents to Jesus Christ and help them grow in their faith.

The need is still there. The news is still good. The feet of those who bring it are still beautiful. And Jesus Christ is still the same, "yesterday, today, and forever."

"THE AMAZEMENT CONTINUES TODAY. THE LORD HAS BLESSED THE MISSION OF YOUNG LIFE IN WAYS NO ONE COULD HAVE PREDICTED, AND ONLY HIS HAND WILL GRANT FAVOR TO THE WORK.

AFTERWORD

> *" AND WHAT MORE SHALL I SAY? I DO NOT HAVE TIME TO TELL ABOUT GIDEON, BARAK, SAMSON, JEPHTHAH, DAVID, SAMUEL AND THE PROPHETS, WHO THROUGH FAITH . . . "*
>
> *HEBREWS 11:32-33A*

Perhaps you've finished reading this book and find yourself wondering why certain people or events weren't mentioned. Maybe the events even involve you.

You are surely not alone in asking this question. In writing about Young Life, a mission more than seven decades old that's currently in ninety-five countries and reaching more than 1.9 million kids this year alone, there were countless names that did not make these pages and even more stories that could not be told.

This is where the words above from the writer of Hebrews prove especially poignant. Like him, we "did not have time" to tell about Pat, Michelle, Mike, Jamie, Erik, Phoebe, and so many others, who through faith . . .

For this we are truly sorry and find great consolation in the fact that the Father knows us and our stories, down to even the smallest detail. As the ultimate Author of history, His records are never lacking!

Thank you for taking the time to read, skim, or just look at the pictures in this book. We are thankful for your Young Life experience and hope you see yourself and your friends mirrored in the many stories here. We truly believe YOU were made for this.

BIBLIOGRAPHY

BOOKS

Andres, Julie. *Malibu: A Celebration of Faith*. Canada: Young Life, 2003.

Cailliet, Emile. *Young Life*. New York, NY: Harper & Row Publishers, 1963.

Campbell, Elsie. *Young Life's Malibu*. Olympia, WA: Good News Book Store, 1984.

Hatasaki, Donna. *Collecting Lost Coins: 21 Days of Celebration with Young Life*. Colorado Springs, CO: Young Life, 2005.

Meredith, Char. *It's a Sin to Bore a Kid*. Waco, TX: Word, Inc., 1978.

Miller, John. *Back to the Basics of Young Life*. Colorado Springs, CO: John N. Miller, 1991.

Milliken, Bill. *From the Rearview Mirror: Reflecting on Connecting the Dots*. Carlsbad, CA: Hay House, 2012.

Milliken, Bill. *The Last Dropout: Stop the Epidemic!* Carlsbad, CA: Hay House, 2007.

Mitchell, Bob. *Letters to a Young Life Leader*. Houston, TX: Whitecaps Media, 2012.

Morse, Toni. *Back at the Ranch*. Buena Vista, CO: Frontier Ranch, 2001.

Munroe, Jeff. *The Power of the Word: The Story of Timber Wolf Lake*. Colorado Springs, CO: Young Life, 2008.

Munroe, Jeff. *Castaway: Celebrating 50 Years of Young Life on Minnesota's Pelican Lake*. Colorado Springs, CO: Young Life, 2012.

Palermo, Nick. *Missing Stars, Fallen Sparrows: A Capernaum Story*. San Jose, CA: Goehner Publications, 2013.

Rayburn III, Jim. *From Bondage to Liberty: Dance, Children, Dance*. Colorado Springs, CO: Morningstar Press, 2000.

Scott, Charlie. *The Story of Southwind*. Greenville, GA: Signal Strength, Inc., 2011.

Scott, Charlie. *Windy Gap: The Best Week of Your Life*. Maitland, FL: C. Scott Publishing, 1997.

Starr, Bill. *The Season for Reflection: Stories from Bill Starr's Life*. CreateSpace Independent Publishing Platform, 2013.

Sublett, Kit. *The Diaries of Jim Rayburn*. Houston, TX: Whitecaps Media, 2008.

Trenner, Ed, editor. *Every Kid: Touching Stories of Real Kids in Urban America Today*. Denver, CO: Young Life Urban Ministries, 1984.

Windahl, Stacy. *Build it Here: Celebrating 50 Years at Trail West Lodge*. Colorado Springs, CO: Young Life, 2014.

PERIODICALS

Focus on Youth, 1967-1975

Relationships, 1987-Present

The Saturday Evening Post, October 1975

Time, January 4, 1960

Young Life magazine, 1944-1964; 1975-1979

Young Life Outlook, 1977-1984

NOTES

Young Life would like to express special appreciation to Kit Sublett and Dan Dyer who, from 1998-2000, conducted many of the interviews referenced here.

THE 1940s: A PERFECT CONVERGENCE

5	"I don't know . . . "	Interview with Murray Smoot, June 22, 1998
6	"Which way shall . . . "	*It's a Sin to Bore a Kid*, Char Meredith, p. 16
6	"I remember [Dr . . . "	Interview with Wally Howard, July 21, 1998
7	"He was pushing . . . "	*From Bondage to Liberty: Dance, Children, Dance*, Jim Rayburn III, p. 34
7	"When he had . . . "	Interview with Wally Howard, July 21, 1998
7	"They'd get down . . . "	*From Bondage to Liberty: Dance, Children, Dance*, Jim Rayburn III, p. 36
7	"There's no way . . . "	Interview with Add Sewell, January 8, 2000
7	"We didn't have . . . "	Interview with Wally Howard, July 21, 1998
8	"I first met him . . . "	Interview with Bob Mitchell, April 12, 1999
8	"On Thursdays . . . "	*The Diaries of Jim Rayburn*, edited by Kit Sublett, p. 64
9	"If you were . . . "	Interview with Tom Raley, July 13, 1998
9	"A great day . . . "	*From Bondage to Liberty: Dance, Children, Dance*, Jim Rayburn III, p. 44
10	"The reason . . . "	Interview with Bob Mitchell, April 13, 1999
10	"You could see . . . "	Interview with Bob Mitchell, April 12, 1999
10	"I got the . . . "	Picture and quote from *Young Life* magazine, September 1945, p. 17
10	"Where I was . . . "	Interview with Wally Howard, July 21, 1998
10	"Real live-wire . . . "	*Young Life* magazine, May 1945, p. 2
11	"High school isn't . . . "	*From Bondage to Liberty: Dance, Children, Dance*, Jim Rayburn III, p. 52
11	"You can't have . . . "	Interview with Add Sewell, July 8, 1998
12	"Our message is . . . "	Interview with Wally Howard, July 21, 1998
12	"I think I was . . . "	Interview with Add Sewell, July 8, 1998
13	"The early leaders . . . "	*Letters to a Young Life Leader*, Bob Mitchell, p. 23
14	"I guess Jim . . . "	Interview with Bob Mitchell, November 17, 2011
14	"It wasn't the . . . "	Ibid
14	"You'll have to go . . . "	*It's a Sin to Bore a Kid*, Char Meredith, p. 30
14	"There was not . . . "	Ibid, pp. 40-41
15	"Maxie, I have . . . "	*Inside the Mission*, September 1991, p. 1
15	"I know now why . . . "	*It's a Sin to Bore a Kid*, Char Meredith, p. 41
15	"[Mr. Taylor] said . . . "	*The Diaries of Jim Rayburn*, edited by Kit Sublett, pp. 167-168
16	"Best investment I . . . "	*It's a Sin to Bore a Kid*, Char Meredith, p. 45
16	"We weren't asking . . . "	Interview with Roy Riviere, April 12, 1999
16	"Every night when . . . "	Interview with Murray Smoot, June 22, 1998

16	"Howard came and . . . "	Interview with Frog Sullivan, June 23, 1998
17	"...and Frog Sullivan . . . "	Interview with Murray Smoot, June 22, 1998
17	"He said there was . . . "	Interview with Frog Sullivan, June 23, 1998
19	"I really don't . . . "	*Monday Morning*, June 17, 1968
19	"The whole business . . . "	Interview with George Cowan, January 8, 2000
19	"Mr. Rayburn, we . . . "	Interview with Frog Sullivan, June 24, 1998
19	"I was there . . . "	*From Bondage to Liberty: Dance, Children, Dance*, Jim Rayburn III, p. 36

Sidebars:

6	**1940s Slang**	Various sources
10	***Young Life* magazine**	
	"We want it . . . "	*Young Life* magazine, May 1945, p. 15
17	**Silver Cliff Ranch**	
	"I called it . . . "	*Camping Philosophy and History* document, George Sheffer, p. 4
18	**Going Where They Are**	
	"I was active . . . "	*Inside Young Life*, February/March 2001, pp. 1-2

Rayburn-isms

20	"I do not want . . . "	*From Bondage to Liberty: Dance, Children, Dance*, Jim Rayburn III, p. 60
20	"The best Young Life . . . "	*Letters to a Young Life Leader*, Bob Mitchell, p. 9
20	"Jesus did somethin' . . . "	Club talk at the Swan Funeral Home, 1952, *From Bondage to Liberty: Dance, Children, Dance*, p. 109
20	"Young Life is a . . . "	*Back to the Basics*, John Miller, p. 82
20	"Who started the idea . . . "	*From Bondage to Liberty: Dance, Children, Dance*, Jim Rayburn III, p. 64
20	"Jesus is the only . . . "	*Selected Quotes from Jim Rayburn*, compiled by Kit Sublett, p. 18
20	"You know, gang, . . . "	*Back to the Basics*, John Miller, p. 92-93
20	"Most kids haven't . . . "	*Young Life* magazine, December 1949, p. 4
21	"That's not just . . . "	Asilomar Staff Conference, 1970
21	"Christ is the . . . "	*From Bondage to Liberty: Dance, Children, Dance*, Jim Rayburn III, p. 151
21	"Everyone has the . . . "	Asilomar Staff Conference, 1970
21	"I always feel a . . . "	Asilomar Staff Conference, 1970
21	"Don't ever let . . . "	Interview with Bob Mitchell, April 12, 1999

21	"When you talk . . . "	Star Ranch, 1946 Young Life staff conference, *Back to the Basics*, John Miller, pp. 74-75
21	"There are thousands . . . "	*From Bondage to Liberty: Dance, Children, Dance*, Jim Rayburn III, p. 37
21	"It's a sin . . . "	*Back to the Basics*, John Miller, p. 74
21	"We're never going . . . "	*Selected Quotes from Jim Rayburn*, compiled by Kit Sublett, p. 10

THE 1950s: AN ABSOLUTE DREAM

23	"For a Young . . . "	Interview with Bill Starr, July 20, 1998
23	"We named the . . . "	*Young Life Informer*, August 2005
24	"We had huge . . . "	Interview with Tom Raley, July 13, 1998
24	"They actually prayed . . . "	*It's a Sin to Bore a Kid*, Char Meredith, p. 55
24	"Max, these folks . . . "	*From Bondage to Liberty: Dance, Children, Dance*, Jim Rayburn III, p. 87
25	"We prayed in . . . "	*It's a Sin to Bore a Kid*, Char Meredith, p. 57
25	"From beginning to . . . "	*Young Life*, Emile Cailliet, p. 26
25	"Next thing you . . . "	*Hurrah for Goldbrick!* Scrapbook, p. 19
25	"Jim, Goldbrick, and . . . "	Interview with Frog Sullivan, June 23, 1998
26	"Goldbrick and Jerry . . . "	*Relationships*, June/July 1996, p. 13
26	"Oh I loved . . . "	Interview with Frog Sullivan, June 23, 1998
26	"There will never . . . "	Interview with Roy Riviere, April 12, 1999
27	"When you're talking . . . "	Interview with John Miller, June 1, 1998
27	"We didn't learn . . . "	*It's a Sin to Bore a Kid*, Char Meredith, p. 61
27	"In fun, at . . . "	Interview with Bill Starr, July 20, 1998
27	"I remember . . . "	*It's a Sin to Bore a Kid*, Char Meredith, p. 58
28	"We didn't talk . . . "	Interview with John Miller, June 2, 1998
28	"Jim and the . . . "	Interview with Bob Mitchell, April 12, 1999
28	"Tom was an . . . "	Interview with Bob Reeverts and Mal McSwain, July 20, 1998
28	"Program was the . . . "	Interview with Bill Starr, July 20, 1998
29	"The progression of . . . "	Interview with Bob Mitchell, April 13, 1999

29	"Well those of . . . "	Ibid
29	"One of the . . . "	Interview with Roy Riviere, April 12, 1999
29	"John had a . . . "	Interview with Tom and Recie Raley, July 13, 1998
30	"Not simply outside . . . "	Interview with Bill Starr, July 20, 1998
31	"We're going to . . . "	Interview with Wally Howard, July 21, 1998
31	"The institute had . . . "	Interview with Mary Stam, June 1, 1998
32	"Rod was a . . . "	Interview with Chris Cook, April 9, 2013
32	"What has saddened . . . "	*Young Life* magazine, June 1953, p. 9
32	"They were pioneers . . . "	Interview with Bob Reeverts and Mal McSwain, July 20, 1998
33	"One hymn the . . . "	Interview with Tom and Recie Raley, July 13, 1998
33	"And I think from . . . "	Ibid
33	"Little did we know . . . "	*Young Life's Malibu*, Elsie Campbell, p. 18
33	"After clearing his . . . "	Ibid, p. 27
36	"There was no . . . "	Interview with Bob Mitchell, April 12, 1999
36	"Tom Hamilton and . . . "	*Young Life's Malibu*, Elsie Campbell, pp. 32-33
36	"Was configured for . . . "	*The Season for Reflection*, Bill Starr, p. 48
36	"In order to own . . . "	*It's a Sin to Bore a Kid,* Char Meredith, p. 66
37	"The church looked . . . "	Interview with Tom and Recie Raley, July 13, 1998
37	"It had no . . . "	Interview with Bob Mitchell, April 13, 1999
37	"I'll never forget . . . "	Interview with Roy Riviere, April 12, 1999
37	"The Special Agent . . . "	Interview with Don Jones, February 17, 2000
37	"Don went to . . . "	Interview with Bob Stover, February 17, 2000
37	"They didn't want . . . "	*It's a Sin to Bore a Kid,* Char Meredith, p. 75
38	"We were building . . . "	*Urban Warriors*, Tom Austin, Chapter 2, p. 1
38	"When Dr. John . . . "	*The Diaries of Jim Rayburn*, edited by Kit Sublett, p. 378
39	"Jim said, 'Don't . . . "	Interview with John Miller, June 1, 1998
39	"Pagan kids would . . . "	Interview with Martie Sheffer and George Sheffer III, June 2, 1998
39	"I heard Jim . . . "	Interview with Annie Cheairs, June 4, 1998
39	"All of us . . . "	Interview with Bob Reeverts and Mal McSwain, July 20, 1998
40	"He liked his . . . "	Interview with Bob Mitchell, April 12, 1999
40	"When I think . . . "	Ibid
40	"These were the . . . "	Ibid

Sidebars

27	**1950s Best Pictures**	oscars.org
41	**A Mission that Camps**	
	"Since Young Life . . . "	Camping Philosophy and History Paper, George Sheffer Jr., 1982, pp. 2-3
	"Why should we . . . "	Ibid, p. 4

46	"When Vinnie and . . ."	*The Last Dropout,* Bill Milliken, pp. 13-14
47	"I was leery . . ."	Interview with Bo Nixon, June 2, 1998
47	"Christ made me . . ."	*Young Life,* Emile Cailliet, p. 102
48	"If you did . . ."	Interview with Bo Nixon, June 2, 1998
49	"Bringing our kids . . ."	Interview with Bob Mitchell, April 12, 1999
49	"Nub of the . . ."	*Time,* January 4, 1960, pp. 54-55
51	"It was very . . ."	Interview with Bill Starr, July 20, 1998
51	"Until then . . ."	*It's a Sin to Bore a Kid,* Char Meredith, p. 104
52	"An accumulation of . . ."	Interview with Bill Starr, July 20, 1998
52	"It was real . . ."	Interview with Bob Mitchell, April 12, 1999
53	"Of course it's . . ."	Interview with Bill Starr, July 20, 1998
53	"The real question . . ."	Interview with Bill Taylor, April 14, 1999
56	"Roy had vision . . ."	Interview with Mal McSwain, July 13, 1998
56	"Then in one . . ."	Interview with Roy Riviere, April 12, 1999
58	"Harry found out . . ."	*It's a Sin to Bore a Kid,* Char Meredith, p. 86
58	"Jim said we . . ."	Interview with Hal Merwald, July 7, 1998
58	"We went into . . ."	*Relationships,* March/April 1996, p. 4
59	"This isn't right . . ."	*History of Young Life International* document, p. 5
59	"When I saw . . ."	*Inside Young Life,* June/July 2001, p. 4
59	"There are eleven . . ."	Letter from Rayburn to Roy Riviere, dated March 17, 1959
60	"Dr. Martin Luther . . ."	*The Season for Reflection* Bill Starr, pp. 65-66
60	"That issue was . . ."	Interview with Bob Mitchell, April 12, 1999
61	"Young Life has . . ."	*Focus on Youth,* July 1968, p. 32
61	"George earned the . . ."	Interview with Rudy Howard, October 5, 1999
61	"If there wasn't . . ."	Interview with Bo Nixon, June 2, 1998
62	"There was a push . . ."	Interview with Bill Starr, July 20, 1998
62	"Carl Nelson was . . ."	*Relationships,* Spring 2014, p. 12
64	"When I was . . ."	Interview with Ted Johnson, May 26, 1999

Sidebars

46-47	**#1 Albums of the Year**	List of Billboard Year-End number-one albums
50	**Trail West Lodge**	
	"There was just . . ."	*Build It Here: Celebrating 50 Years at Trail West,* Stacy Windahl, p. 6
	"It was a small . . ."	*It's a Sin to Bore a Kid,* Char Meredith, p. 120
	"Jim Rayburn's last . . ."	*Back to the Basics,* John Miller, p. 144
51	***Young Life* book**	
	"Anyone who wants . . ."	*Christianity Today,* March, 1964
54-55	**Castaway Club**	
	"Rayburn is a . . ."	*Castaway,* Jeff Munroe, p. 10
	"SID went HOME . . ."	*The Diaries of Jim Rayburn,* edited by Kit Sublett, pp. 175-176
	"Too valuable to . . ."	*Castaway,* Jeff Munroe, p. 18
	"Bill [Starr] and I . . ."	Ibid, pp. 19-20

63   **Woodleaf**
        "Have you considered . . . "   Interview with Bob Stover, May 21, 2014
        "Young Life had . . . "   *Back to the Basics,* John Miller, p. 148

65   **Give Us the Teenagers**
        "Good Lord, give . . . "   *The Diaries of Jim Rayburn,* edited by Kit Sublett, p. 409

67   **Saranac Village**
        "Dr. Bill Keisewetter . . . "   *Monday Morning,* July 28, 1969
        "At that time . . . "   *Relationships,* Fall/Winter 1999, p. 15

THE 1970s: A CONTINUING EDUCATION

71   "To readily accept . . . "   Asilomar Staff Conference, 1970

71   "I've always felt . . . "   Ibid

72   "He was dying . . . "   Interview with Bob Mitchell, April 12, 1999

72   "Everyone thought Jim . . . "   *It's a Sin to Bore a Kid,* Char Meredith, p. 117

73   "Jim was passionate . . . "   Interview with Wally Howard, July 21, 1998

73   "Jim was a . . . "   Interview with Bob Mitchell, April 12, 1999

74   "Our staff have . . . "   *1971 Young Life Annual Report,* pp. 4-5

74   "We discovered that . . . "   *Windy Gap, The Best Week of Your Life,* Charlie Scott, p. 110

74   "Would not respond . . . "   Interview with Char Meredith, June 25, 1998

74   "One group is . . . "   Internal memo, 1970, Kit Sublett manuscript, p. 293

75   "Traditional Young Life . . . "   Interview with George Sheffer III, June 2, 1998

75   "Under experienced . . . "   *It's a Sin to Bore a Kid,* Char Meredith, p. 133

75   "My time spent . . . "   *Young Life Outlook,* January 1978, p. 7

79   "For the specific . . . "   *Young Life Outlook,* October 1978, p. 3

79   "Star Ranch lost . . . "   Interview with Bob Mitchell, April 13, 1999

80   "It took about . . . "   Email from Ed Winkle to his daughter, Vanessa, September 10, 2013

80   "Which for the . . . "   Interview with Larry Entwistle, October 20, 2012

80   "Many Young Life . . . "   email from Ed Winkle to his daughter, Vanessa, September 10, 2013

80   "Those buses covered . . . "   Interview with Larry Entwistle, October 20, 2012

82   "In the late . . . "   Interview with George Sheffer III, June 2, 1998

82   "Umbrella of Young . . . "   Circle C website (circlec.net/timeline)

82   "I love it . . . "   Interview with George Sheffer III, June 2, 1998

83   "Our urban staff . . . "   *History of Young Life's Middle School Ministry (WyldLife)* notes

83   "Two years later . . . "   *The Story of Southwind,* Charlie Scott, p. 23

83	Keith Swagerty history	Interview with Keith Swagerty, January 31, 2014
84	"All that time . . . "	Kit Sublett manuscript, pp. 287-288
85	"I shared with . . . "	*Young Life Outlook*, October 1979, p. 12
85	"During the early . . . "	*German American Partnership*, Char Meredith, p. 8
86	"Staff and leaders . . . "	*Letters to a Young Life Leader*, Bob Mitchell, pp. 94-95
86	"It's easy to . . . "	*It's a Sin to Bore a Kid*, Char Meredith, p. 124
87	"Where else do . . . "	Interview with Donna McClellan, October 7, 1999
87	"We did not . . . "	Kit Sublett manuscript, p. 300
88	"I thank God . . . "	Interview with Rudy Howard, October 5, 1999
88	"When the Bible . . . "	Interview with Bo Nixon, June 2, 1998
88	"For a while . . . "	Interview with Rudy Howard, October 7, 1999
88	"In the early . . . "	*It's a Sin to Bore a Kid*, Char Meredith, p. 128
89	"During my tenure . . . "	*Letters to a Young Life Leader*, Bob Mitchell, pp. 104-105
89	"Emphasized that . . . "	*Young Life Outlook*, October 1978, p. 14
90	"By 1977, I . . . "	*The Season for Reflection*, Bill Starr, p. 72
90	"You had a . . . "	Interview with Bob Reeverts and Mal McSwain, July 20, 1998
90	"People didn't know . . . "	Interview with Bill Starr, July 20, 1998
90	"Bill [hoped] Young . . . "	Interview with Doug Burleigh, May 25, 1999
90	"The positions of . . . "	*The Season for Reflection*, Bill Starr, p. 67
91	"Billy Graham Story"	Interview with Bob Mitchell, April 13, 1999
91	" 'Headquarters . . . "	Bob Mitchell interview, Young Life Service Center, May 29, 2013
92	"It is one . . . "	*Young Life Outlook*, May 1978, p. 13

Sidebars

72	**#1 Singles of the Year**	List of Billboard Year-End number-one singles
78	**Southwind**	
	All excerpts	*The Story of Southwind*, Charlie Scott, pp. 1-2
81	**"Tomorrow is in Their Hands"**	
	All excerpts	*The Saturday Evening Post*, October 1975, pp. 21-23
84	**All Kinds of Leaders**	
	"God is preparing..."	A. B. Simpson (1843-1919), founder of the Christian and Missionary Alliance

86	*Young Life* **magazine**	
	"Aimed to give you . . . "	*Young Life* magazine, Volume 1, Number 1, Spring 1975
92	*It's a Sin to Bore a Kid*	
	"It's a Sin . . . "	Interview with Char Meredith, June 25, 1998

THE 1980s: BRANCHING OUT

97	"I remember Harry's . . . "	Interview with Bob Reeverts, July 20, 1998
98	"It's incredible to . . . "	Ibid
98	"Of the forty kids . . . "	Bob Reeverts letter, September 2, 1987
98	"A kid in Oxford . . . "	Interview with Arnie Jacobs, June 3, 1998
99	"One year later . . . "	First Staff Conference—*Nexus 86*, October 1986, p. 24
99	"Africa has the . . . "	*Inside the Mission*, Volume 6, Number 8, May 1987
100	"We felt the . . . "	*Young Life Outlook*, Volume 4, Number 1, February 1980, p. 11
100	"Amicus completed . . . "	*International Ministry of Young Life Workbook*, p. 47, 1988
101	"It was a history . . . "	*A Narrative History of Military Community Youth Ministries*, p. 10
101	"All present felt . . . "	Ibid, pp. 10-11
102	"In 1982 Young . . . "	Global Newsletter, August/September 1987, p. 2
103	"We started a . . . "	Interview with Jim Meredith, May 26, 1999
103	"Within five years . . . "	email with Jim Meredith, May 3, 2015
103	"By the end of 1981 . . . "	*Urban Warriors*, Chapter IV, p. 5, 1988, Published by the National Urban Office of Young Life
104	"Doug Burleigh said . . . "	*Inside the Mission*, Volume 8, Number 11, October 1989
104	"The Lord has . . . "	Board of Trustees Report, September 10, 1982, p. 3
104	*"Christianity Today . . . "*	*Young Life Outlook*, Volume 6, Number 2, January 1982, p. 11
105	"The next year . . . "	*1983-84 Young Life Annual Report*
105	"I was nervous . . . "	*German American Partnership*, Char Meredith, p. ii-81
108	"Jack, it doesn't . . . "	Interview with Bo Nixon, June 2, 1998
108	"I couldn't believe . . . "	Interview with Doug Burleigh, May 25, 1999
109	"Joe was the first . . . "	Interview with Dave Carlson, July 22, 1998
109	"I'll never forget . . . "	Interview with Doug Burleigh, May 25, 1999; [Fifty] kids—*1985-86 Young Life Annual Report*
110	"To be comfortable . . . "	*Missing Stars, Fallen Sparrow*s, Nick Palermo, p. 7
110	"It was with . . . "	Ibid, p. 43
110	"This ministry was . . . "	Ibid, p. 71
110	"Kids who happened . . . "	Ibid, p. 8
110	"When I conduct . . . "	Ibid, p. 149
110	"The crazy . . . "	Ibid, p. 12
110	"As we involved . . . "	Ibid, p. 33
110	"In the last . . . "	Interview with Bob Mitchell, April 13, 1999
110	"By following the . . . "	*Ventures*, May 1981, p. 1
111	"If there was . . . "	Interview with Doug Burleigh, May 25, 1999
111	"Effort to provide . . . "	Young Life Foundation, *1988-1989 Annual Report*, p. 6
111	"Hal has faithfully . . . "	Interview with Doug Burleigh, May 25, 1999

112	"Well his mother . . ."	Interview with Tom Raley, July 13, 1998
112	"I started coming . . ."	Interview with Doug Burleigh, May 25, 1999
112	"Obviously Young Life . . ."	Interview with Donna McClellan, October 7, 1999
113	"I've never marketed . . ."	Interview with Ty Saltzgiver, April 22, 2014
113	"Because of a . . ."	Email from Doug Burleigh, April 23, 2015
113	"Towards the end . . ."	*Inside the Mission*, Volume 8, Number 10, September 1989
114	"The talks about . . ."	Ibid
114	"It was a thrill . . ."	Interview with Doug Burleigh, May 25, 1999
114	"When you were . . ."	Interview with John Miller, June 2, 1998

Sidebars

98-99	**Fashions, Fads, and Phrases**	Various sources
102	**Oakbridge** "Four years later . . ."	Oakbridge Master plan, p. 5
104	*Every Kid* Entire poem	*Every Kid: Touching Stories of Real Kids in Urban America Today*, 1984

THE 1990s: WHATEVER . . . IT TAKES

119	"I felt it was . . ."	Interview with Doug Burleigh, May 25, 1999
120	"An unprecedented . . ."	*Inside the Mission*, April 1990, p. 1
120	"As I look . . ."	*Relationships*, Winter 1990, p. 2
121	"I think meeting . . ."	Interview with Verley Sangster, October 7, 1999
121	"I felt like my . . ."	*The History of Young*Lives, (Young*Lives* manual), 2002, p. 8
122	"Young Life has . . ."	*Inside the Mission*, September 1992
122	"In the end . . ."	Ibid
122	"The camp was . . ."	*Build it Here, Celebrating 50 Years at Trail West Lodge*, Stacy Windahl, p. 19
122	"We sit down . . ."	Interview with Dave Carlson, July 22, 1998
122	"Field staff would . . ."	Ibid
122	"I believe we . . ."	Senior staff's January 10, 1992, letter in response to a survey of Doug Burleigh and Verley Sangster's "Listening Group" meeting
124	"I think we . . ."	Interview with Doug Burleigh, May 25, 1999
125	"Doug came in . . ."	Interview with Bob Reeverts, July 20, 1998
125	"When Doug left . . ."	Interview with John Miller, June 2, 1998
125	"This experience . . ."	Email from Doug Burleigh, April 23, 2015
125	"Look I'm going . . ."	Interview with Ted Johnson, May 26, 1999
125	"I think these . . ."	Interview with Bob Reeverts, July 20, 1998
125	"Over the course . . ."	*Inside the Mission*, November 1992, p. 6
126	"I thought the . . ."	Interview with Bill Garrison, June 22, 1998
126	"Denny had to . . ."	Interview with Greg Kinberg, May 26, 1999
127	"I believe the . . ."	Interview with Doug Burleigh, May 25, 1999
127	"I was confident . . ."	*Inside Young Life*, May 1993, p. 6
127	"I think what . . ."	Interview with Bill Garrison, June 22, 1998
128	"The first year . . ."	Interview with Denny Rydberg, May 26, 1999

129	"Denny made a . . ."	Interview with a senior leader, May 26, 1999
129	"Now we have . . ."	Interview with Denny Rydberg, May 26, 1999
130	"I'm glad Young . . ."	A favorite saying of Chuck Reinhold
130	"We want to . . ."	*Inside Young Life*, February/March 1996
130	"I realized they . . ."	*Inside Young Life*, November 1994
131	"It's a great . . ."	Interview with Denny Rydberg, May 26, 1999
133	"Common statement of . . ."	Denny Rydberg's letter to the board, April 3, 1998
133	"A mission statement . . ."	Denny Rydberg's letter to National Field Leadership Team and the senior staff, May 4, 1998
133	"The people were . . ."	*Relationships*, Spring 1998, p. 12
136	"He would sit . . ."	Ibid, p. 13
136	"We found it . . ."	*Relationships*, April/May 1997, p. 12
137	"Touch a kid . . ."	*History of Small Towns* document by Don Stuber
137	"History supports . . ."	Ibid
137	"A one-high . . ."	Five-Year Overview document by Don Stuber
138	Thurston High story	*Relationships*, Fall/Winter 1998, pp. 4-5
140	"Full- and part-time . . ."	1988-89 and 1998-99 Annual Reports
140	"Numbers represent . . ."	Interview with Denny Rydberg, May 26, 1999
140	"We know that . . ."	*Inside Young Life*, February/March 1997, p. 3

Sidebars

120	**Top TV Shows**	Various Sources
123	**Rockbridge Alum Springs**	
	"Boarding is 10 . . ."	Letter: Thomas J. "Stonewall" Jackson to his sister Laura Jackson Arnold, quoted in part; archives, Preston Library, Virginia Military Institute
	"Dave Carlson . . ."	Email from Lee Corder, June 11, 2015
124	***Back to the Basics***	
	All excerpts	Interview with John Miller, June 1, 1998
127	**Crooked Creek Ranch**	
	"We felt it . . ."	Interview with Bruce Kramer, July 22, 1998
	"We build these . . ."	Interview with Dave Carlson, July 22, 1998
132	**SharpTop Cove**	
	"Lavelle was the . . ."	Interview with Dave Carlson, July 22, 1998
134-135	**Lost Canyon**	
	"We'd like to . . ."	Interview with Marty Caldwell, September 25, 2014

138	*Christ in the Cafeteria at Columbine*	
	Entire text	*Collecting Lost Coins*, Donna Hatasaki, 2005, pp. 17-18
139	**Timber Wolf Lake**	
	"Rick, more kids . . ."	*The Power of the Word: The Story of Timber Wolf Lake*, Jeff Munroe, 2008, pp. 1-2
	"A void with . . ."	Timber Wolf Lake brochure, 1999
140	**Pico Escondido**	
	"I literally converted . . ."	Interview with Scott Steele, July 25, 2014
141	**When God Wants to Teach You Something**	
	"When God wants . . ."	Bruce Larson (1925-2008), senior pastor of University Presbyterian Church in Seattle, Washington

THE 2000s: READY!

146	"On Wednesday . . ."	*Relationships,* Fall 2001, p. 13
147	"One thing I love . . ."	*Relationships,* Winter 2006, p. 15
147	"One staff person . . ."	*Monday Morning* June 22, 2009
148	"From my experience . . ."	*History of Young Life's Middle School Ministry* Paper
148	"From now on . . ."	Ibid
148	"Veteran staff member . . ."	Ibid
149	"In 2006, nine of . . ."	*Young Life Board Report,* Fall 2006, p. 43
149	"The Asian culture . . ."	*Inside Young Life,* September 1995, p. 1
149	"It's not to be . . ."	*Relationships,* Fall 2005, p. 18
150	"There's a lot . . ."	Ibid
150	"Now we're in . . ."	*Relationships,* Winter 2006, p. 2
151	"The Bible says . . ."	*Relationships,* Winter 2004, p. 15
151	"We always ask . . ."	*Relationships,* Fall 2006, p. 17
152	"An African proverb . . ."	Young Life Africa website, October 7, 2014
152	"Perhaps it shouldn't . . ."	"African Youth, Innovation and the Changing Society," Harry, Njideka, *Huffington Post,* September 2013
152	"In recent years . . ."	Young Life's Proclamation Paper, p. 1
152	"As a mission . . ."	Ibid, p. 8
152	"It took us . . ."	*Inside Young Life,* January 2009
153	"We brought fifty-five . . ."	*Young Life Board Report,* Spring 2009, p. 6
153	"There is anticipation . . ."	*Young Life Board Report,* Spring 2008, p. 40
154	"I believe Young . . ."	*Monday Morning,* October 19, 2009
154	"It gave me . . ."	*Here and Now: Young Life Latino Initiative,* p. 7
155	"Find, thank, encourage . . ."	Email from Pete Fritsch, April 16, 2015
155	"There is a group . . ."	*Monday Morning,* September 26, 2011
155	"I loved my . . ."	*Relationships,* Spring 2011, p. 5
156	"Our main aim . . ."	Ibid
156	"I was really . . ."	*Relationships,* Spring 2011, p. 6
156	"Did you ever . . ."	*Relationships,* Spring 2013, p. 7
157	"It's three hundred . . ."	Ibid
157	"We were able . . ."	*Small Towns Jumpstart Brochure,* August 1, 2007
157	"A jumpstart builds . . ."	Ibid
157	"We can't afford . . ."	*Relationships,* Fall 2011, p. 6

157	"We hope in . . ."	Ibid
160	"I am seeking . . ."	*The Campership Legacy Fund Donor Summary Package*, 2013
160	"In the Campership . . ."	Ibid
160	"We're internet people . . ."	*Relationships*, Spring 2004, p. 15
161	"The goal of the . . ."	*Monday Morning*, June 15, 2009
162	"Whether I presented . . ."	*Relationships*, Spring 2008, p. 6
162	"A new logo . . ."	Ibid, p. 7
162	"The tagline begins . . ."	Ibid
162	"Growth spurts have . . ."	*Relationships*, Summer 2001, p. 17

Sidebars

146	**Technological Innovations**	Various Sources
159	**Creekside at Washington Family Ranch**	
	"This is without . . ."	*Creekside at Washington Family Ranch Press Release*, June 2009
161	***Monday Morning***	
	"We echo the . . ."	*Monday Morning*, June 8, 2009

THE 2010s: THE NOW AND THE NOT YET

169	"Meanwhile, social . . ."	adweek.com/socialtimes/social-media-statistics-2014/499230
172	A New Camp in Armenia	Armenia Case Statement, 2015
173	Creative Camps	Young Life Board Report, Fall 2013, p. 21
173	"Decontee Davis . . ."	Young Life Africa website, December 16, 2014
173	"I overheard them . . ."	*Monday Morning*, October 22, 2012
176	"This summer, twenty . . ."	Board Report, Fall 2011, p. 29
176	"The New Believer's . . ."	Ibid, p. 12
176	"Jesus suffered. He . . ."	*Relationships*, Spring 2012, p. 1
177	"Over my twenty-nine years . . ."	*Monday Morning*, March 26, 2012
177	"What Brian does . . ."	Young Life Board Report, Fall 2011, p. 7
178	"I see a lot . . ."	Picture and caption from *Relationships*, Winter 2012, p. 22
178	"In 2014 Young*Lives* . . ."	Young Life Board Report, Fall 2014, p. 37
178	"With Capernaum, I . . ."	Interview with Nick Palermo, July 14, 2010
179	"It's just amazing . . ."	Email from Pam Harmon, March 3, 2015
179	Young Life College	*Monday Morning*, March 16, 2015
180	"The remarkable . . ."	*Monday Morning*, June 7, 2010
180	"I can think . . ."	*Monday Morning*, November 29, 2010
180	"From the moment . . ."	Young Life Board Report, Fall 2010, p. 19
181	"We will walk . . ."	*Monday Morning*, February 3, 2014
181	"We found leaders . . ."	*Monday Morning*, August 4, 2014
181	"The Freedom Walk . . ."	Ibid
181	"Each kid was . . ."	Young Life Board Report, Fall 2011, p. 37
183	"We placed the . . ."	Young Life Board Report, Spring 2012, p. 21
183	"The rooftop allowed . . ."	*Relationships*, Winter 2012, p. 10
185	"It's been said . . ."	Ibid

185	"It was unbelievable . . ."	Ibid
185	"But maybe the . . ."	Young Life Board Report, Fall 2013, p. 12
186	"Young Life is . . ."	2015 Spring statistics
186	"As we near . . ."	Interview with Josh Griffin, April 24, 2015
186	"Population predictions . . ."	*A Special Anniversary Booklet commemorating the first 25 Years [of] Service of Young Life*, 1965, p. 30
186	"You compare this . . ."	*Relationships,* Fall 2013, p. 6
186	"Young Life will . . ."	*Inside Young Life*, July 1994
187	"As I travel . . ."	*Monday Morning*, April 2, 1953

Sidebars

170	**Notable greats from 1941 still going strong!**	Various sources
171	**Carolina Point**	
	"On June 30 . . ."	Board Report, Fall 2013, p. 17
175	**Cairn Brae at Loch Monzievaird**	All excerpts Interview with Randy Nickel, December 23, 2014
182	**Social Media**	
	"Young Life leaders . . ."	Interview with Josh Griffin, April 24, 2015
	"I've been reading . . ."	*Young Life*, October 1949, p. 2
	"I think 'Say, Gang' . . ."	*Young Life*, December 1949, p. 2
	"Beyond excited to . . ."	*Twitter*, January 6, 2015
	"@YoungLife has . . ."	*Twitter*, December 9, 2014
184	**The Future of Young Life**	
	"Population predictions . . ."	*A Special Anniversary Booklet commemorating the first 25 Years [of] Service of Young Life*, 1965, p. 30

INDEX

bold denotes photograph

A

Abel, Dick, 120, **120**
adult guests, 50, 122, 139, 142, 155
Afghanistan, Young Life work in, 178
Africa, Young Life in, 41, 84, 98, 99, 151–152, 180
Africa All Staff Conference (2008), 151
African-Americans, 61, 65, 78, 84, 88, 103, 185
African Young Life Staff Conference (1986), 99
"All Kinds of Kids" (Rydberg), 65
"All Kinds of Leaders" (Rydberg), 84
All Staff Conference
    (1996), 130
    (2000), 148
    (2008 in Africa), 151
    (2008 in Florida), 160, **165**
    (2012), 176, **176**, **181**, 183, **185**
"All Staff Conferences," overview, 164
Alumni and Friends, 153, 155
Alumni department, 155
Alvo da Mocidade (Target for Youth), 58
Amen, Henry, 59, 101
Amicus ministry, 59, 98, 100, **100**, 142
Amidon, Doug, 82
Anderson, Al, 155
Anderson, Cliff, 162
Anderson, Johan, 73
Anderson, Stacy, 155, **155**
Annemasse, Switzerland, Young Life in, 98
Anthony, Jim, 171
Area Director School, 84, 129
Armenia, Young Life in, 172–173
Armenian Young Life camp, **95**, 172–173, **173**
Asfahl, Marv, 140

Ashburn, Mike (Ash), 105, **117**, **167**, 176, **176**
Asian Young Life, 149–150
Asilomar conference (1970), 71–72, 93, 164
assignment team, 142, 152
Atger, Marc, 58
Atkinson, Margie, 128
Atkinson, Neil, 122
Australia, Young Life in, 83, 98
Austria, Young Life in, 101, 103
Azios, Cristina, 147

B

Back to the Basics of Young Life (Miller), 124, **124**
backpacking, **75**
Bade, Tom, 28, **166**
Balkans, Young Life camp in, 174
Baltimore, Maryland, Young Life in, 13
basketball, 46, **46**, 59, 83, **83**, 102, 131, 136, **166**
Bean, Lavelle, 132
Beckwith, Rick, 148
Bellingham, Washington, Young Life in, 13
Benevolence Fund, 147
Benson, Ted, 7, 9, 14, 24, 186
Berassa, Moges, 84
Bermuda, Young Life in, 58
best week of your life, 69, 108, 115, 142, 151
Beyond Malibu program, 75, **75**, **95**
Biehl, Bobb, 104
Big Muddy Ranch, 131
"The Big Dream" speech, 71–72
Bigkis (bind together), 85

Birmingham, Mississippi, Young Life in, 88

"The Black Manifesto," 62

Block, John and Margie, 102

blogs, 160

Board of Directors
    change of name to Board of Trustees, 91
    first woman member, 89
    formation of, 9, 186
    role of, 9

Board of Trustees
    change of name from Board of Directors, 91
    first member from outside of North America, 152
    first minority member, 103
    number of members, 186

Bobby the hapless matador (program character), 116, **117**

Borgman, Dean, 46, 48, 67

Boston, Massachusetts, Young Life in, 88

Branch, Billy, 123

Branham, Sam, 146

Brazil, Young Life in, 58, **94**

Breakaway Lodge (camp), **95**

Bright, Bill, 120, **120**

Broadmoor Hotel (1979 Staff Congress), 92, **93**, 164

Broyles, Bob, 101

budget
    for 1952, 43
    fiscal year 1982, 43
    for original staff, 9
    Rayburn as raising all on his own, 29-30

regional and area staff as responsible for raising, 142
    trouble in meeting, 14

Buena Vista, Colorado, Young Life in, 17, 40, 49, 50

Build It Here: Celebrating 50 Years at Trail West Lodge (Windahl), 50, 122

Burleigh, Debbie, 112

Burleigh, Doug, 90, 104, 108, 109, 111, 112, **112**, 113, 114, 119, 120, **120**, 121, 122, 124–125, 126, 127

Burnt Mountain Assembly, 132

Burress, Cy, 24

buses, purchase of, 80, **80**

Buttercreek Lodge (camp), **95**

"Buy an Acre" campaign, 123

Cailliet, Emile, 25, 51, 92

Cairn Brae at Loch Monzievaird (camp), **95**, 175, **175**

Caldwell, Marty, 135, 150, 183

Cambodia, Young Life in, 133, **144**, 150

camp counselors, 27

Camp Navarac, 67

Camp On Wheels, 170, **170**

Camp Video Scrapbooks, 182

Campaigners, 12–13, 32, 82, 103, 115, 128, 140, 142, 148, 156, 177, 178, 179

Campaigners song book, **12**

Campbell, Elsie, 33, 36

Campbell, Jim, 33

Campership Legacy Fund, 160

Camping department, 122

camps
    alternative approach to, 74
    brochure, **39**
    creative, 173-174, **174**
    current number of, 41
    impact of, 160
    marketing films for, 79–80
    meaningful conversations at, **87**
    as one of five C's, 128, 142
    Rayburn's commitment to, 41
    Rayburn's dream of, 14, 15
    traditional approach to, 75

Canada, Young Life in, 36, 45, 79, **94**, **95**, 111, 183

Canton, Ohio, Young Life in, 88

Capernaum, 109, **109**, 110, 142, **149**, 156, 176, 178–179, **179**, 183

Carlson, Dave, 109, 122, 123, 124, 127, 132

Carlton, Greg, 139

Carolina Point (camp), **94**, 171, **171**

Carpenter, Jack, 108

Carpenter, Reid, 67

Carter, John, 29, 50, 53

Carter, Millie (Sisco), **40**

Castaway Club (camp), 55, **54-55**, 95

celebration (AKA All Staff Conference), 142, 176

Centurions (gang), 46

Chafer, Lewis Sperry, 5, 6, 9, 186

Champion, George, 108

Chardonnens, John and Mitsy, 58

Chatelain family, 102

Cheairs, Annie, 13, 39

Chesemore, Jeff, 184

Chester, Pennsylvania, Young Life in, 13

Chicago, Illinois, as part of mission field in 1945, 13

Chicago Fellowship, 49

Christian Workers Foundation, 14

Christianity Today, 51, 104

Chung, Mr., 83

Chung, Steve, 149, **149**

Church Relations Advisory Committee, 104

churches
as one of seven commitments of mission, 92
as wrestling with how to care for kids outside their doors, 49
Young Life's relationships with, 49, 85–86, 104–105

Circle C Project, 82

Clearwater Cove (camp), **94**, 172, **172**

Cleveland, Ohio, Young Life in, 88

Climb for Change, 180, 181

Club Beyond, 59, 101, **101**, 146, 156

club
definition of, 142
7, 9, 11, 13, 24, 27, 38-39, 42–43, 45, 62, 71, 73, 83, 104, 128

Coe, Doug, 24, 101

Collecting Lost Coins (Hatasaki), 138

color, kids of, 80, 87, 142. *See also* African Americans; Hispanic community; Latinos

Colorado Springs, Colorado
camp location in, 15, 17, 29
club locations in, **24**
Dale House Project, 61, 82
headquarters location in, **16**, **52**
Service Center location in, 130-131

Columbine High School (Littleton, Colorado) shooting, 138

Combes, Tom, 160–161

Comee, Les, 83

committee, 30, 40, 121, 125, 128, 140, 142

committee members, 84, 115, 125, 185, 186

communism, suspicions of, 36–37

Contact Jeunesse, 98

contact work, 12, **12**, 37, 42, 45, 59, 104, 109, 115, 126, 128, 142, **144**, 155

Cook, Chris, 32, 98, **99**

Corder, Lee, 123, 150, 180

Costa Rica, Young Life in, 98, **170**

Coty, Paul, 183, **183**

counterculture members, 82

Covenant for Ministry, 92

Cowan, George, 7, 9, **9**, 19, 186

Creede, Colorado, backpacking/camping near, 75, **76-77**

Creekside at Washington Family Ranch, 158-159, **158-159**

Crofton, Michael, **167**, 176, **176**

Crooked Creek Ranch (camp), **94**, 124, 127, **127**

Cross Carriers, 48, **48**

Crystal Park, Colorado, camp location in, 15

C's (of Young Life), 128, 142

Culp, Larry, 31

cultural turbulence, 82

D

Dale House, 61, 82, **82**

Dallas, Texas
as part of mission field in 1945, 13
presence of Young Life Campaign in, 9
tent meeting, 7, 8

Dallas Theological Seminary (DTS), 6, 7

Dance, Children, Dance (Jim Rayburn III), 7, **101**

Davis, Decontee, 174

Davis, Fred, 103

Davis, James, 84

Day, Cecil, 132

Daystar University, 99

Delaney, Andy (Goldbrick), 25, 26, **26**

Delaney, Jerry, 25, 26

Developing Global Leaders (DGL) program, 153, 155–156

Di Pasquale, Vinnie (Diablo), 38, **44**, 45, 46, 48, 83, **167**

The Diaries of Jim Rayburn (Sublett), 8, 156, **156**

Dirty Bert (program character), 116

disabilities
kids with, 62, 65, 69, 97, **109**, 110, 114, 142, 170, 171, 179. *See also* Capernaum
leaders with, 84

discipleship, 13, 27, 75, 92, 103, 125,

133, 152, 178

diversity, 71, 80, 84, 93, 128, 149

division organization, 124

divisional conferences, 83, 119

Dobson, Barney, 75

Dominican Republic, Young Life in, **95**, 98, 124, 140

donors, 15, 24, 25, 67, 122, 142, 160, 169

Douglas, Ilene, 56

Douglas, Lawrence, 56, 78

Douglas, Sara, 23, 56, 78

drug addiction, 48

Duct Tape Man (program character), 116

Dustin, Ollie, 13

Dyer, Dan, 161

E

Eareckson, Joni, 3, **3**, 62, **62**, 64

earning the right to be heard. *See* right to be heard, earning/winning

Ebola outbreak (2014), 174

Edson, Jim, 83

Edwards, Chad, 156

Edwards, Mike, 147

electronic communications, 161

eNewsletter, 161

England, Young Life in, 8, 98. *See also* United Kingdom, Young Life in

Entwistle, Larry, 80

environmental issues, 74

every kid, 142

Every Kid (book), **104**

"Every Kid" (poem), 104

Expeditions, 103, 143, 147

F

Facebook, 146, 160, 169, 182

family camp, 122

Fast Track positions, 129

Fazenda Salto (camp), **94**

Federal Bureau of Investigation (FBI), 36–37

Fernandez, Anthony, **178**

field games, **89**

Five C's, 128, 142

Flagler College, 86

Focus on Youth magazine, 60–61, **60**, **86**, 114, **166**

football, 12, **12**, 59, 67, 115, 137, **166**, **167**

foreign exchange students, 59, 100

Forward Fund, 67

Fountain Valley School (Colorado Springs), 31, 87

Foxworthy, Gregg, **160**

Foxworthy, Jeff, **160**

France, Young Life in, 31–32, 56, 58, **94**

Frasher, Clara, 5, 6, 19, 88

Freedom Walk, 181

Fritsch, Pete, 155

From Bondage to Liberty: Dance, Children, Dance (Jim Rayburn III), 101

Frontier Ranch (camp), 19, **22**, 25, **25**, **29**, 38, **94**, **95**

Fuller Theological Seminary, 86

fundraising, 24–25, 29–30, 49, 56, 67, 122, 123, 142, 147, 150, 156

furthest-out kid, 142

"The Future of Young Life," 184

G

Gaffney, Mike, 153, 179, 180

Gainesville, Texas
Clara Frasher's prayers for teenagers in, 5, 19, 109
presence of Young Life Campaign in, 9, 19
start of MBC chapter in, 6
tent meeting, 7, 8

gangs, 38, **44**, 46–47, 48

Garcia, Gerald, 157

Garrison, Bill, 126, 127

Geneva, Switzerland, Young Life in, 98

Germany, Young Life in, 59, 174

Giusta, Randy, 148

"Give us the teenagers" prayer, 65

Gloag, Ann, 175

global leaders, 142. *See also*
　　Developing Global Leaders
　　(DGL) program

glossary, 142–143

Goers, Patsy, 157

"Going Where They Are" (Rydberg),
　　18

Goldbrick (Delaney, Andy), 25, 26, **26**

Good News, 5, 65, 120, 136, 138, 143,
　　184

Gordon-Conwell, 86

Gosling, Francis (Goose), 58

Gospel, 29, 30–31, 41, 42, 48, 50, 60,
　　61, 62, 82, 100, 114, 116, 133,
　　147, 148, 152, 161, 163, 176

Graff, Stu, 135

Graffiti camp, 173, **174**

Graham, Billy, 13, 91, 108, 125

greatest week of their lives, 102, 160,
　　169, 174, 182

Greece, Young Life in, 102, 103, 174

Green, Lee, 103

Greensboro, North Carolina, Young
　　Life in, **70**, 114

Griffin, Josh, 182, 186

Grimstead, Jay, 28, **28**, 82

Guder, Darrell, 86

H

Hall, Brian, 149

Hamilton, Tom, 33, 36

Hammon, Tom, **117**

Happiness Is Malibu
　　(marketing film), 80

Harlem, New York, Young Life in,
　　146, **46**

Harmon, Pam, 179

Harris, Harlan, 72

Harvey Cedars, New Jersey, Young
　　Life weekend in, 25

Hatasaki, Donna, 138

Hautt, Bill, 122

Hayner, Steve, 120, **120**

He That is Spiritual (Chafer), 5

headquarters, change in name, 91

healthy families, building of, 92

Heim, Pamela, 111

HELPERS, 98, 103

high school assembly meetings, 11

Hill, Carol, 99, 113

Hill, Nobie, 99, 113

Hispanic community, 65, 103, 157
　　See also Latinos

Holy Spirit, 5, 9, 19, 63, 101, 125, 130,
　　157, 163, 179

Hoover, J. Edgar, 37

Hornsby, Jim and Sarah, 75, 136

horse program, **17**, **25**, 39, 50

Houston, Texas
　　as part of mission field in 1945,
　　13
　　presence of Young Life
　　Campaign in, 9
　　tent meeting, **7**, 8, 9
　　Young Life in, 88

Howard, Rudy, 61, 88

Howard, Wally, 6, 7, 8, 9, **9**, 10, 12,
　　13–14, 31, 37, 73, 88, 186

humor, 8, 10, 11, 27, 28, 40, 64, 72,
　　74, 111, 116, **116–117**, 143,
　　164, 176

Hurricane Ike, Young Life response
　　to, 147

Hurricane Katrina, Young Life
　　response to, 147

Hurricane Recovery Fund, 147

I

"I'm Not a Problem, I'm a
　　Man" (*Focus on Youth*
　　issue), 60, **60**

incarnational, 18, 88, 92, 124,
　　133, 143, 170

India, Young Life in, 83, 133

Indianapolis, Indiana, Young
　　Life in, 88

inerrancy, 87

Inner-City Young Life, 61

Instagram, 146, 169, 182

institute, Young Life, 31. *See also*

Institute of Youth Ministries (IYM)

Institute of Youth Ministries (IYM), 86, 105, 110, 129

International Schools, 98, 102–103

international work
growth of, 133, 145, 150

Ireland, Young Life in, 150, 180

It's a Sin to Bore a Kid (Meredith), 14, 51, 72, 75, **92**

J

Jacobs, Arnie, 10, 98, 99

Jacobs, Mary Lou, 98

Jamaica, Young Life camp in, 174

Japan, Young Life in, 133

Jenkins, Leonard (program character), 116

Jessup, Dan, **114**

Jesus
mission statement, 105, 133
Rayburn quotes about, 20, 21, 43, 71, 72, 143
reflections of, 97–100
with skin on, 151

Jeunesse Ardente (Youth Aglow), 58

Johnson, Cliff and Liz, 83

Johnson, Nancy, 125

Johnson, Tate, 174

Johnson, Ted, 64, 125, **125**, 160

Johnston, Art, 31

Johnston, David, **99**

Johnston, Fran, 31–32, **32**, 58, 98, **99**

Johnston, Pam, **99**

Johnston, Rod, 31–32, **32**, 58, 98

Jones, Don, 37

Judy Makes a Date (film), 161

Jump Mountain, 123

jumpstart, 157

junior high kids, programs for, 148–149
See also middle school ministry

K

Kaiser, Dale, 50

Kamau, Mungai, 84

Kamgaing, Moyo, 152

Kee, Howard, 16–17

Keisewetter, Bill, 67

Keller, Tim, 180

Kennedy, Clyde, 6, 7

Kenya, Young Life in, 61, 99–100

Kesler, Jay, 101

Khalil, Yousef, **181**, 183

Kim Jong Dal, 83, **85**

Kinberg, Greg, 122, 126, 164

King, Martin Luther, Jr., 60, 62, 87

Kirk, Jerry, 24

Koerner, Diether, 59

Koop, C. Everett, 58

Koop, David, 58

Kough, Jack and Arlene, 63

Kramer, Bruce, 127

Kvasnickova, Tyna, 155–156, **155**

Kwamy, Alexis, 84

Kyrgyzstan, Young Life camp in, 173, **174**

L

La Finca (camp), **94**, 137, **137**

La Salle Street Young Life, 103

La Vida (at Saranac Village), 74, 75

Lake Champion (camp), **95**, **106–107**, 108–109, 122

Lake Cliff Dude Ranch, 75

Lambeth, Hunter, 181, **181**, 183

Lambeth, Lauri, 183

Larmey, Dyan, 151

Larmey, Steve, 151, 152, 174, 181

Larson, Bruce, 141

Larson, Norman, 18

Latino Student Staff Initiative, 153, 154. *See also* Texas Latino Initiative

Latinos, 84, 103, 185. *See also* Hispanic community

leadership
"All Kinds of Leaders" (Rydberg), 84
as key, 27
changes in, 87–88
development of, 153
diversity in, 84
global leaders, 142. *See also* Developing Global Leaders

(DGL) program

Leland, Mississippi, Young Life in, 37–38

Lewisohn, Adolph, 67

Lilly Endowment, 82, 103

Lin, Tony, 149

Little Rock, Arkansas, as part of mission field in 1945, 13

logos, **162**, **168**

Lost Canyon (camp), **95**, **134–135**, 135

Lowey, Dick, **28**, **116**

Luther Seminary, 86

lyrichord book, **73**

M MacDonald, Harry and Hope, 58

Macedonia, Young Life camp in, **174**

Mackay, John A., 38

magazines, **166–167** *See also Focus on Youth*; *Relationships* magazine; *Young Life* magazine

Malibu Club (camp), 33, **33**, **34–35**, 36, **36**, 41, 75, **75**, **95**

Malibu Princess, **35**

Marquard, E. Alfred, 25

Mays, Annie, 157

McCarthyism, 36–37

McCarty, Marty, 176

McClellan, Donna, 86, 112–113, **112**

McClusky, Evelyn MacFarlane, 6

McDonald, Harry, 83, 97

McDonald, Kay, 13, 15

McDonald, Phil, 28, **28**, 51, 55, **116**, **117, 166**

McDougal, Bouton, 56

McGonigal, Terry and Suzette, 92

McKenzie, Bobby, **10**

McSwain, Mal, 26, 28, 39, 40, 56

MCYM (Military Community Youth Ministries), 59, 98, 101–102

media coverage
    The Saturday Evening Post, 81, 84
    Time magazine, 49, 81

Meirelles, Iberê, 58

Memphis, Tennessee, as part of mission field in 1945, 13

Memphis, Tennessee, Young Life work in, 88

Mentor Moms, 121

Mercer, Wanda Ann, 13

Meredith, Char, 14, 36, 50, 51, 58, 72, 74, 92

Meredith, Jim, 102–103

Merrick, Gail, 128

Merwald, Hal, 58, 59, 111, **111**, 125

Merwald, Judy, 58, 111

Mexico, as part of mission field in 1945, 13

Middle East, Young Life in, 181, **181**, 183

middle school ministry, 82–83, 102, 148–149. *See also* junior high kids, programs for

Mike Edwards Motorsports Team, 147, **147**

Military Community Youth Ministries (MCYM), 59, 98, 101–102, 142

Military Weeks, 122

Miller, Beverly, 38

Miller, John, 28, 37, 38, 39, 50, 63, 98, 114, 124, 125

Milliken, Bill, 45, 46, 47, 48, **48**, 83

Minneapolis/St. Paul, Minnesota, Young Life in, 88

Miracle Book Club (MBC), 6, 7–8, 9

Miranda, Jay, 154

Missing Stars, Fallen Sparrows (Palermo), 110

mission, seven commitments of, 92

mission field, as of 1945, 13

mission statement, 105, 133, 148

"A Mission That Camps" (Rydberg), 41

Mitchell, Bob, 8, 10, 13, 14, 24, 29, **30**, 33, 36, **36**, 37, 40, 52, 60, 63, 72, 75, 79, 86, 89, 91, **91**, 97, 101, 104, 105, 110–111, **116, 117**, 161

Mitchell, Claudia, 75, 91

Mitchell, John E., 9, 186

Monday Morning (eNewsletter), 161, **161**, 180, 187

Mongolia, Young Life in, 133

Morgan, Rocky, **10**

Morristown, New Jersey, Young Life in, 38

Mountain Lodge (camp), **95**

movies, of 1950s, 27

Mt. Kilimanjaro, **180**

Multicultural/Urban, 156

Muncie, Frank, 63

Murphy, Donna, 128, 133, 150

Murphy family, 127

music, 8, 23, 27, 39, 45, 47, 71, 72, 73, 74, 88, 97, **108**

My First Thirty Quiet Times (Saltzgiver), 113

N

Nairobi, Kenya, Young Life in, 61, 99

Nall, Van, 10

National Urban Conference, 87

National Urban Office, 88

The Navigators, 12, 13, 19, 99, 120

Nazism, suspicions of, 10

Nelson, Carl, 62

New Believer's Walk, 176

New Canaan, Connecticut, Young Life in, 49

New Staff Training, 129

New York City, Young Life in, 46–47, 183, 185

Newark, New Jersey, Young Life in, 38, 45

The New Yorker magazine, 24

Nicaragua, Young Life in, 98, 133, 136–137

Nickel, Randy, 175

night that never ends, 143

Nixon, Bo, 46–47, **47**, 48, 61, 87, 108, 183

Nixon, Mary, 183

Nixon, "Tap," 47

North Park Theological, 86

O

Oakbridge (camp), **95**

Oakbridge Christian Family and Sports Camp, 102

October 16, 1941 (date of incorporation), 10

O.K. Dude Ranch, 78

Okiria, Simon, 84

O'Leary, Mike and Carol, 183

O'Neil, John, 59

Ongley, Arthur, 83

Oostdyk, Harv, 38, **38**, 45, 46, 48

opera, 143

Operation Flex, 23

Oraker, Jim, 82

"Outreach '80s," 103

Outward Bound, 74

ownership, sharing of with youth, 177

P

Page, Mae, 89, 112, **112**

Palermo, Nick, 109–110, **109**, 179

Palestinian Young Life, **181**

Paolella, Joe, 109

Paris, France, Young Life in, 31–32

Parker, Ken, 79

Parker, Kevin and Kerry, 138

Parsons, Gary, 114, 125, 133, 136, 173

Parsons, Jeanne, 114, 133, 136

Patak, John and Christine, 82

Patchell, Lindsey, 178

Pelican Lake, Minnesota, **55**

Peru, Young Life in, 59

Peterson, Marge, 89

Philadelphia, Pennsylvania, Young Life in, 88

Philippines, Young Life in, 58, 59, 84, 85, **94**

Phnom Penh Young Life, 150

phrases, 98-99

Pico Escondido (camp), **95**, 124, 140, **140**

Pinterest, 146, 182

Pioneer Plunge (camp), 75, **94**, 136

Poll, Rick, 139

Porter, John, 87, 88

Portland, Oregon
    as part of mission field in 1945, 13
    Young Life in, 30, 88

Portugal, Young Life camp in, 173

Postigo, José, 140

prayer, 7, 24, 39–40, 56, 65, 88, 109, 115, 125, 157, 164, 177

Praz de Lys (camp), **58**, **94**, **99**

Presbyterian Board of National Missions, 5

presidents
    Bill Starr (second). See Starr, Bill
    Bob Mitchell (third). See Mitchell, Bob

Denny Rydberg (fifth). *See* Rydberg, Dennis I. (Denny)

Doug Burleigh (fourth). *See* Burleigh, Doug

Hal Merwald (interim), 111

Jim Rayburn, Jr. (first). *See* Rayburn, Jim, Jr.

Ted Johnson (interim), 125

Proclamation Paper, 152

program, 116-117, 143

   See also humor

Properties department, 122, 124

property staff, 143

Prospect Point, New York, 67

Pustoshkina, Zhenya, 84

Pynn, Vern, 63

pyramids, **70**

racial issues, 26, 37, 62, 78, 80

racism, 23, 60, 73

Rajneesh, Bhagwan Shree, 131

Raley, Recie, 33

Raley, Tom, 9, 23, 24, 29, 33, **36**, 37, 67, 112

rappelling, 77, 143, 172

Rary Mountain Boys, 28, **28**

Rayburn, Bob, **12**

Rayburn, James, Sr., 5

Rayburn, Jim, III, 7, 59, **101**

Rayburn, Jim, Jr.

   amazement of, 187

   "The Big Dream" speech, 71–72

   on camping, 24, 41

   cancer diagnosis, 71

   chronic pain of, 40

   death of, 72

   declining health, 49, 51

   desire to spur on church in outreach to kids, 49

   early efforts of, 5–11

   friendship with Dawson Trotman, 12-13

   as introducing kids to outdoors, 14

   leave of absence, 51–52

   no request ever too big for, 33

   as one of original staff, 185

   photos of, **7**, **9**, **15**, **20**, **24**, **36**, **40**, **72**, **117**

   prayer, 50, 65

   summary of, 73

Rayburn, Maxine (Maxie), 5, 6, 15, 24, 40, 41, 49, 101

Rayburn-isms, 20–21, 26, 127

Reaching a World of Kids (RWOK), 152–153, 156, 163, 169, 178, 180, 186

rebranding, 162, **162**

Recruiting, Training, and Deploying (RTD), 128–129

Reeverts, Ann, 100

Reeverts, Bob, 32, 89, 90, 97, 98, 100, 101, 125, 150

Reeves, Angela, 121

Reinhold, Chuck, 127, 129, 130, 151, 164

Reinhold, Linda, 151

Relationships magazine, 114, **114**, 160, **167**

Relevant Youth Ministry, 99

revivals, 7

Rhodes, Sarah, 117, **117**

right to be heard, earning/winning of, 12, 18, 38, 61, 124, 126, 128, 142, 153, 184, 186

Riviere, Doris, 29

Riviere, Roy, **inside front cover, 12,** 16, 19, 25, 26, 29, 37, 51, 56, 57

RMR Backcountry (camp), **95**

Roche, Gladys, 13

Rockbridge Alum Springs (camp), **94**, 123, **123**, 124, 132

RockRidge Canyon (camp), **94**

Rod and Fran fund, 32

Rodgers, Aaron, **167**

Romans (gang), 38

Romanyuk, Sergie, 84

Romine, Ernie, 63

Round-Up Lodge for Boys, purchase of, 24–25, 41

R

RTD (Recruiting, Training, and Deploying), 128–129

run-on, 143

rural areas, kids in, 119, 137

Rural Conference (1999), 137

Russia, Young Life in, 133, **136**
See also Soviet Union, Young Life in

Rydberg, Dennis I. (Denny), 18, 41, 65, 84, 115, **117**, 126, **126**, 128–129, 133, 141, 148, 152, 153, 154, 159, 164, 176, 177, 181, 184, 186

Rydberg, Marilyn, 115, 126, 127, 141, 181

S

Sadler, Shelley, **117**

Sailing Beyond, 79

Salem, Oregon, Young Life club in, 24

Saltzgiver, Ty, 113

"A Salute to Our Volunteers" (Rydberg), 115

San Francisco Bay Area, Young Life in, 88

San Francisco Theological Seminary, 6

Sangster, Verley, 83, 87, 88, 103, **103**, 104, 121

Saranac Village (camp), 67, **67**, 74, **95**, 105

The Saturday Evening Post, 81, **81**, 84

Sauer, Ron, 138

Say-So tradition, 16, 17, 19, 109, 138, 143

scholarships, 146, 155, 160

school shootings, 138, 140, 145

Schultz, Earl, 101

Schultz, Jonathan, 155

Scotland (camps), **95**, 175, **175**, 180

Scott, Charlie, 74, 78, 103

Scott, Chuck, 171

Scripture References
1 John 5:12, 10
1 Thessalonians 2:8, inside front cover
2 Timothy 2:15, 31
Acts 1:8, 9
Colossians 4:5, 124
Hebrews 11:32–33a, 189
Hebrews 13:8, 187
John 1:14, 133, 143, 151, 180, inside back cover
John 14:6, 9
Luke 9:23, 48
Mark 2:1–12, 110
Mark 10:45, 110
Nehemiah 2:11-18, 127-128
Psalm 107:2, 16, 143
Romans 10:15, 187

Scripture Union, 99

Seattle, Washington, Young Life in, 23, 112

Second Wind positions, 129

segregation, 37

September 11, 2001, Young Life response to, 145–146

September 11th Camp Scholarship Fund, 146

Service Center, 91, 130-131, **130, 177**

Sewell, Addison (Add), 7, 9, **9**, 11, 12, 13, 14, 33, 37, 186

Sewell, Loveta, 13

SharpTop Cove (camp), **95**, 132, **132**, 176

Sheffer, George, 17, 39, 41, 47, 61, **61**, 75, 82, 98, 99, 100

Sheffer, George, III, 74, 82, **82**

Sheffer, Martie, 39, 61, 75, 82, 99

Shelly, Joe, 80

Shively, Scott, 87

Siegle, Dave, 64

Silver Cliff Ranch (camp), 14, 17, **17**, 24, **29**, **95**, 105

Silver Dollar City amusement park (discipleship program), 92

Simpson, A. B., 84

Sin, Jaime, 85

Sing with Young Life, **73**

skits, 14, 28, 40, 74, 143

slang, 6, 23

Small Town Jumpstarts program, 156–157

Small Towns/Rural Initiative, 137, 156

Smith, C. Gordon, 55

Smith, Mr. and Mrs. Sidney, 55

Smith, Stan, 102

Smith, Tarneisha, 147

smoking pit, 28

Smoot, Murray, 16, 17

social media, 160, 169, 182

Somerville, Mary, 121, **121**

song book, Campaigners, **12**

Sor, Pyneath, 150, **150**

Souter, Calum, 175

Souter, Lady, 175

Souter, Sir Brian, 175

Souter Charitable Trust, 175

South Korea, Young Life in, 83, 85

Southwind (camp), 78, **78**, **95**

Soviet Union, Young Life in, 84, 113–114, 125. *See also* Russia, Young Life in

specialty conferences, 119

Spencer, Jim, 83

Spooner, Harold, 103

Squinty Newton (program character), 116

staff

growth of, 13, 125, 128, 140, 186

original five, 6, 9

staff conferences, 13, 119-120, 164. *See also* All Staff Conferences

Staff Congress (1979), 92-93, **93**

Stam, Mary, 31

Star Ranch (camp), **4**, **13**, 15–16, **15**, **16**, **29**, 31, 41, 79, **94**

Starr, Bill, 10, 23, 27, 28, 30, 33, 36, **36**, 38, 51, 52, 53, **53**, 55, 56, 60, 62, 67, 74, 83, 85, 90, 92, 105

Starr, Ruth, 53

Statement of Faith, 87

Station Wagon Grad School, **31**

Steele, Scott, 140

Stephens, Don, 175

The Story of Southwind (Scott), 78

Stover, Bob, 37, 63

Street Academies, 48

Stretar, Betsy, 121, **121**

Stuber, Don, 137, 156–157

Sublett, Kit, 8, 156

Sullivan, Frog, 16, 17, 19, **19**, 25, 26

summer staff, 143

Summerall, Brian, 177

Sun, Mr., 83

Sundberg, Beth, 83, 84

Sundberg, Bruce, 83, 84, 85

Swagerty, Keith, 83

Swan Funeral Home, as club location, **24**

Swenson, Terry, 162

Switzerland, Young Life in, 83, 98

Sylte Sisters (Deanna, Joan, and Deanda), **28**

tableau, 143

Tacoma, Washington, Young Life in, 88

Tada, Joni Eareckson, 3, **3**, **62**, 64, **167**. *See also* Eareckson, Joni

tagline, 162

Taking Donors Seriously (TDS), 122

Tankersley, Ken, **167**

Tanzania, Young Life in, 180–181

Taylor, Bill, **52**, 53, 99

Taylor, Gloria, 14–15, **14**

Taylor, Herb (H. J.), 14–15, **14**

Teachers in Mission project, 153, 155

"A Team on a Mission," 147

technological innovations, 146, 160–161

Teen Challenge, 108

teen moms, 119, 121, 142, 170, 178

tent meetings, 7, **7**, 8, 13

terrorist attacks, Young Life response to, 145–146

Texas Latino initiative, 157

Thomas, John, 87

Thompkins, Bernard, 87

Thurston High School (Springfield, Oregon) shooting, 138

Timber Wolf Lake (camp), **94**, 139, **139**

Time for Living (film), **79**, 80, 161

Time magazine, 49, 81

"Tomorrow is in Their Hands" (*Time* magazine article), 81

Towson High School (Baltimore), 13

tragedy, walking with teens through, 138, 140

Trail West (camp), 49, 50, **50**, **94**, 122

training, 30–31, 43, 82, 86–87, 92, 103, 105, 128

See also New Staff Training; Recruiting, Training, and Deploying (RTD)

Trinity Ranch (camp), **94**

Trotman, Dawson, 12, 13

T-shirts, **68–69**

Tulsa, Oklahoma, as part of mission field in 1945, 13

Turkey, Young Life camp in, 174

Turner, Eddie, 87

TV shows, 23, 119, 120

twenty minutes, 29, 75, 143

Twitter, 146, 169, 182

Tyler, Texas

as part of mission field in 1945, 13

presence of Young Life Campaign in, 9

presence of Young Life clubs in, 11

T

U

Ukraine, Young Life in, 136

United Kingdom, Young Life in, 180. *See also* England, Young Life in

United States, ten regions of Young Life in, 73

University of Washington, Young Life leadership program at, 13

urban ministry, 38, 45, 60–61, 62, 83, 87, 88, **88**, 90, 97, 103, 104, 137

Urban Primus Council (UPC), 87, 88, 104

U.S. basketball team, **83**

Utkin, Sasha, 84

V

Van Dyke, Dick, 64, **64**

Vancouver, British Columbia, Young Life in, 79

Vaus, Jim, 108

Velilyayev, Stepa, 84

Ventures, 110–111, **111**

Vicary, John, 171, 176

Video Scrapbook Program, 161. *See also* Camp Video Scrapbooks

videos, 161–162

Vik, Dave, 79

Vik-Winkle Productions, 80

volunteer leaders
  in camps, 27
  defined, 143
  growth of, 125, 140, 186
  introduction of, 13–14
  quality and training of, 42. *See also* training teachers as, 155

volunteers, 115

W

Wagner, John, 183, 185

Wallace, Chad, 140

Wamalwa, Martin, 84

war, 10, 23, 36, 101, 113, 146, 178

Ward, Pete, 98, 99

Warden, Nancy, 112

Warner, Mariah, **inside back cover**

Washington, D.C., Young Life in, 88

Washington, Dennis and Phyllis, 131, 159

Washington Family Ranch, 124, **131**, 133

Washington Family Ranch Canyon (camp), **95**, 133

Washington Family Ranch Creekside (camp), **95**, **158–159**

Weaverville, North Carolina, 56

website, 128

Welcome Center, **177**

Wetmore, Ernest, 137

Wheaton, Illinois, Rayburn's travels to, 13

Wheaton College, 13, 98, 99, 132

"When God Wants to Teach You Something" (Rydberg), 141

Whipple, Grant, 13

White, Jerry, 120, **120**

White, Joe, 62

Whitelock, Gordon, 9, **9**, 186

Wichita Falls, Texas, presence of Young Life Campaign in, 9

"Wild Life" program, 83

wilderness experiences, 74, 75, 79

Wilderness Ranch (camp), 75, **76-77**, 92, **94**

Wildhorse Canyon (camp), 133

Windahl, Stacy, 50, 122, 162

Windy Gap (camp), 56, **56**, **57**, 75, 78, **89**, **94**, 105

Winkle, Ed, 79, 80

Winston-Salem, North Carolina, 113

Winter Park, Florida, Young Life in, 83

women, roles of, 88–89, 112, 128

women's conference, 89, 112

Women's Ministry Council, 112

Woodleaf (camp), 63, **63**, **94**, **149**

work crew, 143

Wright, Gene, 83

Wright, Ken, 59

Wyatt, Will and Betty, 75, 92

WyldLife, 115, **133**, 142, 148–149, 159, 160

Wynn, Dick, 120, **120**

Y

Yakima, Washington, as part of mission field in 1945, 13

Yasi, Eli, 59, 84, **85**

you were made for this, 162, 189

Young Life
  corporate model, 53
  date of incorporation, 10
  headquarters of, **16**, **52**
  logos, **162**, **168**
  Rayburn's request for permission to use name, 8
  tagline, 162

Young Life buses, 80, **80**

Young Life (Cailliet), 25, 51, **51**, 92

Young Life Campaign
  first use of name, 8
  name shortened to Young Life, 10

Young Life camps. *See* camps

Young Life College, 153–154, **154**, 178, 179–180

Young Life Expeditions, 143, 147

"The Young Life 50th Celebration" (1990), 119–120

Young Life Foundation, 90, 111, 122, 125, 160

Young Life International, 98

Young Life magazine, 10, **11**, **86**, 114, **166**, **167**, 182

Young Life Manhattan Project, 146

Young Life Military, 59, 156, 176

Young Pioneer camp, 172, **173**

Younger Life program, 82

Young*Lives*, 121, 156, 178, **179**

Youth Development International, 108

Youth for Christ, 59, 99, 101, 120

Youth Research International, 59

BECOMING YOUNG LIFE

A timeline of highlighted events.

THE
GOLDEN
AGE OF YOUTH
MINISTRY

'33
• Miracle
Book Club
• Navigators

'41
• InterVarsity
Christian
Fellowship/USA
• YOUNG LIFE

'44
Youth for
Christ

≈ '44
Young Life CAMPAIGN

'33
Ladies start
praying across from
Gainesville *(Texas)*
High School

'40
• "Miracle Book Club"
becomes the "Young Life
Campaign" • Tent meetings
• Young Life Board of
Directors forms

'42
Campaigners
begins

'44
Contact work
begins

'49
Silver Cliff
acquired

1930s

'37 **AMELIA EARHART'S PLANE**
DISAPPEARS
'38 ***SUPERMAN* DEBUTS**
'39 **WORLD WAR II BEGINS**

1940s

'41 **PEARL HARBOR**
'44 **D-DAY**
'45 **WORLD WAR II ENDS**
'47 **DEAD SEA SCROLLS DISCOVERED**
'48 **MODERN STATE OF ISRAEL CREATED**

'39
Rayburn
begins Gainesville
club

'41
• Young Life
incorporated October 16
• Rayburn becomes first
president

'46
• Volunteer leaders
come on board at Wheaton
• Star Ranch acquired *(also
serves as new headquarters
until '61)*

1941
2,400 KIDS
REACHED PER
YEAR

NUMBER OF KIDS REACHED PER YEAR

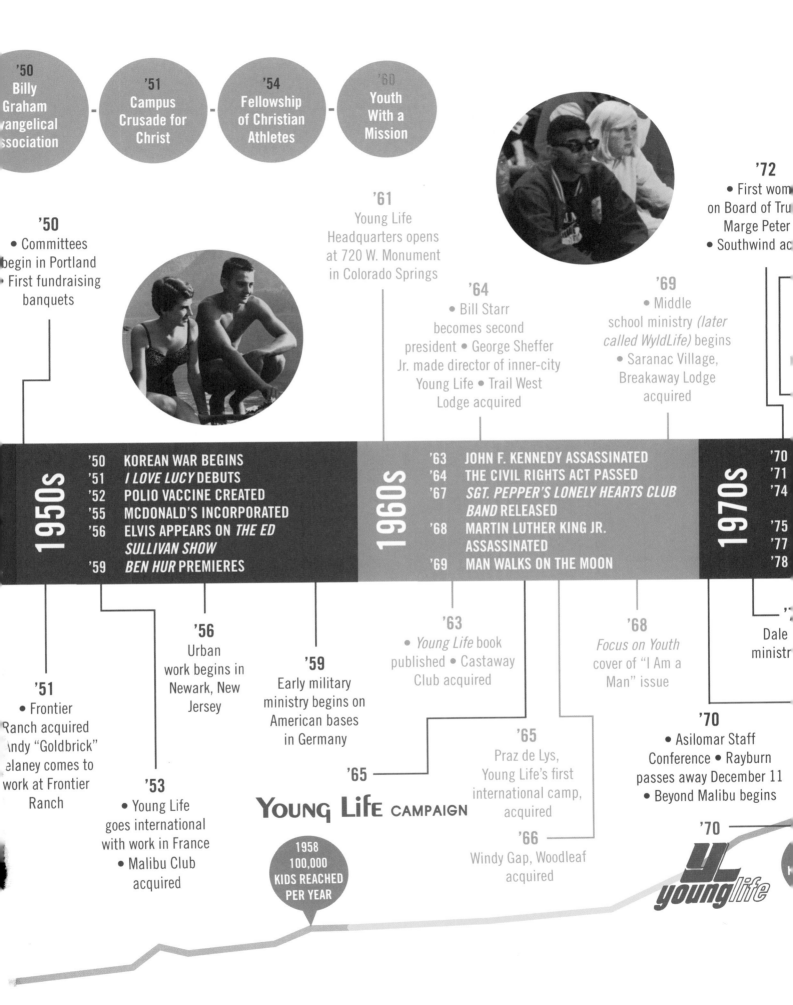

'50
Billy Graham
Evangelical
Association

'51
Campus
Crusade for
Christ

'54
Fellowship
of Christian
Athletes

'60
Youth
With a
Mission

'50
• Committees
begin in Portland
• First fundraising
banquets

'61
Young Life
Headquarters opens
at 720 W. Monument
in Colorado Springs

'72
• First wom
on Board of Tru
Marge Peter
• Southwind ac

'64
• Bill Starr
becomes second
president • George Sheffer
Jr. made director of inner-city
Young Life • Trail West
Lodge acquired

'69
• Middle
school ministry *(later
called WyldLife)* begins
• Saranac Village,
Breakaway Lodge
acquired

1950s

'50	KOREAN WAR BEGINS
'51	*I LOVE LUCY* DEBUTS
'52	POLIO VACCINE CREATED
'55	MCDONALD'S INCORPORATED
'56	ELVIS APPEARS ON *THE ED SULLIVAN SHOW*
'59	*BEN HUR* PREMIERES

1960s

'63	JOHN F. KENNEDY ASSASSINATED
'64	THE CIVIL RIGHTS ACT PASSED
'67	*SGT. PEPPER'S LONELY HEARTS CLUB BAND* RELEASED
'68	MARTIN LUTHER KING JR. ASSASSINATED
'69	MAN WALKS ON THE MOON

1970s

'70	
'71	
'74	
'75	
'77	
'78	

'56
Urban
work begins in
Newark, New
Jersey

'59
Early military
ministry begins on
American bases
in Germany

'63
• *Young Life* book
published • Castaway
Club acquired

'68
Focus on Youth
cover of "I Am a
Man" issue

**'7
Dale
ministr

'51
• Frontier
Ranch acquired
• Andy "Goldbrick"
Delaney comes to
work at Frontier
Ranch

'53
• Young Life
goes international
with work in France
• Malibu Club
acquired

YOUNG LIFE CAMPAIGN

'65

'65
Praz de Lys,
Young Life's first
international camp,
acquired

'66
Windy Gap, Woodleaf
acquired

'70
• Asilomar Staff
Conference • Rayburn
passes away December 11
• Beyond Malibu begins

'70

1958
100,000
KIDS REACHED
PER YEAR

**yl
young life**

THE FIVE C'S

Throughout the mission's history, Young Life has refined its methods to ensure we continue reaching kids with excellence. Those methods are anchored by a set of best practices that have stood the test of time. We call these practices the Five C's (contact work, club, camp, Campaigners, and committee) and on these pages we take a closer look at some images and insights associated with them.

As you unfold these pages, you'll also find a timeline of specific events that shaped the course of the mission, and where they fit in a larger historical context.

CAMP

CONTACT WORK

CAMPAIGNERS

CLUB

COMMITTEE

'30s Club moves from classroom after school to kids' homes at night

'40s "'V' is for Victory!" a favorite club song

'43 Duct Tape invented

'48 Reddi-wip Whipped Cream invented

'50 Water balloons first marketed

'58 *The Phillips New Testament* published

'60s Guitars replace pianos in club

'61 "Barbara Ann" / "The Lion Sleeps Tonight" / "Sing Hallelujah!" / "Stand by Me" all released

'67 "Brown-Eyed Girl" / "I Am the Resurrection" both released

'69 "Build Me Up, Buttercup" / "One Tin Soldier" / "Sweet Caroline" all released

'70s "King Jesus is All" a favorite club song

'72 First *Young Life Song Book* published by Johann Anderson

'80s Overhead projectors begin to replace songbooks and lyrics on poster board

'82 Super Soaker water gun invented

'87 "Lean on Me" (upbeat version) / "Light the Fire" both released • First "Mr. Christmas Tree Pageant"

'89 "Free Fallin'" song released • First car windows shoe polished "YL 7:29"

'90 "It's Amazing" written

'93 PowerPoint begins to push out transparencies

'01 The iPod is invented; club mix tapes and CDs eventually fade out

'02 *The Message* translation of the Bible published

'04 Facebook launches, soon becomes modern version of club flyers

'10 "Firework" released • Instagram and mass text messaging soar, new means of reminding kids about Young Life events

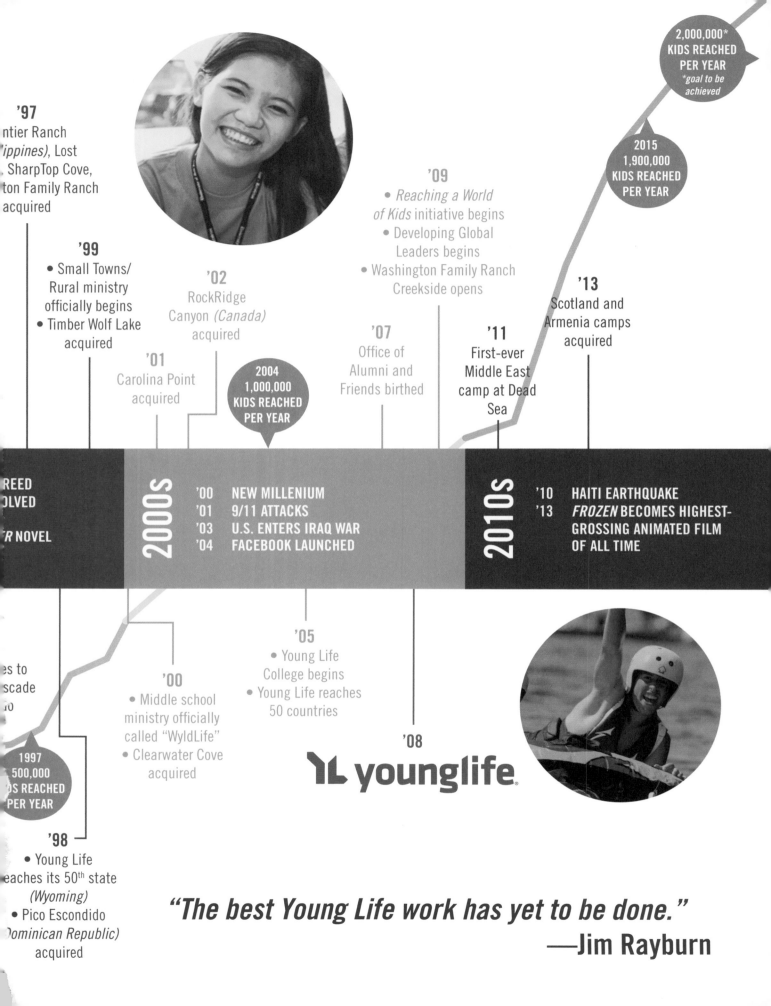

'97
ntier Ranch
ippines), Lost
SharpTop Cove,
ton Family Ranch
acquired

'99
- Small Towns/
Rural ministry
officially begins
- Timber Wolf Lake
acquired

'02
RockRidge
Canyon *(Canada)*
acquired

'01
Carolina Point
acquired

**2004
1,000,000
KIDS REACHED
PER YEAR**

'09
- *Reaching a World of Kids* initiative begins
- Developing Global Leaders begins
- Washington Family Ranch Creekside opens

'07
Office of
Alumni and
Friends birthed

'11
First-ever
Middle East
camp at Dead
Sea

'13
Scotland and
Armenia camps
acquired

**2,000,000*
KIDS REACHED
PER YEAR
goal to be achieved*

**2015
1,900,000
KIDS REACHED
PER YEAR**

REED
OLVED

R NOVEL

2000s
'00	NEW MILLENIUM
'01	9/11 ATTACKS
'03	U.S. ENTERS IRAQ WAR
'04	FACEBOOK LAUNCHED

2010s
| '10 | HAITI EARTHQUAKE |
| '13 | *FROZEN* BECOMES HIGHEST-GROSSING ANIMATED FILM OF ALL TIME |

es to
scade
o

**1997
500,000
S REACHED
PER YEAR**

'98
- Young Life
eaches its 50th state
(Wyoming)
- Pico Escondido
ominican Republic)
acquired

'00
- Middle school
ministry officially
called "WyldLife"
- Clearwater Cove
acquired

'05
- Young Life
College begins
- Young Life reaches
50 countries

'08

⅄⅃ younglife.

"The best Young Life work has yet to be done."
—Jim Rayburn

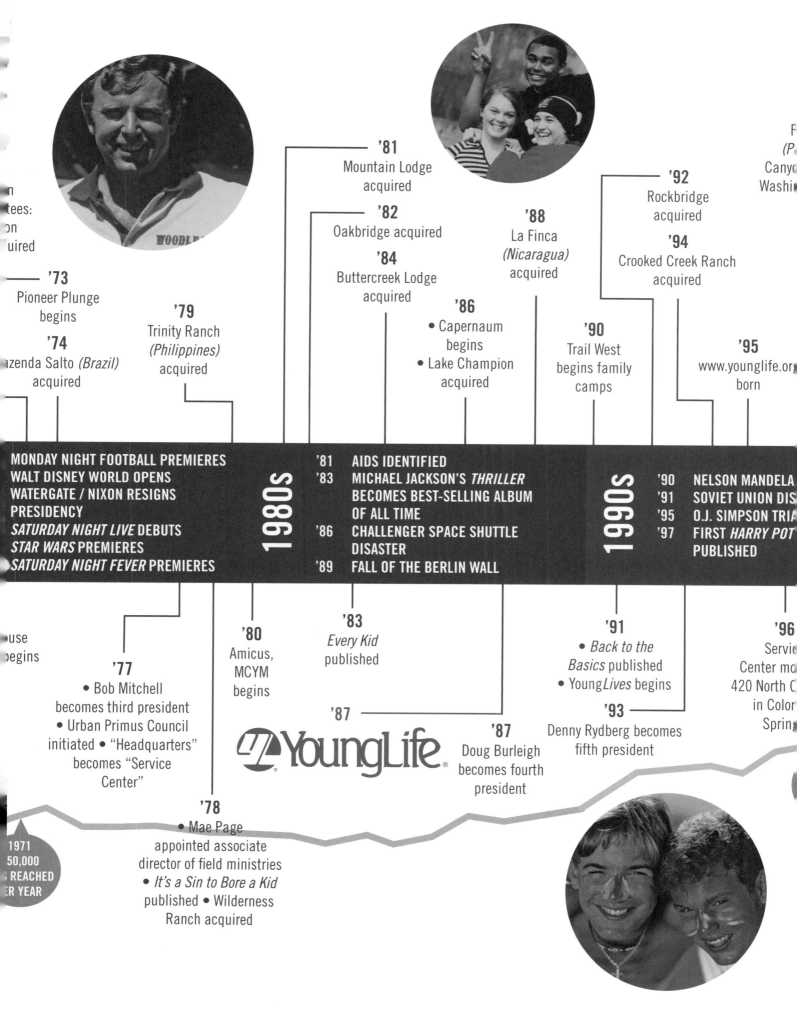

'73
Pioneer Plunge
begins

'74
azenda Salto *(Brazil)*
acquired

'79
Trinity Ranch
(Philippines)
acquired

'81
Mountain Lodge
acquired

'82
Oakbridge acquired

'84
Buttercreek Lodge
acquired

'86
• Capernaum
begins
• Lake Champion
acquired

'88
La Finca
(Nicaragua)
acquired

'90
Trail West
begins family
camps

'92
Rockbridge
acquired

'94
Crooked Creek Ranch
acquired

'95
www.younglife.org
born

1980s

MONDAY NIGHT FOOTBALL PREMIERES
WALT DISNEY WORLD OPENS
WATERGATE / NIXON RESIGNS
PRESIDENCY
SATURDAY NIGHT LIVE DEBUTS
STAR WARS PREMIERES
SATURDAY NIGHT FEVER PREMIERES

'81 AIDS IDENTIFIED
'83 MICHAEL JACKSON'S *THRILLER*
BECOMES BEST-SELLING ALBUM
OF ALL TIME
'86 CHALLENGER SPACE SHUTTLE
DISASTER
'89 FALL OF THE BERLIN WALL

1990s

'90 NELSON MANDELA
'91 SOVIET UNION DIS
'95 O.J. SIMPSON TRIA
'97 FIRST *HARRY POT*
PUBLISHED

use
begins

'77
• Bob Mitchell
becomes third president
• Urban Primus Council
initiated • "Headquarters"
becomes "Service
Center"

'78
• Mae Page
appointed associate
director of field ministries
• *It's a Sin to Bore a Kid*
published • Wilderness
Ranch acquired

'80
Amicus,
MCYM
begins

'83
Every Kid
published

'87

YoungLife

'87
Doug Burleigh
becomes fourth
president

'91
• *Back to the
Basics* published
• YoungLives begins

'93
Denny Rydberg becomes
fifth president

'96
Servic
Center mo
420 North C
in Color
Sprin

1971
50,000
REACHED
R YEAR

THE EVOLUTION OF YOUNG LIFE CAMPING

'30s-'40s

» Jim Rayburn takes kids camping in the East Texas Hills; "program" consists of hunting rattlesnakes, armadillos, and hiking. In what is essentially the first Young Life skit, Rayburn falls into a campfire while performing "Little Red Riding Hood."

» Leaders bring kids to rented camps in Texas; professional recording artists like The Sylte Sisters and The Gut Bucket Four provide entertainment. Program also includes "resort-quality" melodramas and skits.

» The Say-So begins in the early forties.

» Young Life acquires its first camp, Star Ranch. (1946)

'50s

» The Role Play first appears, where leaders portray what they see in kids, sparking discussion and helping kids see themselves more realistically. (1954)

» The "Twenty Minutes of Silence" begins in the mid-fifties.

'60s

» "The night that never ends," which usually includes a tableau (still life), an opera, a carnival, and a square dance, first appears. Jay Grimstead, longtime staff member in the San Francisco Bay Area, was the mastermind behind so many of these ideas. (1968)

» Young Life-owned buses come and go. (1968-1975)

'70s

» The film *Time for Living* becomes Young Life's first professionally designed marketing piece for getting kids to camp. (1971)

» Music evolves into a combination of the sacred/spiritual and the secular, with more guitar accompaniment.

» Wilderness camping emerges around the country.

» Entertainment night features more leaders (not just camp staff) in skits so kids can see and cheer on their leaders up front.

'80s

» More adventure activities are added to the camp week (zip line, ropes course, Blob, go-karts, rappelling) ... something with an element of challenge, but that all kids could accomplish and receive the sense of adventure, overcome fears, and build self-esteem.

» The speaker-kid relationship decreases, placing more emphasis on leader-kid relationships. Every program event measured by the standard: Does this enhance the leader-kid relationship?

» In the mid- to late-eighties, dramas like "The Broken Heart" added to the Gospel presentation.

'90s

» Eight camps acquired—the most by far in a single decade.

» The Role Play evolves more to a Life Signs style where leaders play themselves in high school and their own life experiences.

» The camp musician role grows in usage and importance, as music further enhances the Gospel presentation.

» *The Journey* Bible given to new believers at camp. (1995) As of 2014, 350,000 had been given away.

» Video Scrapbook program begins. (1998)

'00s

» Five-day WyldLife camping employs more rental camps located across the country to decrease travel time/cost.

» The Role Play/Life Signs continues to be refined and Cardboard Testimonies first appear. (2009)

'10s

» Camp On Wheels brings camp to international kids. (2013)

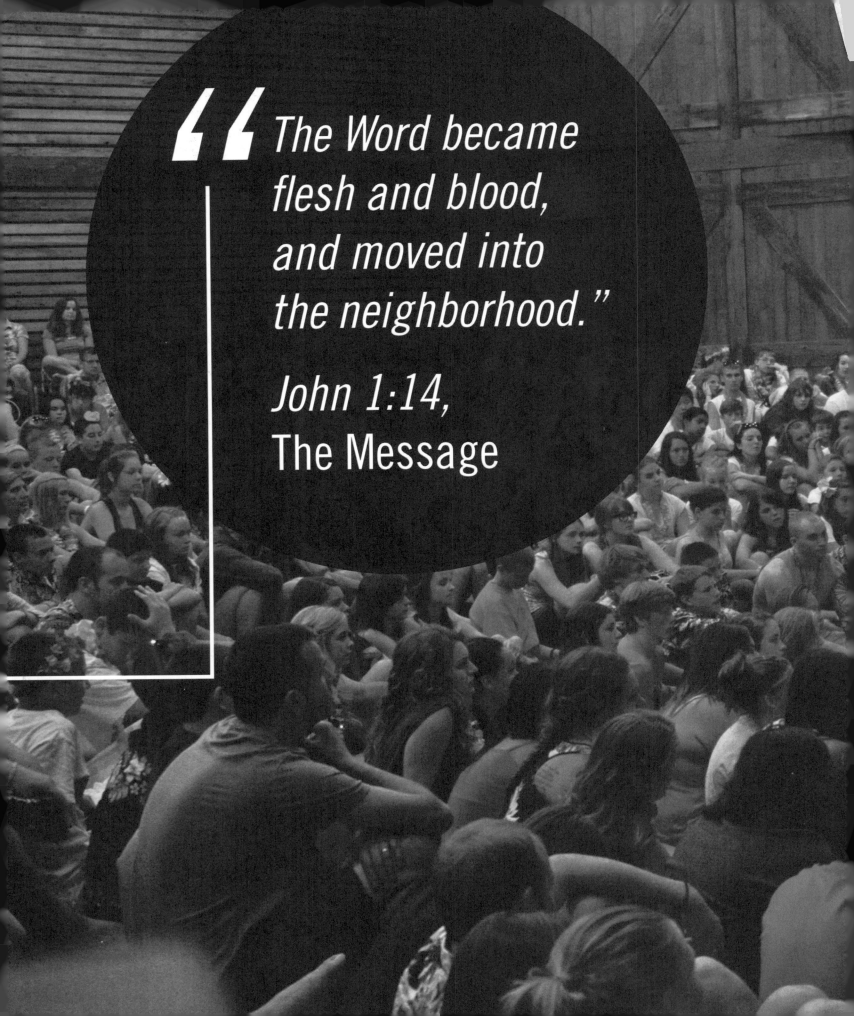

The Word became flesh and blood, and moved into the neighborhood."

John 1:14,
The Message